COME WALK THE NARROW PATH WITH ME

Stories Along My Journey

Betsy Tacchella

Unless otherwise indicated, Bible quotations are taken from The New American
Standard version of the Bible. Copyright © 1995 by The Moody Bible Institute
of Chicago. Other versions used are the KJV and the NIV Copyright © 2005 by
Zondervan. Also, the Living Bible, Copyright © 1971 by Tyndale.

ISBN: 197965834X
ISBN 13: 9781979658348

Psalms 16:11, "You will make known to me the path of life; In Your presence is fullness of joy; In Your right hand there are pleasures forever."

ACKNOWLEDGEMENTS

There are three people who have consistently and sacrificially helped me by editing all of my books. These three are very dear to me and I truly could not have undertaken the task of writing a book without their help. Each one offered a unique area of expertise and I am indebted to them for the hours of support, suggestions, changes, reading and re-reading that they happily gave me over the course of my writing. Their editing skills have been invaluable.

My husband, Bill Tacchella, facilitated the context of the book. After all, he lived many of my stories with me, listened to me tell and retell them over the years, and patiently encouraged my writing. Bill sometimes remembered details I had forgotten. He also offered some of his own stories which I was delighted to include. With a quick mind when it comes to the practical side of our faith, he often added appropriate verses or better ways of getting my point across. Bill is a measured person who can catch errors or tones that might not reflect what I'm trying to communicate. He often helped me reword and refresh a story. I've given Bill free reign to truly critique each story. At times, it was brutal, but I've learned much from his critiques and feel he has made me a more sensitive writer. I love you, Bill, and I'm forever grateful for your footprint in my writing.

My daughter, Kim Hapner, has been another tireless assistant as my book unfolded. Always eager to read my stories, I think she has not only gotten to know her mother better during the process but has added her own strengths to my book. Kim is an amazing woman of God who demonstrates in many venues her wonderful gift of organization. She can look at a story and immediately see if it flows, if the order of events makes sense. Her re-arrangements have always been spot on and I think I have used just about all of them. If I send her a story that seems kind of lopsided, within a short time, she will shift four or five paragraphs or sentences and suddenly, it makes perfect sense. Her suggestions have been priceless and incredibly useful. I love you, Kim, and appreciate all the time you have taken from your busy schedule to invest in my books.

My dear friend, Sue Werschky, continues to be my third helper. Sue gets so excited when I tell her I have another story for her to read and correct. In fact, without needing to, she recently decided to re-read the whole book, again showering me with positive comments. She is a whiz when it comes to grammar and punctuation and tells me I am improving in that area. I'm now seeing fewer red marks on each page. It has been a pleasure to work with Sue as she champions my stories, building me up as she exhorts me to keep going. I'm thankful for her commitment to me as a friend and an author. I love you, Sue, and appreciate you endlessly for your contribution to my books.

A special thank you to my sweet granddaughter, Laura Davis, who lent her expertise in creating the beautiful cover for this book. I am so grateful for your help.

CONTENTS

INTRODUCTION

*W*hat is life all about? Why am I here? Is there any meaning or purpose? These were questions I pondered and even labored over, always hoping that someone could give me answers. Yes, I went to church but I always felt something was missing. It seemed there had to be more than attending services. Coming to Christ in my mid-twenties led me on an adventure in God that continues to shape my life, my identity, my relationships, my purpose and so much more. It is my heartfelt desire for others to also discover this most amazing gift of salvation that Jesus Christ offers.

Before I begin, I need to tell you something. I am not an evangelist. Although I very much admire those with this gift, and at times, have wished I had it too, it is not one of my spiritual gifts. There was a period in my life when I truly longed for this gift. In fact, I took a course on evangelism at our church, Walnut Creek Presbyterian, in California. While in that class, I pretty much memorized how to bring a person to Christ. We studied a wonderful book called, "Evangelism Explosion," by Dr. James Kennedy, out of Florida. Maybe you've heard of him.

Our church had evangelism teams who regularly called on people who had visited the church. Chuck Joplin was the head of the Evangelism Department and he definitely had the gift. Chuck, a man of tall stature with a thick head of wavy white hair, always carried a warm smile and sincere enthusiasm. He was a man who would walk into a restaurant and almost begin to cry as he looked over the sea of faces. His comment to those dining with him would remind his companions of what is really important in life. "Look at all these people who may spend eternity apart from God. My heart is broken that some of them may not know Jesus yet." Now, that is the heart of a true evangelist.

Don't get me wrong. I have a heart for people, but when I go to a restaurant, I'm not thinking of souls dying without Jesus. I am thinking of what is on the menu. I greatly admired Chuck's attitude and his consuming sense of purpose in sharing the gospel with as many people as possible. His passion, his purpose in life, his reason for living and his heart for people's salvation definitely had an impact on me.

When Chuck and our team called on homes, I literally sat on the edge of my chair, drinking in the gospel message afresh each time it was presented. Mesmerized, I watched Chuck share from his heart the love of Christ. His selfless love for people and longing for their salvation was palpable. Eagerly watching for people's response, I sat almost breathless, never tiring of hearing the good news of Jesus over and over again. Each time was like the first for me and my heart thrilled with every person who acknowledged their need and prayed the sinner's prayer. What a privilege to be part of leading someone to their Savior. Many accepted the Lord under Chuck's guidance and many also went on to serve Christ and grow in faith.

Probably the most fun I had as a result of Chuck's ministry was a Bible study I began. It was for new believers and people who didn't know Christ yet but were seeking to know more about God. Since my gift is teaching, that role suited me perfectly. Chuck would bring people to the Lord or share his faith in such a way that people were interested in knowing more about the Bible. He would then filter those who showed interest into my Bible study. A Bible study full of baby Christians and people searching for answers made for a very exciting class. I fondly remember the amazed looks on the faces of participants as they learned of God's love, goodness and holiness, Jesus' miracles, and His teachings. Everything was new to them just as it had been for me when I first met Him. My heart was warmed as I observed their eagerness to grow and mature in Christ.

As the years have moved on, although I'm not an evangelist, I have had some unique experiences sharing Christ. We are all called to be witnesses for Jesus and I believe every Christian has a personal testimony to share. A witness is simply one who gives a firsthand account of something seen, heard or experienced. While sharing my faith with others may not be a daily occurrence or, at times, even monthly, occasionally God has called me to give testimony of His goodness. I have found these opportunities both enriching and exhilarating. I think you will understand why as you read some of my stories. They are stories that only God by His Holy Spirit could have orchestrated, each one fine tuned to fit His purpose.

It is such a blessing to see how God uses each of our gifts to further His Kingdom. He knows each one of us individually and He loves to play to our uniqueness. He knows that I love adventure, so some of the openings He has given me are perfectly suited to my desire for variety and diversity in my journey of sharing my faith. There is nothing boring about Jesus, and I believe He loves to fit us into situations like perfectly matched puzzle pieces. God's heart is for people, all people. He loves every one of us with a passionate love, enough that He sent His son to die for us. He cares deeply about lost people and will even seek them out over and over as He endeavors to save their souls for eternal life.

This book is full of stories, first of how my father and I found Christ and then how God has used me over the years to share the good news of Christ with others. Some of the names in my stories are real and some are changed to protect privacy. I hope that, in the process of reading, you will be inspired to hear God's voice and respond when He holds opportunities out for you to be a witness. We each have a story of how we came to the Lord, a story of our own redemption and the difference He has made in our lives. Let's start with that.

CHAPTER 1

OUT OF DEATH, INTO LIFE

"It's cancer and it's all through his body. There's nothing we can do for him. It's too late. We just sewed him back up so in a few days you can take him home to die," were the insensitive, words blurted out by my father's doctor as my mother and I stood numb in the hospital corridor. Stunned, my mother gasped for breath and almost lost her balance. We were speechless as shock waves rippled through both of us. We were not used to such poor bedside manners from a doctor, especially at such a critical and life changing moment.

Time seemed suspended as my mother, in her fragile emotional state, wept softly. I helped her to a chair but any words of comfort seemed empty. Her worst fears were being realized as my father slowly slipped away from her.

Daddy had been ill for two years but refused to see a doctor. In his heart, he feared he had cancer and was afraid to face treatment. The thought of chemo or radiation terrified him. Now, he looked feeble and vulnerable laying there in a hospital bed and now it was too late for any help at all.

I had not seen my parents in a year or so but had been called to his bedside for the impending operation. Mother had warned me on my approaching visit, "Your father doesn't look like himself, Betsy. Don't be too shocked at his appearance. He's very weak and frail."

But I was stunned. My once robust father looked so emaciated, his body wasted away, so thin and gaunt. Overcome with emotion, I fled the room unable to hold back my tears. It was obvious my relatively young, sixty one year old father was facing certain death, probably a very painful death, leaving my mother to live out her senior years alone.

As the days went by, when I visited Daddy in his hospital room, he would ask me to read something to him from the Bible. "Read to me from Romans 8, Betsy. That's your favorite chapter." So, I gladly read a few verses to him. Many of them seemed to fit his circumstances and give him comfort in the midst of excruciating pain.

Such verses as Romans 8:18-19, 22-23, 26 seemed to speak to his situation. *"For I consider that the sufferings of this present time are not worthy to be compared with the glory that is to be revealed to us. For the anxious longing of the creation waits eagerly for the revealing of the sons of God. For we know that the whole creation groans and suffers the pains of childbirth together until now. And not only this, but also we ourselves, having the first fruits of the Spirit, even we ourselves groan within ourselves, waiting eagerly for our adoption as sons, the redemption of our body. In the same way the Spirit also helps our weakness; for we do not know how to pray as we should, but the Spirit Himself intercedes for us with groanings too deep for words;"*

My father gave his life to the Lord when I was a teenager. A dynamic preacher, Dr. Donald Grey Barnhouse, was a visiting pastor for our church mid-winter Bible conference. At this conference, the congregation was somewhat stunned when Barnhouse began to gently call the parishioners sinners in need of a Savior. One elderly lady was incensed, got up from her seat and huffed her way out mumbling arrogantly, "I will not sit here and be called a sinner!"

That same preacher, however, had a different effect on my father who was one of several who responded favorably to the message and embraced Christ. Likely, this was my father's first exposure to the gospel message and he was radically saved that night. Like Paul, he became zealous about his new found faith. From then on, every evening meal at our house was prefaced and concluded with Bible talk, that is, Daddy talking about the Bible and Jesus, and me squirming, hoping to leave quickly. My heart was not ready to respond but Daddy faithfully planted seeds which would later sprout into my own personal faith. He had been so pleased the day I had told him of my salvation. After many years of resistance, his prayers had been answered. We now had common ground for spiritual conversation.

One afternoon as we sat together after he had left the hospital, he began to share a verse with me with emphatic authority. *"Truly, truly I say to you, he who hears my word and believes Him who sent Me, has eternal life and does not come into judgment; but has passed out of death into life,"* (Jn. 5:24).

Although we didn't talk about it, Daddy knew he was dying and this was his way of reassuring me of his destiny. I was deeply touched. This was his favorite verse, he told me, and I felt that day that God had given me that verse, too, as reassurance of my father's future with Jesus. He truly loved the Lord and now our bond was sealed for eternity, both of us in Christ.

After several agonizing months, my father passed away. That is…his physical body ceased functioning. But assuredly, his soul and spirit passed right out of death into eternity just as Jesus promised in John's gospel. Daddy's earlier decision to follow Christ afforded him a guarantee of eternal life. It was such a soothing consolation for me to know that he was now in God's presence. What joy, what comfort and security to know the assurance that only Christ can give. *John 10:27-28, "My sheep hear My voice, and I know them, and they follow Me; and I give eternal life* to them, and they will never perish; and no one will snatch them out of My hand."

Again in John 6:37, *"All that the Father gives Me will come to Me, and the one who comes to Me I will certainly not cast out."* What a blessing, what freedom, what assurance comes in knowing that my father is eternally secure.

Even today, I believe Daddy is part of that great cloud of witnesses spoken of in Hebrews 12:1-2, cheering me on as I run the race. *"Therefore, since we have so great a cloud of witnesses surrounding us, let us also lay aside every encumbrance and the sin which so easily entangles us, and let us run with endurance the race that is set before us, fixing our eyes on Jesus, the author and perfecter of faith, who for the joy set before Him endured the cross, despising the shame, and has sat down at the right hand of the throne of God."*

"Our verse," John 5:24, sustained me through the funeral with an inner peace as I envisioned Daddy resting from his pain racked body, now enveloped in the love of Jesus, a smile returning to his face, even a thunderous laugh of delight. I picture him exuberantly proclaiming to me the wonder and beauty of being in Jesus' presence. Today, I still cling to John 5:24. I will see Daddy again someday and we will rejoice together as we sit at the feet of our Savior singing praises to our Lord.

I often think as I see our three children and nine grandchildren that my father was the start of a whole new generation. One by one, they have given their hearts to the Lord. It is a wonderful heritage. My guess is that my father may have prayed that future generations would also put their trust in the One who gave His life for him and our family. I know that I also pray for future generations. I want them all to embrace the eternal promises of God.

CHAPTER 2

MISSING LINK

Understandably, some of my father's testimony overlaps my own but come along with me for a brief walk down memory lane, with all the nostalgia I can muster, as I tell you about my early years and, later, how Christ entered my life. Even as a youngster, the Lord was setting the stage for my salvation, the redemption of my lost soul.

I've never really felt like a Texan, but by birth, I am one having been born in Terrell, Texas, a small town between Fort Worth and Dallas. Because of my father's work, we only lived there until I was six weeks old. Then we transferred to West Virginia where three years later, my sister, Cynthia, was born. Since I was so young and we moved again when I was three, I have no memory of these two places.

According to my mother, while living in West Virginia, at the age of three, I disappeared from our yard one afternoon. Frantic, thinking of the river that ran through our neighborhood, my mother called neighbors but no one had seen me. With dread, she and my father phoned the fire department to come and help with the search. Consumed with fear, my parents imagined the worst scenario. Could I have wandered down to the river, just a block away, and somehow fallen in? I imagine my mother was hysterical by then. Just as the fire department began talking about dragging the river, a neighbor who lived several blocks away up a steep hill, called to say I had wandered up to her house.

What relief my parents must have felt, yet with my mother's panic, I'm sure I must have picked up her emotional upheaval because, into adulthood, I had a fear of getting lost. When God later revealed to me that this incident was the core of my fear, through prayer, I soon found peace and no longer carried that foreboding.

While still pre-school age, we moved again, this time to Pennsylvania where we settled in a cozy, hilly neighborhood, great for sled riding in the winter. We remained in Johnstown, Pennsylvania until I was in seventh grade. During those early years, my life was good. I had neighborhood friends, a sense of community, a good school, parents who loved me, and lots of fun activities. For the most part, I was genuinely happy.

I remember well the pleasant times with neighborhood friends. Besides sledding in winter until our hands and feet froze, we roller skated all the sidewalks in the summer. In those days, we slipped our shoes into the metal skates and adjusted them with a key. If we weren't roller skating, we were riding our bikes. Playing dolls was also a highlight and we had a nearby wooded area where we pushed dolls in their strollers along a path to what we called "Big Rock" where we spent many hours in carefree play.

Paper dolls were another hit, and happily, an artistic neighbor drew and dressed them in the latest styles. I used to love watching her draw and cut out a dress or a skirt. All the little girls gathered around in awe of her talent. In those days, I was definitely a girly girl.

On summer nights, neighbor children could be found playing dodge ball or tag in the street. At Christmas, the whole neighborhood went caroling, picking up people at each house and ending the evening with cocoa and cookies. Life was carefree back then.

I was popular in elementary school and had loads of friends. Of course, there was a pecking order and I think I was near the top. But even then, I was somewhat shy and afraid of boys. My worst memory of grade school was of a boy in the neighborhood chasing me home from school lighting matches as we ran up the steep hill to my house. All the while, he threatened to light my pants on fire. I was just glad it wasn't an icy winter day because I recall having trouble getting home from school on those occasions as I kept slipping back down the hill. There were times my father even had to park at the bottom of the long hill we lived on because it was too treacherous to drive up.

A hard worker, my father's job caused him to be absent three or four nights each week with traveling. In part, because of that, I never felt I had a relationship with him. From the time I was young, when he came home each weekend, my first words were an excited, "What did you bring me, Daddy?" He always brought a present or took Cynthia and me to the candy store to appease his absence. When he was home, he was tired and spent his time watching sports on TV or reading the Wall Street Journal and he did not appreciate any interruptions. His tired, leave me alone attitude, played into my growing shyness and fear of men.

While most of my grade school memories are good, some memories puzzle me. For instance, when I was five, I was hospitalized for a week because I wouldn't eat. Finally, the doctor said if I would eat one thing I could go home. So, I asked for a popsicle and home I went. I have no idea what might have caused me to stop eating.

I do know, however, that throughout elementary school, I had to come home every day for lunch because I was obsessively concerned about my mother's well being. My emotional state of mind left me overly sensitive to my mother's needs. Looking back, I believe she was depressed and I somehow internalized her emotions. Because of this, I endured a lot of separation anxiety when I was away from her. Going to camp was a nightmare for me and going away to college was completely unbearable.

Although I have no memory of my family attending church until I was in about fifth grade, it is possible we did. My most poignant memory was when my fifth grade Sunday school teacher heard I was taking piano lessons. One Sunday, she insisted I play hymns while the class sang along. Too shy to disobey her, but knowing this was not going to end well, shaking like a leaf, I approached the organ. If ever there was cause for me to abandon church forever, that day was it. Mortified that I had no idea how to play the organ, much less hymns I had never practiced, I slogged through accompanied by the snickers of my classmates. Head down, I stumbled back to my seat convinced that I couldn't do anything right. Looking back, I realize her goal was not to hurt me, of course, but it was one of the events in my early life that left a wound of self doubt that was not healed until many years later when I came to know Jesus.

My piano teacher, being a perfectionist, did not help matters either. For one solid year, she had me play, "Carry Me Back to Old Virginny". To this day, I cringe at the thought of that song. Of course, I never got it right because I was traumatized at my lesson each week, nerves on edge, knowing I had to perform it perfectly if I wanted to move to the next song. Finally, after a year, I begged my mother to let me quit. Mercifully, she agreed.

Despite my bad experience with the organ, my parents loved that church and we soon joined. It met my mother's desire to further her social life and my father was quickly put in charge of the finances, a job he enjoyed for many years. My sister and I joined youth group and choir, and at the proper time, we partook of catechism and joined the church. I can still envision my lovely white confirmation dress with its crisp, fresh smell.

In that church, we were, if nothing else, hobnobbing with society people in the most prestigious location in town. For me, it was just a boring place to go on Sunday mornings. If the preaching was ever about Jesus, I somehow missed it as I yawned through every hymn and sermon, truly bored to tears. A sermon title I still remember was, "Why I Like Johnstown". Not exactly a spiritual lesson, as I recall.

When I was in junior high, my family moved to another part of town, a community closer to our church and more suited to boost my mother's social aspirations. We joined the country club and now spent summer days sunbathing and swimming at the pool. Still, I had a hard time adjusting to this move. Making friends in my new school was difficult and I longed for my old, comfortable relationships. I even remember hugging my old brick house goodbye the day we left, somehow knowing a new chapter of my life was about to begin. I think many young teens find those years difficult and I was no exception.

While I had felt mostly secure and happy in my childhood, as a teenager, I became increasingly timid and awkward, so shy that I hardly spoke at all. My grades dropped, and I remember being unbearably lonely.

Sometimes, boys would tease and taunt me, look at me and snicker, whisper about me and laugh, sometimes right in front of me. I felt mocked and rejected. When some of them started a conversation with me, I felt their purpose was to find something to laugh at. How much of this was actually true, I don't know, but this was my perception of my life at that time and it only sealed in my heart that boys were mean, even cruel and to be feared. I already felt distant and fearful of my father. This only added to my growing, negative feeling towards all males.

Then to top it all off, my parents announced that they wanted me to be a debutante. Of all things, me, being presented in the top social circles. I was horrified and after much discussion, I refused and thankfully, they accepted my, "No". I had already joined Rainbow Girls for my mother, but being a Deb was too much. Even so, although I agonized, in the back of my mind, I always felt that someday a knight in shining armor would come and rescue me from all the torment in my soul.

Once in high school, my parents didn't encourage me to do extracurricular school activities and it actually never occurred to me that I should. I felt stupid at sports and was usually the last one picked when teams were chosen.

In my parents' thinking, young ladies didn't work so I was not encouraged to get a job either. I was often bored and spent a lot of time in my room feeling depressed, helpless, worthless and ugly. I had no idea how to cope with life and no one to talk to about it. I was brought up not to share feelings so I was often left alone with my personal anguish. Although I did date some, I never felt I really fit in. While we attended church regularly, I didn't know Christ in a personal way. I only knew "about" Him so I had no comfort or direction in my life. Who would rescue me from all this sadness?

It was during this time that my father accepted Christ and became ardent, if not zealous, about his new faith. I remember many nights around the dinner table hearing Bible verses or things he was learning. Since my relationship with him was minimal, all this new found religious stuff was irritating at best. Excusing myself from the table each evening, I couldn't get away fast enough. He had not won a hearing with me. Yet, today, I believe it was his prayers that were later instrumental in my own decision to follow Christ.

After graduation from high school, we moved to Kansas. It was another traumatic move as I had to leave a boyfriend behind. He did take a train out to visit me that summer but later, after an initial flurry of letters, we eventually realized distance was a serious obstacle to our relationship. It soon ended, and in the fall, I was off to Texas Christian University, a college I had chosen as a way to reconnect with my birth state. It was amazing to me that I had been accepted because, after having taken the ACT, my high school counselor had looked at me and said, "You might as well not even try to go to college, Betsy. With this score, you will never make it." Another rejection in life, another hit to my waning confidence, another confirmation that I wouldn't amount to anything.

Fortunately, that advice was not heeded because my parents told me I was going to college. It was part of the plan. Case closed. Besides, I had maintained acceptable grades in my class work through high school. Looking back, I'm glad my parents didn't let that counselor's words impact that future decision. I have used her words instead as a caution concerning what I say to people. Words can be powerful. They can leave a lifelong impression for good or for bad.

I lasted only one semester at TCU but not because of grades. After an almost fatal bout with homesickness, still dealing with separation anxiety, I transferred to the University of Kansas which was in Lawrence, the town where my parents now lived. After living at home for a year, I pledged a sorority, made some friends and felt a little more secure. I found a sense of community on campus and enjoyed the rest of my college years.

Actually, in college, I went berserk. When I joined the Alpha Chi Omega sorority, I also joined the party life where I drank on weekends and majored in getting my MRS. I was there to find a husband and if I got an education along with it, great.

One evening, one of my sorority sisters yelled down the hall that someone she knew was looking for a blind date. I was within hearing distance, and since I wasn't dating anyone seriously at the time, I agreed to go. Through this date with a man named Ed, I eventually ended up meeting my future husband, Bill.

Since Ed and Bill were friends and lived in the same apartment building, I got to know Bill who asked if I would fix him up with some of my sorority sisters. He had just moved from Kansas City in hopes of meeting some college girls. After arranging several dates for him where Ed and I double dated with them, I began to think, *hmmm, maybe I would like to date Bill.* So, one night when Ed was busy, I got word to another of Bill's friends that I was free.

Bill was extremely good looking and also loved to party. He was as shallow as I was, and like me, had no direction in life. A perfect match, although with some wisdom, he did convince me to change my major from social work to elementary education. That turned out to be a prudent move because, at that season of my life, trying to deal with other people's problems would, no doubt, have overwhelmed me.

Within three months, we were engaged and six months later, we were married. Bill, to me, was that knight in shining armor, the one who had come to rescue me. While today, I do not recommend that people jump into marriage that quickly, for us, because of God's later intervention, we have remained married now for over fifty years. We married in December during Christmas break my junior year at KU. For our honeymoon, we spent only a few days in Kansas City because, due to my continuing separation anxiety, I had to be home for Christmas.

Life should have been great. But it wasn't. We had no communication and each of us was a mess. We were two broken people trying to start a life together, each tapping in to the other's ragged edges, neither of us having maturity, stability, or direction in life. I was twenty-one and Bill was twenty-four. Whatever happened to my fairy tale knight in shining armor? Today, we're thankful that God had a plan even though at that time, we were both disasters.

In my mid-twenties, I began to feel something was really missing from my life. By then, I had finished college, married and started a family. We were blessed with two adorable little blond girls, Kim and Laurie, born two years apart. We had moved to Oklahoma with Bill's work, away from both of our families. My separation anxiety had diminished and I was fully engaged with my own family. Yet, I had no idea how to raise our children. When they were still young, I admit, I spent more time thinking of myself than about them. Looking back, I'm sure that if I had continued on that trajectory of selfishness, my children would have endured a more difficult and painful life.

Although Bill and I attended church, neither of us knew the Lord yet. A number of questions began to form in my heart and I found myself pondering and contemplating deeper issues of life. *What is the meaning of life? Why am I here? Is there more purpose to life than what I'm experiencing?*

My parents had set goals for me – go to college, get married, have children. By my mid-twenties, I had accomplished all of their goals and now floundered as to where to go from there. *Surely, there had to be more but what could it be?* Having survived my troubled teen years, I now felt a new gnawing emptiness in my heart. Something seemed to be missing but I had no idea what.

There I was in Oklahoma, involved in yet another church, attending regularly, a church where Bill and I were even youth group leaders. But I was now enduring an increasing restlessness of soul. Convinced that I just needed to read the Bible, I began reading everyday but I had no idea what it was talking about. Later, I learned that the Bible is a spiritually discerned book and that without the guidance of the Holy Spirit, it can't be fully understood. 1Corinthians 2:14, *"But a natural man does not accept the things of the Spirit of God, for they are foolishness to him; and he cannot understand them, because they are spiritually appraised."* The more I read, the more questions I had and the more confused I became. I didn't understand a thing the Bible was saying. It made no sense to me at all.

In my frustration, I decided that the problem was that I needed a Bible study group with someone to teach me. So, I asked the pastor if he would lead a study. With great expectancy, I attended the first class, but sadly came out greatly disappointed, so much so that I never returned. It was like a history lesson and I had always found history extremely boring. He lost me on the first day. So much for that idea.

What was it I was longing for? We attended a Sunday school class that was about as edifying and informative as the Bible study had been. Often, one of the members of the class would walk out with me. Turning to each other, together, we puzzled over what life was all about. Neither of us had any answers. The class and our discussions only added to my frustration.

Then, after four years in Oklahoma, instead of being fired, which Bill in hindsight felt should have been his company's decision, they transferred him to the best territory in the U.S., Northern California.

By any standard, we had it all in the world's eyes... a healthy family, two darling daughters, a good job, and a lovely new home in beautiful California. Yet, the nagging in my soul continued to escalate. Somehow, these outward benefits were not bringing me the fulfillment, peace or satisfaction I was looking for. I longed for something more, something I could not yet identify. Something was definitely missing and no matter how I tried to fill the void, nothing made me feel whole. Looking back, I know that God was in the process of wooing me to Himself.

Years later, I learned that by design, God has placed this kind of longing for more in each of us. Romans 8:20-21 says, *"For the creation was subjected to futility, not willingly, but because of Him who subjected it, in hope that the creation itself also will be set free ...."* I find it interesting that God has actually put in each human being a sense of pointlessness, a sense of futility, lacking in meaning and purpose until we turn to Christ. Many people keep their lives so busy that they numb themselves to God's nudges. At this time though, He was surely giving me an insatiable hunger and thirst for something that the world could not satisfy.

Being church goers, it was important for us to find a new church as soon as we moved to California. The one we settled in was much larger than the small one we had left, but for the first time, we began hearing things in church that we had never heard before. We joined an adult Sunday school class of about a hundred people and were impressed with their knowledge of the Bible. Discussion was often animated, genuine and pertinent to our daily lives. People even seemed excited about Jesus. This was a new concept for us.

For the first time, going to church became a highlight in our week. We began learning things that made sense. One Sunday after class, as I spoke to some of my new friends, I decided to test them to see if they would judge our lifestyle. I practically flaunted that we spent weekends in bars. I wondered what their response would be, but interestingly, no one judged us. Instead of reacting or shunning us, they reached out and warmly accepted us. They showed us the love of Christ which quickly won a hearing. I was increasingly puzzled and began to want whatever it was that they all had. Whatever it was, I knew that I didn't have it. *Could this be what I've been longing for? But what exactly is it?*

From time with our new friends and from Sunday school lessons, we began to understand how much God loves us and that He is not only the One who created us but that he has a plan for our lives. It made sense. Who would have a better plan than the One who created us? I saw that, from God's point of view, we are all sinners and fall short of perfection. I learned that what defines us as sinners is merely the fact that we all fall short of God's perfect standard of holiness. We all miss the mark. No one is faultless. So, whether we exist in debauchery or live the best we can, in God's sight, we are all sinners. Maybe that's why no one at church judged us. We were all sinners in one way or another. I learned that Jesus wanted to forgive me and to have a personal relationship with me. During this time, I could actually feel Him drawing me to Himself.

After much wrestling and thought, at the age of twenty-six, I made what I consider the most important decision I had ever made, a decision that has had a profound impact on every area of my life. As I grappled with God one night, I decided it was time to take the leap and invite Jesus into my heart. I agreed with God that I am a sinner, asked for forgiveness and invited Jesus to be my Lord. This one remarkable decision set my life on a course that changed everything. I had finally met and embraced my true Knight in shining armor, the One who loved me unconditionally and could fill my emptiness.

I began to study the Bible and understand how God wanted me to live, and this time, with the help of other believers, I understood the Bible. With the Holy Spirit living in me, I was promised truth. John 16:13, *"But when He, the Spirit of truth, comes, He will guide you into all the truth...."* I could see that the Holy Spirit had been wooing me from the moment my search had begun, probably even before that. He put the desire for God in my heart and led me until I was ready to accept Christ. What a comforting thought. Interestingly, I never had to make decisions about getting certain bad habits out of my life. They just fell away by neglect as I filled my time and thoughts with new relationships, Bible studies, and meaningful activity. An evening with Christian friends became so much more fulfilling than one at a bar. Being a Christian benefited my marriage, my children, my friendships, indeed, every aspect of my personal life.

When the Lord came into my life, one of the first things He began to work on was my lack of self worth. We had volunteered to host a missionary in our home who had a profound impact on me personally. Out of the blue, she wanted to share a verse with me that had meant a lot to her. She had no idea that it would be a life changing verse for me. As she shared Isaiah 43:4, a light shone in my heart and my soul began to heal from all the torment, rejection, and worthless feelings from my past. *"Since you are precious in My sight, Since you are honored and I love you, I will give other men in your place and other peoples in exchange for your life."* I began to understand at a deep level that I was precious, honored and loved by God. He was telling me that He delighted in me, that He felt affection for me, that I was special. Something fresh was birthed in my heart as this kind missionary read this verse and it has continued to grow to this day. Having received this personal word from God, it made a huge difference in my life, in my confidence, and in my personal sense of worth. When God, Himself, tells us who we are, it has the power to mend and heal years of negativity.

Two Bible studies I joined early in my Christian walk, studies that also influenced me in very practical ways, were on marriage and raising children. I had no idea how to make either of these areas of my life work well. With God's help, as I heeded His Word, both areas began to transform into something beautiful. Six months after I accepted the Lord, Bill also committed his life to Christ and we began to communicate and to love each other in new ways. God literally saved our marriage and put Bill and I on a track together on how to build our family life. All things had become new. As we grew together, we attended Christian seminars and conferences which enriched our lives and helped us make godly decisions and choices on a daily basis. As one speaker said, "God doesn't want us to try; He wants us to die." Choosing to die to selfishness was a giant step to moving forward in our marriage and family life. It enabled us to enjoy God's resurrection power on a daily basis.

One book we read said marriage is like a triangle with the husband and wife on the lower two points and God at the pinnacle. The closer the couple moves toward God, the closer they grow to each other. We have found that to be a true principle, one that really works.

Within two years of accepting Christ and spending rich time in Bible Study Fellowship and other studies, I was asked to teach the Bible. What an unexpected honor. From the beginning, I knew this was a calling on my life and I have now been teaching the Bible for over 45 years. God has used me to mentor and disciple young women as well. It is truly a joy to my heart to see others transformed by the power of God.

God is in the business of restoring relationships as He did when my father was in his demise with cancer. He drew us together. I remember so well the day that we shared our favorite verses with one another, his being John 5:24, *"I tell you the truth, whoever hears my word and believes him who sent me has eternal life and will not be condemned; he has crossed over from death to life."* Our hearts were knit together around this verse since he was so pleased that I, too, had made the decision to follow Christ.

God later blessed Bill and me with a late in life son, Mike, who brought much joy to our lives as we raised him, and now, as he raises his own children. When Bill and I had first become Christians, we had attended a week long, life changing, Bill Gothard seminar where we had learned many principles for living our new life in Christ. When Mike was a teenager, we wanted him to share in that experience, so we took him to one of Gothard's seminars. Expecting him to come away filled with the same awe and excitement we had experienced, we were momentarily taken aback when his response was, "Well, I didn't really learn anything new. It's all what you have taught me as you've raised me." At first I was disappointed until I realized the weight of his words. They were testimony to the goodness of God and how far He had brought us and our family. I realized that, of course, Mike would not have the same response we did. Our family had been living these principles of forgiveness, self worth, making appeals, walking in freedom and a good conscience, and choosing good friends for years. Not perfectly, of course, but with God's help. Praise God! Mike had already absorbed these into his own belief system.

When my mother had Alzheimer's, that was another opportunity for me to see the Lord at work. I had decided I would look for Him at every turn. I couldn't imagine either of us going through that ordeal without Him. God even nudged me to write a book on that experience called, "Mother Has Alzheimer's," Hope in the Midst of Loss.

When Bill suffered a stroke and later cancer, it was again God who met us at every turn. He is the one who gave us the grace, the endurance, and finally healing in both cases. His amazing power continues to work in our lives.

Today, almost everyone in our family has accepted Jesus as Lord. Only one is too young yet, but I have no doubt Mike and his wife, Katie, will bring their daughter to the Lord and teach her the same principles throughout her life. She is only three at this writing. What peace and joy that thought brings me. We were thrilled the day Mike called to tell us her older brother, Jacob, had invited Jesus into his heart. III John 1:4, *"I have no greater joy than this, to hear of my children walking in the truth."*

I can look back on my life and see God's hand at every juncture. He revealed to me the futility of life apart from Him and gave me a yearning for something more. He wouldn't let me be satisfied until I found Him, even though it was He who was pursuing me all along. Then, He took my brokenness and exchanged it for His forgiveness and love and began to build fruit into my life. If someone had told me when I was a shy, sad, lonely, wreck of a teenager that I would one day have children and grandchildren devoted to the Lord, teach women the Bible, write several books and do public speaking, I never would have believed it. But God had a plan all along. All glory to Him. My decision to follow Christ set me on a wonderful journey with God, one of peace, love and hope. I am so thankful that I know Jesus and that He not only knows me but can use me for His glory.

So, join me as you read the rest of this book and see how God has given me opportunities over the years to share with others His awesome goodness.

CHAPTER 3
THE BABYSITTER

Janet was the first person I had the privilege to bring to the Lord. A pretty blue eyed, brown haired, vivacious teenager, she was our daughters' favorite babysitter. Our girls were always excited when Bill and I went out because they knew that meant lots of fun with Janet. Always a warm smile on her face, she loved playing games and entertaining them. Definitely a hands-on babysitter, really a perfect companion for the girls on the occasions when we were away. Beyond playing, she also made sure the house was neat and the dishes washed before we arrived home. No wonder we all loved her.

Janet grew up in a Catholic family and we could tell she had been brought up well. Her manners were well taught and her social skills were a delight. She was a people person. With a gentle spirit and a soft heart, God had already prepared her to know Him before she arrived in our lives.

One week, while Bill and I attended a Bill Gothard Seminar every evening, Janet watched our children. Each night we came home with lots of new knowledge to share with anyone who would listen. Being new Christians, we were excited to learn more about God. The week long seminar was feeding us with much new information including principles on forgiveness, having a clear conscience, raising children and so much more.

At the end of the week, we were full to overflowing with all we had gleaned from the conference. With Janet right there in our home when we returned, we just had to share with her some of what we had learned. Her focused attention revealed that she was interested as she attentively listened. From comments she made, we soon realized that, although she attended church, she had not yet received Jesus as her personal Lord and Savior. We explained the gospel message to her and felt prompted to invite her to accept Christ into her life. With a sparkle in her eyes, she broke into a broad smile. God had prepared her heart and we were thrilled when she enthusiastically agreed that she would like to have a personal relationship with Jesus. We held hands as we bowed our heads and led her in prayer. Now, Janet was not only our favorite babysitter, but that evening, she became a sister in Christ.

Bill and I were ecstatic and thankful that our first experience sharing Christ wasn't with a scoffer or critic but that God had led us to someone with whom we already had a sweet relationship. I think friendship evangelism is really the best kind. Janet was comfortable with us and our testimony seemed like a natural step to take in the warm relationship we already had. She trusted us, and of course, we trusted her as well. Bill and I ended that night praising God and thanking Him for the wonder and power of His Son, Jesus, and how He brings people together for His purposes.

CHAPTER 4

A CALL TO MY NEIGHBORHOOD

Around this same time, a friend, Bev, and I decided to hold a neighborhood Bible study on raising children. There were a number of young married couples in our area and we thought it would be fun to get to know some of the wives better, hopefully on a spiritual level. Many of us had already formed relationships through our local pool. In California, many neighborhoods have a common swimming pool, a great way to meet people and form friendships.

I had met Bev previously through a neighborhood get together. Walking into that gathering, having recently moved to California and accepted the Lord, myself, I hadn't known many people. Interestingly, I recall that when I first saw her, I knew instantly that she was a Christian, a kindred spirit in Christ. I guess God must have somehow revealed that to me. Bev and I developed a friendship and soon realized that we shared a passion for God's Word and an interest in teaching others. We were both also involved in Bible Study Fellowship, an international Bible study, where I gained much of my early knowledge as a Christ follower. As we discussed our mutual love for the Word one afternoon at the pool, we agreed that it would be fun to reach out to the ladies in our neighborhood. Perhaps some of them would enjoy a Bible study. We saw it as an opportunity to share our love for God's Word and show them how it can be applied to our everyday lives.

We knew the study would have to be something low key with minimal homework because we didn't know the commitment level of many of our neighbor women. After some discussion, we put together a six week class on the topic of raising children. That seemed like a pertinent subject as all of the women were about our age and had school age children in their homes. It also seemed like a non-threatening topic to use to introduce the women to the Bible. Most women, we decided, are happy for the opportunity to talk about their children and to glean wisdom from one another. After sending out invitations inviting about fifteen ladies, we found a neighbor who was willing to host the group in her home.

When the women arrived for the first meeting, they seemed enthusiastic for the chance to get to know one another and to study child rearing. Bev and I took turns leading the group each week. Discussion came easily as interest was high and everyone was eager to improve their parenting skills. During the study, we shared Christian principles along with appropriate Bible verses. Overall, we felt the class went well.

Near the end of the study, Bev and I had agreed we wanted to give the ladies an opportunity to accept Christ. Even though a little nervous, not knowing how it would be received, we shared the gospel message. We had prayed that God would touch their hearts and that they would see the value of knowing Jesus on a personal level. We also felt sure it was God who had led us to give them an invitation to receive Him. I had not realized how vulnerable I would feel putting my faith out there with people I saw every day, people I didn't know well yet. Of course, we hoped the ladies would be excited and come running into Jesus' arms. But, alas, there was no response. They just sat there politely and said nothing. Yes, they had enjoyed talking about child rearing but the fire of the gospel had not led them to salvation.

Although disappointed, Bev and I chose not to let their lack of response steal our joy. By faith, we decided to continue with another study. Maybe God was still at work in their hearts. We talked about what topic would be of interest and decided on one that discussed women's emotions, another non-threatening subject. As that class formed, we had lost a few of the ladies we had hoped to reach in the first class. This time, however, I knew all the ladies, but there was one in particular whose salvation we were unsure about. Patty had come to the study on raising children and was eager to continue studying the Bible. She had never attended a study before so everything was new to her and she seemed especially responsive to our lessons. Each week she came prepared with answers and entered enthusiastically into the discussion.

At the end of that class, we decided to once again offer an opportunity to anyone who would like to accept Christ. Holding our breath, we waited to see if anyone would respond. This time, we were delighted when Patty indicated that she would like to do that. Our excitement was palpable but we tried not to go overboard and scare her. After the other women made their way out, we talked with Patty and explained what it means to invite Jesus to be Lord. Her broad smile revealed she was ready to make the commitment. With great zeal, we prayed with her and welcomed her to the Kingdom of God.

It was so special for us to know that God was at work. I was reminded of the story of Jesus when He went after the one lost sheep. He cares about each one of us and loves us passionately. I can still imagine the angels rejoicing in heaven over Patty as she received His invitation to eternal life. Luke 15:10 puts it well. *"In the same way, I tell you, there is joy in the presence of the angels of God over one sinner who repents."*

As a follow up, I invited Patty to begin attending Bible Study Fellowship with me. She eagerly agreed to go after which I was blessed to watch her faith grow as she matured in Christ.

Bev and I had planted many seeds in our first study. Most fell by the wayside but praise God, one seed fell on good soil, began to grow and is still firmly rooted. Patty heard the word and it became a part of her life. Luke 8:15, *"But the seed in the good soil, these are the ones who have heard the word in an honest and good heart, and hold it fast, and bear fruit with perseverance."*

Some years later, after we moved away from Walnut Creek, I had an opportunity to return and visit old friends. As I inquired about Patty, I was delighted to hear that she had not only continued in faith but had become a Bible study teacher herself. Once again, I was rejoicing at the goodness of God. He cares deeply about people and has a plan for each one of us. At our little neighborhood study, He had snatched Patty out of darkness into His wonderful light and had started her on a path of purpose as He unfolded His plan for her life. What a thrill to have been a part of her salvation and to see where He had taken her.

CHAPTER 5

LIFE CHANGING PHONE CONVERSATION

When we lived in Northern California, we attended a mega-church of three thousand people. Because of the large size, we divided ourselves into couples groups by age. Bill and I were in charge of about a hundred young adult couples plus a constant flow of new people. Several times each year we met together as one big group, but for our monthly meetings, we divided into smaller groups of about twenty people and met in homes. My job entailed calling the new people and placing them in one of our small groups.

I enjoyed this task as it gave me the opportunity to get to know newcomers and help them to integrate into the life of the church. Because of the popularity of our church, however, not everyone who attended started out as a believer.

One of my phone calls was to a lady named Ann. A friendly conversation developed and she indicated she and her husband would be interested in joining a group. As we talked, it became clear to me that Ann had not yet invited Jesus into her life. However, I began to sense that she was open to talking about God so I watched for an opportunity. The opening came, and I was able to tell her about God's love for her and how Jesus had paid the penalty for her sins. I explained how she could invite Jesus into her life as her personal Lord and Savior.

Sometimes the Holy Spirit nudges me to speak on an impulse. No preplanning occurs, the opportunity just arises. This happened in my conversation with Ann. When I am sharing Christ with someone, I try to be sensitive to the Holy Spirit's leading in what I say. It is also important for me to be sensitive to the person's response. Some people are immediately ready to accept Jesus while others need some time to think it over and still others may show no interest at all. In Ann's case, I felt the thought of a personal relationship with God was so new to her that she needed time to process the idea. It seemed prudent to allow God to work in her heart for a bit, to take time for her to ponder our discussion. I knew I would be calling her again about the next couple's meeting so decided I would wait until then to approach the subject again. When the soil of her heart was ready, I felt she would embrace the Lord. God is a gentleman and more interested in a sincere commitment than in a shallow rushed decision that eventually drifts away.

Intrigued, Ann did agree to think about our conversation. Several weeks passed before I had another opportunity to call her about an upcoming meeting. This time, during the conversation, I asked, "Ann, I was wondering if you have considered the things we talked about in our last conversation. Have you made any decision yet about the Lord?" I was not expecting her enthusiastic response.

"Have I ever!" she exclaimed. "Yes, Betsy, I invited Him into my life that very night. What a difference that decision has made! I was so excited that I told my husband and he also invited Christ into his life. Then, we told the children and they did the same. Since then, we have told several other relatives and they have all made commitments to the Lord too."

Overwhelmed by her enthusiasm, I expressed my own joy to her. All this from one conversation! Just one phone connection with Ann and the Holy Spirit had used it to bring her and several generations of her family to salvation. God's timing was perfect. What could be more exciting than this?

"Ann," I said, "I have to meet you. Can you come for lunch next week?"

Over lunch, we shared more about the Lord. As time went by, Ann continued in faith, got involved in Bible study, and eventually grew into a strong Christian woman.

It was such a blessing that God had allowed me to be a part of this joyful experience. Some years prior, I had learned how to share a simple gospel message with people, so I was glad God had prepared me in advance for my appointment with Ann.

I believe God has opportunities and experiences planned for every believer. In II Corinthians 5:18-20, we are all called to be "Ambassadors for Christ," and "Ministers of Reconciliation". *"Now all these things are from God, who reconciled us to Himself through Christ and gave us the ministry of reconciliation, namely, that God was in Christ reconciling the world to Himself, not counting their trespasses against them, and He has committed to us the word of reconciliation. Therefore, we are ambassadors for Christ, as though God were making an appeal through us; we beg you on behalf of Christ, be reconciled to God."*

An ambassador is a person sent by one sovereign state to another to be a representative of the sending state. They are appointed and sent for the purpose of negotiating treaties. Reconciliation means to win over or restore. As Christians, we are sent from God's Kingdom to be representatives of His kingdom here on earth. Our task is to reconcile people to God, to speak words toward spiritual restoration. It is a Holy Calling and privilege to share God's Kingdom with hungry souls. Unlike earthly kingdoms, where the ambassador travels by himself to a foreign country, our King actually travels with us. That is why, with one simple nudge from the Holy

Spirit, Ann and her family entered God's eternal kingdom. I was simply the vessel God used to bring His message of reconciliation.

To me, God-given opportunities are exhilarating and fulfilling. It's all a matter of expecting God to involve us in His work, watching for opportunities, and allowing the boldness of the Holy Spirit to shine forth. As you can see, this was such a simple witness. It was not planned or contrived. It just happened. Ann's heart was ready to receive, and apparently, so were her family members.

Similar to fear, an area that keeps us from sharing our faith is lack of boldness. Sometimes, it is scary to step out and talk about Jesus and we become timid. For me, it is vitally important to first hear from God, to know that He is prompting me to share my faith. Then, it is essential that I call on the boldness of the Holy Spirit to prompt me to say something. In Acts1:8, there is a clear promise, *"But you will receive power when the Holy Spirit has come upon you; and you shall be My witnesses both in Jerusalem, and in all Judea and Samaria, and even to the remotest part of the earth."* As Christians, we have the Holy Spirit. We are promised that His power is in us and at our disposal to boldly witness. Not only that, but God has also given us the authority to witness. Matthew 28:18, *"Then Jesus came to them and said, 'All authority in heaven and on earth has been given to me. Therefore go and make disciples of all nations, baptizing them in the name of the Father and of the Son and of the Holy Spirit....'"*

If Jesus has all authority and He lives in me, then the authority to witness has been granted and on the basis of that authority, I can be bold. II Corinthians 13:10, *"For this reason I am writing these things...in accordance with the authority which the Lord gave me for building up and not for tearing down."*

Sharing our faith is a matter of being filled with the Holy Spirit. We need only ask, and by faith, He will fill us. Notice the first thing these believers did once they were filled? Acts 4:31 says, *"And when they had prayed, the place where they had gathered together was shaken, and they were all filled with the Holy Spirit and began to speak the word of*

God with boldness." Notice, they *"...began to speak the word of God with boldness."* They had the power and now they had the boldness and authority. They simply had to appropriate these, step out in faith, and open their mouths.

Even knowing that, it is still easy to say that we don't feel adequate to witness to others. We are very aware of our own inadequacy in this area. But the Bible also recognizes that dilemma when it says in II Corinthians 3:5, *"Not that we are adequate in ourselves to consider anything as coming from ourselves, but our adequacy is from God."* We can be assured that God is fully aware that we are not adequate in ourselves to witness in a life giving way. We need Him to help us. Sharing Christ in the power of the Holy Spirit is not about our ability. Paul tells us in II Corinthians 9:8, *"And God is able to make all grace abound to you, so that always having all sufficiency in everything, you may have an abundance for every good deed."* Not just enough, but an abundance, an abundance of everything we need to witness the gospel of Jesus Christ.

The people in the New Testament were just like you and me. We can have the same power and boldness in our lives through the Holy Spirit that they had in theirs. It is just a matter of appropriating the gift. Every Christian has most likely felt some measure of anxiety or fear at the thought of sharing their faith. We all want to be liked and accepted. When fear strikes, we have to ask, "What is the source and why is it there?" If we are trying to witness in our own strength, then fear is natural. Fear is a voice trying to hinder us from God's assignment. Notice the promise in II Corinthians 9:8 again. It is clear that God's grace, strength and sufficiency are readily available for witnessing. So, we must ask, "What voice am I listening to? God or fear?"

One of the things that fear often accomplishes is that we become mute. I have heard people say, "I don't witness verbally. I just want them to see Christ through the way I live." While that is a noble thought, if that were everyone's attitude, then I wonder what the outcome would be. Would anyone ever really know that Christ died for them and offers forgiveness for their sins and eternal life? Can a person figure that core aspect out just by watching someone's life?

While it is vital to live a godly life, I don't see a biblical precedent for the theological view of stopping with that. While we are called to live a life worthy of our calling (Eph. 4:1), that is not an end in itself. It is the proof that we are in a position to share that life verbally with others. When people shared Christ in the Bible, yes, they lived and promoted a godly lifestyle but they also boldly shared their faith verbally.

The disciples were sold out to God. They put their very lives on the line to declare the good news of Jesus Christ. When they were chastised for publicly proclaiming Christ, it didn't stop them. They bravely continued on with these famous words from Acts 4:19-20, *"But Peter and John answered and said to them, 'Whether it is right in the sight of God to give heed to you rather than to God, you be the judge; for we cannot stop speaking about what we have seen and heard.'"* Oh, that we could have the same mindset and be as bold as they were! I struggle with this too so don't feel you are alone.

Although, to me, my simple witness to Ann did not seem nearly as consequential as what the disciples faced, yet God used it to bring her and her extended family to salvation. What an amazing blessing and honor to be used as part of the process! What joy I felt knowing they had found the Savior. Would Ann and her family have come to Christ if I had said nothing? Probably not at that time but I imagine they would have heard the message if they continued attending our church. But think about it...who would have missed a blessing? The answer is...me.

Kingdom work demands that we educate ourselves in how to present a simple gospel message. Several helps are available in Appendix B of this book. May we each move forward courageously in the tasks God calls us to.

CHAPTER 6
A HARD DECISION

Janice was a friend I met through Bible study. Her red hair matched her fiery, sanguine personality. As an eager student of God's Word, she had a sincere desire to grow. But it wasn't long before I learned that she was dealing with a heavy sin issue in her life, one that was keeping her from a full and vital commitment to the Lord. Sin can sometimes put a person on a fence between two worlds and that was where Janice found herself. While she earnestly wanted to walk with God, she also honestly wanted to continue in an adulterous affair with a man she had met in her community. As she confided her secret to me over a cup of coffee one morning, I knew I would have to depend on the Lord to navigate this weighty issue. I didn't want to scare her away from Christianity so I knew an issue of this magnitude had to be dealt with carefully. Of course, the affair was secretive, as affairs usually are, but because of her new life in Christ, she was becoming more and more convicted by the Holy Spirit that she needed to abandon it.

I could tell she was really struggling. Her marriage was not altogether terrible but this new man seemed to be meeting her need for the thrill of adventure. There was an excitement that went with the anticipation of their clandestine meetings, an eagerness that had long ago died in her marriage. By comparison, her marriage seemed flat and boring.

While the draw to the affair was strong, her newfound enjoyment of God was beginning to vie for more attention. The more I shared with her about God's love and forgiveness, back and forth she went, at times wanting to do things God's way and allow her marriage to heal and, at other times, shifting away from God and into the arms of the other man.

During one of our meetings, I shared, "Janice, did you know that Romans 5:8 says, '*But God demonstrates His own love toward us, in that while we were yet sinners, Christ died for us?*'"

She needed to be reassured that God loved her even in the midst of her poor choices that He had not given up on her. "Janice, God still loves you with an everlasting love, a pure love. His arms are reaching out to you right now. He cares so much about you."

Sometimes, our meetings ended with new resolve as she desperately wanted to end the turmoil in her soul. Other times, she slipped back into old and now familiar patterns and again her life became one of emotional torture. All the while, I felt I needed to stay close to her and continue to gently encourage her to make the right decision. Life choices can be very difficult at times. I reminded her that even godly people in the Bible struggled, fell, suffered consequences, repented and made better decisions, ones that led to life and peace.

Affairs are one of Satan's interesting tools. Without any of life's real responsibilities to deal with and no accountability at all, they seem to engage people in a surreal existence. There is a certain excitement that accompanies a secret rendezvous. We have all heard that the grass always looks greener on the other side. I recently heard someone say that if the grass looks greener on the other side, maybe it is time to start watering your own grass.

Janice stayed on the fence for several months. "I just can't give him up, Betsy. I love him," she lamented. And in the next breath she would say, "I have to give him up. I know I do if I want to walk with God." Her inner torment was becoming intolerable.

It was a painful time, yet a time when the "Hound of Heaven" was unquestionably pursuing her. I am reminded of Luke 14:28, *"For which one of you, when he wants to build a tower, does not first sit down and calculate the cost to see if he has enough to complete it?"* Janice was at a point where she needed to count the cost. The cost of continuing the affair would be great probably ending in divorce and her children enduring much suffering. But there was also a cost to following Christ. She would be required to die to her flesh, to give up the very thing that had engaged her heart in a tight soul tie. Even though the affair was eating at her and would eventually destroy her, her marriage and her family, the pull was strong. That is what is so insidious about sin. Once emotionally entangled, without realizing it, people become en-trapped in a snare that is almost impossible to escape from. The anguish can be agonizing.

In the end, Janice decided she couldn't take the torment any longer. She knew in her heart what she had to do. She gave the dangerous relationship up cold turkey. At that point, I led her in a prayer of confession and repentance. God, of course, already knew of her sin, but I wanted her to enjoy the fruit of confession. I John 1:9 says, *"If we confess our sins, He is faithful and righteous to forgive us our sins and to cleanse us from all unrighteousness."* It was a time of cleansing for Janice where she experienced the knowledge that God had instantly forgiven her. There was such freedom in that awareness.

Psalm 124:7 started to become a reality in her life. *"Our soul has escaped as a bird out of the snare of the trapper; The snare is broken and we have escaped."*

Now, the test would come. Going forward would not be easy. You don't just turn off your emotions, especially when you have invested so much of yourself in another person. Would she be able to stand strong? Was she truly repentant? The Bible says in Acts 26:20, *"... even to the Gentiles, that they should repent and turn to God, performing deeds appropriate to repentance."* Could she really change? This would mean that she would not only have to give up the affair but that she would need to begin working on her marriage and at the same time tend to her relationship with the Lord. Janice came to understand that godly repentance is not just being sorry you were caught. With Christ's help, true repentance leads to a change of heart that ends with an abundant life. In II Corinthians 7:10, she learned, *"For the sorrow that is according to the will of God produces a repentance without regret, leading to salvation, but the sorrow of the world produces death."*

I had honestly thought Janice would vacillate in the weeks ahead but she stood firm in her decision. Because her mind was made up, she began to sense the power of the Holy Spirit guiding her each day, each moment, as she moved out of darkness into the light. She confessed her sin to her husband and together they began to restore their marriage. Thankfully, he forgave her and their marriage was saved. She also made a decision to stop playing games with God and made a firm commitment to allow Him to be Lord of her life. She spent time with Him each day and rebuilt that relationship as well.

I mentored Janice for several more months, but being in different churches, our relationship eventually drifted. I felt she would be in good hands in her church with other mature Christian women to disciple her.

Several years passed. Janice and her family were preparing to move out of our area. Her marriage was doing well, and in hindsight, she was so thankful she had counted the cost and made the choice to stay with her husband. With a move pending, she decided to give herself a going away party. Happily, she invited me to come. Of course, I was delighted with the invitation, and since I had not seen her in a few years, I was also interested to see how she was doing in her walk with God.

I was not prepared for what happened at the party. That day, she welcomed me into her home. All of the other guests were already there. As she ushered me into her living room, she looked at me with a sweet smile on her face, then with a sweep of her hand across the whole room, she announced to me, "Betsy, I'd like you to meet your grandchildren."

I was puzzled. "What do you mean by that, Janice? I don't understand."

"Well," she continued, "I have walked the straight and narrow with the Lord ever since the time we used to meet. Over the years, I have had the privilege of sharing Christ with a number of women in my community. Here, today, are the women who have made the decision to follow Jesus. So, Betsy, these are your grandchildren."

I was speechless. My eyes welled up with tears of joy. There were over twenty women in that room, women who had come to the Lord as a result of Janice's obedience. When I had met with Janice in her early Christian days, I had not known that God would give her a gift of evangelism but there before my eyes was the fruit of her ministry.

We never know how God will use the people we bring to His throne of grace, but we can know that being faithful to help them make the hard choices to follow His lead has the potential to bring great reward. God wants to bless us exceedingly, abundantly more than we can ask or think.

God had amazing plans for Janice's life before she ever allowed Him to be Lord of her life. He had already planned for her to be an evangelist bringing many people to the Lord. I can't help but think that Satan also knew the plan and was doing everything he could to thwart God's plan. Tempting Janice with an affair, if it had not been stopped, would have made her miss the sheer joy of walking with Christ and leading other women to the Lord. Just the thought of that makes me shudder.

I have no doubt that Janice is continuing to follow the Lord in her new location. I am so thankful God allowed me to help guide her to the Lordship of Christ. She was truly a gift from God to me and I love that God allows us to have grandchildren, both by birth and through His Spirit by rebirth!

CHAPTER 7
HIGHWAY TROUBLE

It was a holiday weekend and, after a pleasant time away, we were traveling back to our home in California. Barreling down Interstate 5, on a curvy and hilly section, our Volkswagen van was straining to keep up with the eighty mile per hour traffic. A common, but troublesome, malady sometimes occurs with VW's under these conditions and that day, it happened to us. We sucked a valve. Now, I have no idea what it means to suck a valve but that is what Bill immediately knew had happened. Over a hundred miles from home, a holiday weekend, and now a locked engine. With power lost, the van slowly crawled to the side of the road. Once on the shoulder of the interstate, it gradually came to a full stand-still.

Turning the key several times, with no hint of restarting, we quickly determined that the engine was dead and we were going nowhere. It was a helpless feeling especially since cell phones had not yet been invented. There we sat in our car on the shoulder of a very busy highway hoping that help would come soon.

With literally thousands of cars speeding past us at eighty miles an hour, the draft we felt was unsettling. Every time a car passed in the lane next to us, the van shivered and rocked from the wind.

That was not counting the trucks which really jolted us. Although we weren't frightened, we were keenly aware we needed help.

For the first fifteen minutes, we sat and watched the cars go by, hoping a police car might spot us. With the rapid flow of traffic and no sight of police, we soon realized it might be a long wait. Not a great way to end a vacation.

Then Bill and I both had the same thought... to use this time to thank God and sing praise songs. That is not always our first thought so we recognized God was somehow leading us. Bill had brought his guitar along, so we and our girls began to sing choruses and give thanks. One thing we have learned is that it is impossible to be discouraged and upset when you choose thankfulness and praise in any given situation. Sometimes, circumstances make our lives uncomfortable and we tend to easily give in to complaining and grumbling but irritation and thanks just don't go together. I am certainly not always quick to practice a thankful attitude, but this time, we all made the choice together. It was a joyful experience to sing to the Lord but... about two hours later, with no end in sight for our dilemma, we had sung every song we could think of. Even though we continued to pray for help to come, not one car had come to our aid. We were beginning to feel trapped. What should we do now?

We decided to stop and pray once again, only this time we specifically asked God if He would send someone by six o'clock. It was after five and we sure didn't want to be stuck along the road when night came and darkness fell. Time seemed to drag along after that as we chatted and tried to keep a positive attitude. How much longer would we have to wait? Our girls had done incredibly well staying still in the car but even I was beginning to feel a little restless. Tired and hungry, we just wanted to go home. Watching the clock, as the time slowly ticked toward six o'clock, seemed to drag out every minute. Five minutes till six, four, three, two, then one. Every minute seemed to last an hour.

Then, amazingly, at exactly six o'clock, a highway patrol car pulled over and asked if we could use some assistance. After explaining our difficulty, he used his radio to try to contact help for us, but unfortunately, without success. Being a holiday, he explained, it might take some time but he would try to find someone to come for us when he exited the road up ahead.

Wasn't that an interesting answer to prayer? A measure of excitement and even refreshment came upon us as we contemplated how God had answered our prayer exactly as we had prayed, right to the minute, six o'clock. Now, it would seem that He must be up to something more than just a tow truck.

After waiting another hour, a tow truck finally arrived. We were grateful that the patrolman, who had promised to get us help, had been faithful to his word. In short order, our van was attached and our weary, but content, family climbed aboard ready for the two hour trip home. While we thought that the arrival of the tow truck was the big story, this turned out to be the beginning of what God had in mind.

Our driver was a young man, and as we sped along the highway, he began, although unsolicited, to pour out his life story telling us of his many heartaches and disappointments. As we listened to the tangled mess of his life and marriage, we realized the circumstances involved in our meeting were no accident. God was at work. Without our van stalling, we wouldn't have had the opportunity to meet this man who desperately needed someone to talk to. We quickly realized this was a divine appointment.

When he finished his woeful tale, we told him about the love Jesus had for him and how, if given a chance, God could help untangle the muddled web of his life. We shared with him that God had a plan for his life and could be trusted to help restore the damaged relationships. We let him know of God's interest in healing the wounds of his heart. As we traveled down the road together, we were able to speak many words of life to this man's desperate, shattered soul.

Arriving at our destination, we thanked our new friend for the tow and said our good-byes. While he did not make a decision for Christ that evening, we knew God had given him a glimpse of hope and an opportunity to turn his life around. We felt we had accomplished what the Lord asked us to do. We were a cog in the wheel of his life, sent to bring an important message. Perhaps, the next person or the next after that will bring him into God's Kingdom. Our part was to simply be faithful to plant some seeds.

Our circumstance on the road turned out to be an opportunity to listen for God's voice and to co-operate with His plan. Because we heeded God's prodding to thank Him and sing when we first realized we had car trouble, we were in a mindset to flow with God's plan. If we had become disgruntled and angry over our own inconvenient circumstance, I wonder if we would have been in the right state of mind to have ministered to this man's apparent need.

An interesting scripture comes to mind. Romans 8:6 says, *"For the mind set on the flesh is death, but the mind set on the Spirit is life and peace."* As I have thought about what that means, I noticed the verse uses the words "mind set" twice. For practical purposes, to me, that means that I can do a spot check on my mind at any time to see what it is set upon. If I am disgruntled, angry, unthankful or any of the negative traits listed in Galatians 5:19-21, I can immediately know that I am responding in the flesh. The result will be death, which is shutting down to the things of God.

Often when problems or difficulties come into our lives, the first thing we want to do is deny them or get angry. If something is uncomfortable, we think, how could God have allowed this? Inconvenient interruptions, in truth, are really a normal part of life. But since comfort and convenience are considered an American entitlement, we have been brainwashed into thinking we deserve them.

On the other hand, if my mind is focused on the Lord and thereby on positive things such as being thankful, choosing joy, patience, kindness, and other fruit of the Spirit mentioned in Galatians 5:22-23, then the results are life and peace. While the flesh shuts us down, the Spirit expands and stretches us into God's plan.

Surely, being in a stalled car was minor compared with some of life's more serious difficulties, but we can remember that troublesome circumstances provide an opportunity to be led by the Spirit, to hear God's voice. And isn't that how we grow in our walk with the Lord?

It wasn't an accident that we were in that particular tow truck. We all agreed it was God's appointment, a result of hearing God's voice and responding in the Spirit. The result was an opportunity to share life and peace with a struggling soul. In a sense, we cried out for help with our stalled car and God led us to a man who was crying out for help with a stalled life.

I have learned from James 1:2 that when I consider my trials with joy, I can know that the test is producing the valuable quality of endurance in my life. The blessing of the opportunity to share Christ with the young man outweighed the tiresome wait and the $1600 bill for the tow and the motor rebuild.

CHAPTER 8

ANOTHER TOW TRUCK

Unfortunately, this was not the only incident where we needed tow truck service in our travels. One night, after we had moved to Michigan, our son, Mike and I had been shopping in Kalamazoo which was about an hour from our home. As we traveled down the highway toward home, I noticed the charge battery light had come on. Pulling into a gas station, I retrieved the car manual from the glove box and read that it sometimes comes on if a certain belt in the engine breaks. Lifting the hood of the car, I inspected what looked like the belt in question and it appeared to be fine. Unbeknownst to me, I had looked at the wrong belt.

We decided to drive on. Continuing our journey, we prayed and trusted God to get us home safely. Though it was dark out now and the only light came from cars passing on the other side of the highway, I felt at peace and sensed the Lord had a plan. *"Don't fret, Betsy; I have everything under control,"* He seemed to whisper to me.

Driving on a long, unpopulated section of the highway, the car suddenly began to sputter. Within seconds, the motor died and the car gradually decreased in speed as we coasted to a stop on the shoulder of the road. Interestingly, I felt God was with us in our predicament as Mike and I quietly prayed for help. We were in God's hands and trusted He would somehow come to our rescue.

I admit, though, that I did have a twinge of trepidation being a woman alone with a child, stalled on a highway at night. As I tried to focus up and down the dark, desolate stretch of road we were parked on, I imagined we would be sitting there for some time as we had in California. Only this time, it was night and a very dark one at that. Time to hunker down and continue to pray for help to arrive in a timely manner.

Peering out into the darkness, we saw no houses, buildings, or phones and cell phones had not yet been invented. We were truly in the middle of nowhere on a pitch black night, and seemingly, all alone. What should we do?

Shortly after we stopped, I turned around and squinted into the darkness behind our car and onto the other side of the highway. Something was out there. What was I seeing? At first, I couldn't tell for sure but then, to my amazement, it looked like it was a tow truck parked about a hundred feet up the road. Absorbed in their work, I could see from their headlights and flashlights that two men were busily attaching a car to the truck. With possible help so close, Mike and I bolted out of our car. This could be our only chance to get a tow. It seemed too much of a coincidence that a tow truck "just happened" to be sitting along the highway at the very time and in the very place we needed assistance. I had to be sure we caught them before they headed off into the night.

After waiting a minute for an opening in the traffic, we darted across the highway and ran along the shadowy shoulder, only lit momentarily by passing cars. We reached the tow truck just before they were about to leave. I am sure they were taken off guard to have an out of breath woman and child suddenly appear out of no-where. Panting for breath, I explained that our car was stalled and we, too, could use a lift. Having noticed the other car was already hooked to the tow, I thought perhaps the driver would be willing to come back later and pick us up.

I noticed the man whose car was about to be towed was listening intently to our conversation. Before we had even caught our breath, he turned to the driver and suggested that we be towed first, that he didn't mind waiting. Surprised by his generosity, we marveled at how incredibly kind it was of him to forfeit his tow and defer to us, especially when his car was ready to go. When he heard how far away we lived, he still insisted that we take my car first. He even decided to ride with us to keep the driver company on the return trip. I was amazed by his gracious attitude.

After detaching his car, we all headed over to my car which was then attached to the tow truck. We climbed into our seats in the truck and were on our way. Although, at first, I felt a bit apprehensive getting into a truck with two men who were strangers to us, I decided that it would probably be ok, that clearly God had put the tow truck in our path. It was too much to just be happenstance.

As we traveled toward Sturgis, we quickly became absorbed in animated discussion. The driver was a talker and was glad to have company on this journey. It was clear he was a people person. Unlike our last towing experience, this driver enjoyed talking about world affairs and social issues rather than his personal problems. Soon, he turned the conversation to the topic of drug use in the United States. I asked the Lord what I should say regarding this subject and a question came to mind, so I proceeded. "How do you think the drug problem can be solved?" I asked. For ten minutes he explained every solution he could think of concerning drugs, everything from better education to "just saying no".

Having exhausted his opinions, he quieted, waiting for my response. I paused, and then offered my thoughts, "Those are all good ideas, but may I share with you another answer?" He was all ears. I could tell he was stymied and couldn't imagine what further solution existed. Certainly, he had exhausted all viable options.

I knew this was an opportunity from God so I plunged in with a different perspective. "When people choose to turn their back on God," I said, "they open themselves to many things. It seems to me that the drug problem has its roots in a spiritual issue." I could tell his interest was piqued so I continued. "Perhaps, you have noticed that at the same time there has been a rise in drug use, people also seem to be moving away from God. People are frustrated with their lives. They don't have answers for issues they are facing so some turn to drugs. Could it be that the answer to moving away from drugs lies in coming into a personal relationship with Jesus Christ? Maybe, if people had something higher and more meaningful in their lives, using drugs would become a less satisfactory option."

I went on to explain a simple gospel message to him of how a person can come to Christ, have their sins forgiven and enter into a personal love relationship with God. "Once a person has Christ in their life, He can guide them to better, more productive choices."

"Interesting perspective," he said, "one I hadn't considered." His tone softened as he explained, "You know, I was raised in a church, but I haven't gone in years. When I was young, I gave my life to Jesus. I guess I am not a very good Christian."

I reassured him that wherever he was in his life, God still loved him and would gladly welcome him back anytime he chose to renew his relationship with Him. "God wants to have a close, personal relationship with you," I explained.

Arriving at our destination, I could tell he was seriously thinking about our conversation. As we waved good-bye, I pondered my awareness that God had set up this whole scenario. He had given me peace in the situation with my car so that I could lay aside anxiety about my dilemma in time to remind a stray sheep that his Father loved him and had a better plan for his life. For the first time in years, this tow truck driver had just received a fresh awareness of

God's presence and love. Although the man who was also a passenger didn't contribute much to the conversation, I suspect he was also thinking about what had been spoken in his presence.

Some of the most gratifying experiences in life are when I am aware that God is setting up a situation and even revealing what I am to say. Witnessing is like being on God's turf, His territory, knowing that He is moving in a person's heart to draw them closer to Him. It reminds me of Henry Blackaby's words from his book, "Experiencing God," that we are to "watch for where God is at work and join Him." I am convinced that God was at work in the lives of two men I met in the shadows one dark night, a tow truck driver and his passenger. I was glad for the opportunity to join Him.

While the tow truck driver was open and receptive to conversation about God, sometimes people aren't so eager. In the next story, you will see the difference between scoffers, skeptics, and seekers.

CHAPTER 9

THE TYPIST

I had finished the manuscript for my first book and was ready to hire a typist. This was before computers and I didn't trust I could do a perfect job of typing on my own. Maybe some of you recall the frustration of using "white out" to make corrections. The manuscript was a Bible study for women called, *"I'm a Woman, I Have Needs,"* but was never actually published.

Having prayed about whom to use for the typing job, I looked through the phone book under secretarial help. I came across a woman who only typed manuscripts. Sensing this was the one God wanted to type my work, I made arrangements to drop it off at her home.

When I met Glenna, I immediately liked her. She was warm and friendly, accepting and interested in my work. After talking with her and agreeing on a price for her labor, I felt confident she would do a good job. I also sensed that God was up to something that was more than a typing job. When I arrived back home, I felt led to pray for her. Considering that Glenna may not be a believer yet, I asked God to touch her heart and to draw her to Jesus as she read my manuscript.

After a few weeks, Glenna called to let me know my book was ready to be picked up. On the phone she expressed how much she had enjoyed reading it. From the tone of her voice, I noted that she had a soft heart, open to spiritual truth. Before heading to her house, I prayed that God would give me an opening to share Christ with her. An eager expectation rose up in my heart that an opportunity would indeed be forthcoming. God reminded me of I Peter 3:15, "... *Always be prepared to give an answer to everyone who asks you to give the reason for the hope that you have. But do this with gentleness and respect,*" (NIV).

For years, I thought I was supposed to work all conversations around to spiritual things. I felt compelled to share my faith with non-Christians whether they wanted to hear it or not. Needless to say, I was frustrated and on edge much of the time. This philosophy also interfered with my ability to love and accept people. I recall a book I read about a man who made a commitment to share Jesus with at least one person every day. One night as he prepared for bed, he remembered he had not shared Christ with anyone that day. So, he dressed and went out to find someone. Because of his obsession, his family suffered and often felt neglected as he seemed to put his ministry ahead of them. I have to wonder if that commission was really from God or was it a "law" he had put on himself.

When I felt under compulsion to constantly share Christ, it made me a nervous wreck. Then one day, I poured out my anxiety to a dear friend, Pat Churchill. She looked me in the eye with great compassion and said, "You mean you have been carrying that kind of burden around all these years? Oh, honey, that's not how God wants it to be."

Through prayer, she proceeded to help me lift this great load from my heart. That day, I gained a new freedom in the area of witnessing. I realized from I Corinthians 3:5 that it is God who gives people opportunities to believe, not me. "*What then is Apollos? And what is Paul? Servants through whom you believed, even as the Lord gave opportunity to each one."*

From verses six and seven, I learned that God may use one person to sow His seed, to share the basic message, and another to water or expound on the message, but it is God who causes the growth. I Corinthians 3:6-7 *"I planted, Apollos watered, but God was causing the growth. So then neither the one who plants nor the one who waters is anything, but God who causes the growth."* It was so freeing to know that I'm not responsible for anyone coming into the Kingdom of God. God is solely responsible for those accepting Him. My responsibility was to be available if He decided to use me as a vessel for His message and to be prepared with an answer to anyone who showed interest. Of course, this required me to be sensitive to His voice, to listen for when He prompted me to speak and also to when He said, *"Not now."*

We know from the Gospel of John that Jesus did nothing of His own initiative but only what He saw or heard the Father doing. Five times, He declared that He only spoke or did what the Father initiated, (Jn. 5:30, 8:28, 8:42, 12:49, and 14:10). My favorite is John 12:49, *"For I did not speak on My own initiative, but the Father Himself who sent Me has given Me a commandment as to what to say and what to speak."*

Nowhere in Scripture do I find anyone forcing the message of Christ on another person. In fact, as I look at Christ's life, the norm for Him was for people to come to Him seeking what He had to say, especially after He had given a public message. They saw peace, strength and character in Him and were also attracted by His words. They saw a life that stood for truth and righteousness and they hungered for it just as we do today.

Colossians 1:10 is a good reminder of the connection between our call to walk with the Lord and the fruit that will naturally follow as a result. *"So that you will walk in a manner worthy of the Lord, to please Him in all respects, bearing fruit in every good work...."* Jesus also said, in John 15:16, *"You did not choose Me but I chose you, and appointed you that you would go and bear fruit...."* Do you notice that He said He "appointed" us to bear fruit? Another way to put it would be to say that He has ordained us to bear fruit and part of bearing fruit comes with sharing our faith.

When I arrived at Glenna's home, I quickly realized that God had prepared her heart to hear His message of truth. She shared with me, "Betsy, I have this empty spot in my heart that nothing seems to fill. I find myself searching for the answer to life. I've been so frustrated and confused. Then, as I typed your manuscript, something began to happen in my heart. I became hungry as I read about Christ and what He offers. Can you tell me how a person finds God on a deeper level?"

Glenna was asking me for the source of my hope and I praised God that He had prepared me with the answer. It was the same question I had asked many years ago, wanting to really know God personally, not just know about Him. Glenna and I talked for over an hour about what it means to have a relationship with God through Christ. When we were done, I asked her if she would like to have Christ in her life. She eagerly affirmed that indeed she would so we prayed the sinner's prayer and she became born again that day. (See Appendix B)

I thank God for this dear lady, for her openness to God, for her soft heart in wanting to know Him that He might be real in her life. I also thank God that He entrusted me with the great privilege of sharing His word with a hungry soul.

As I drove home and reviewed the evening, tears streamed from my eyes as I realized anew the magnitude of the glory of God, how wonderful He is and how He delights in giving me the desires of my heart. Not because I deserve special times like that night, but simply because He loves me and loves blessing His children. God especially loves having His children bring others to sit at His feet.

I had thought I was just moving forward with my manuscript toward publishing. God had other plans. He knew that book would not be published but He also knew there was a hungry heart out there that needed to hear the encouragement of the gospel message. I have to ask myself: Which is more important…getting a book published or helping a lost soul find her way to Jesus? I think God accomplished His work that day. It is a privilege to be used by God. II Corinthians 4:5-7 says it well, *"For we do not preach ourselves but Christ Jesus as Lord, and ourselves as your bond-servants for Jesus' sake. For God, who said, 'Light shall shine out of darkness,' is the One who has shone in our hearts to give the Light of the knowledge of the glory of God in the face of Christ. But we have this treasure in earthen vessels, so that the surpassing greatness of the power will be of God and not from ourselves."*

God pours into us so we are able to pour out to others.

CHAPTER 10

SCOFFERS, SKEPTICS, AND SEEKERS

Scoffer #1

When Bill worked in California, occasionally there were parties we attended with his co-workers. At one of these events, I ventured in conversation to mention to one of them that I had prayed about something and God had answered. I don't recall exactly what I said but I do remember his mocking eyes and sarcastic response that was meant to make me feel like an idiot for praying and even more so for telling someone about it. My faith was literally laughed at. It wasn't a pleasant feeling. At that time, my self-worth was not exactly at its highest point and I just wanted to crawl away. He had put me in my place and I had absorbed his scorn.

One of the things I have learned is that I need to be sensitive to people, especially when speaking of my faith. Remembering Colossians 4:2-6 has been a good reminder. *"Devote yourselves to prayer, keeping alert in it with an attitude of thanksgiving; praying at the same time for us as well, that God will open up to us a door for the word, so that we may speak forth the mystery of Christ, for which I have also been imprisoned; that I may make it clear in the way I ought to speak. Conduct yourselves with wisdom toward outsiders, making the most of the opportunity. Let your speech always be with grace, as though seasoned with salt, so that you will know how you should respond to each person."*

In pondering those verses, it seems good to pray that God will not only open opportunities to share our faith, but to remember to ask Him to make it clear how we ought to speak. That Scripture is a good reminder to be gentle, prayerful, and loving. We don't always know where people are coming from or what their world view may be. It may be completely different from our biblical world view. We also don't know what hurtful life experiences they may have endured that could have jaded their response to God. It is possible the words we use may be foreign to them, like we are speaking a different language.

Scoffer #2

An incident arose during a visit by Bill's parents, Carmen and Lou. While they were out running errands, I accidently spilled boiling water on my arm. Painful would mildly describe that experience as I watched my arm turn bright red and an ugly crimson blister rise up. I had recalled a friend, Loretta, who had once told me that God had instantly healed her in a similar situation so I grabbed the phone and punched in her number. Breathing a sigh of relief when she answered, she was happy to pray for my arm over the phone. Incredibly, as she sought God's healing touch, I witnessed my own healing. My eyes were wide with wonder as I watched the blister shrink away. Next, as she continued to pray, all the stinging and redness disappeared. In a few minutes time, as I turned my arm from side to side, I could not detect that it had even been burned except for a small remnant of fading pink. I had just observed a miracle. "Loretta," I yelled into the phone, "my arm is healed! There is no sign of the burn." It was an awesome experience for which I thanked both

God and Loretta. Together, we rejoiced and gave God praise for His healing touch.

Shortly after I hung up the phone, Bill's parents walked in the door. Years before, they had dictated to us that we were never to speak of our faith in their presence. Their hearts were hardened toward God and any mention of Him was beyond irritating. For Lou, the subject of faith was downright infuriating. Intimidated by his wrath, I feared Lou and was usually very careful to abide by his wishes. But with my obvious excitement about this undeniable miracle, I could not keep silent. My enthusiasm in that moment was unrestrained with joy. With great passion and excitement, I gave God glory as I told them the story of my burn and the quick healing. Upon finishing, Lou literally stomped out of the room. He was so irate with my testimony that his face flamed red with rage. Never mind an incredible and marvelous wonder had just occurred. His scoffing was more than apparent. Although his response did not dampen my exhilaration, I chose to say no more. The door was closed.

On another occasion, Billy Graham came to our area and we took the chance of asking Carmen and Lou if they would attend a meeting with us. We were thrilled when they agreed to go and we prayed God would touch their hearts. As I listened to Graham's message, I was trying to hear it through the grid of their thinking. The message was wonderful, so inspiring and just what they needed to hear. I was sure they would be touched and run to the front for salvation but it was not to be.

Undaunted, with my own enthusiasm soaring from the fabulous message we had just heard, as we left the arena, I asked what they thought of it. My balloon of excitement popped when they answered with indifference, "Oh, it was a nice talk." A nice talk like any talk on any subject. Nothing special about it.

In his later years, Lou became a victim of Alzheimer's. While in the early stages, Carmen asked if she could fly him up to visit us so she could have a break. As I anticipated a week with him, I decided that I would commit to showing him God's love at every turn. During his visit, I drove him two hours north to visit our daughter, Laurie, and two hours south so he could visit our other daughter, Kim. He had a soft heart toward his grandchildren so I felt it would please him to see them once again. As we drove, I noticed Lou seemed a bit restless. Then he began to sob and in the midst of tears, he asked me, "Why are you being so nice to me?"

What an interesting question. I had to answer honestly. "Lou, I love you and we are family. I want you to have a nice visit while you're here. As a Christian, God has given me a special love for you and I want to serve you while you are with us."

No response was forthcoming but I knew God had sewn a seed. Regardless of how Lou had treated me over the years and regardless of turning his back on God, God had given me a genuine love for him and he noticed it. One baby step at a time.

As Lou's Alzheimer's progressed, he was put in an Alzheimer's unit in a nursing home. During that time, Laurie, flew to Arizona for a visit. Moved by her love for her grandfather, she wanted one more chance to share the good news of Christ with him before Alzheimer's completely took over his mind. It is such a wretched, destructive disease.

When she arrived, Lou was in a wheelchair sitting in a hallway. It was hard for Laurie to see her once active grandpa now confined to a wheelchair. They chatted awhile and then she boldly, yet tenderly, shared the gospel message with him. Surely, being so close to his eternal destiny, he would now relent and fall into Jesus' loving arms. Surely, his days of scoffing God were past. But sadly, again, it was not to be. When Laurie asked him if he would like to accept Jesus into his heart, he replied with a sharp, "No!" Again, she asked, "Are you sure, Grandpa? Don't you want to know you are going to heaven when you die? You just need to accept Jesus." Again, his quick negative response was emphatic.

Laurie left feeling dejected that her grandfather was so adamant in not wanting Jesus. But our gracious Lord saw her discouragement and gave her a ray of hope. As she walked down the hallway, an elderly lady in a wheelchair pulled up beside her. With a twinkle in her eye, she whispered, "I heard everything you said to your grandpa, and I want you to know that I will be praying for him every day." What sweet words for Laurie to hear. Just knowing someone in his facility would be praying brought her a measure of peace. God, in His great mercy and grace, was on top of this situation and would woo Lou giving him every opportunity to come to Him for salvation.

Although Lou was a generous man who lived an upright life, we do not know if he ever accepted Christ. As a family, we had entrusted him to our gracious Lord knowing that He *"...desires all men to be saved and to come to the knowledge of the truth,"* (I Tim. 2:4). Perhaps, God reached him before he died. While we don't know for sure, we are at peace that he was clear as to the choice set before him.

Scoffer or Skeptic
Bill's co-worker and Lou were both scoffers. A scoffer can be defined as one who speaks with disdain, who mocks or has a scornful attitude. On the other hand, a skeptic is a person who questions the validity or authenticity of something reported as factual. A skeptic is a doubter. Let's face it...if we speak out regularly about our faith, at some point, we will meet up with a skeptic or a scoffer. In truth, probably one of the main reasons we are hesitant to voice our faith in Christ is because we fear the rejection we know we will feel in the face of either of these kinds of responses. No one likes to be ridiculed and we are not crazy about the validity of our faith being questioned. We don't want to be thought of as fanatics and human nature is to avoid being mocked at all cost. It can feel so demeaning. Why would we want to place ourselves in that situation? Many of us have long ago memories of being jeered at in some childhood

situation. It was painful. We wanted to hide. Unfortunately, for this very reason, we tend to stay clear of any situation that might cause waves that rock the boat of our security.

Skeptic #1

I once had a neighbor who, like Lou, was also offended by anything about God. He was probably a skeptic though, because he didn't demean my faith. He just didn't want it for himself. One day, we were out in our yard talking. Being elderly, and with some physical issues, I wondered if he had secured his eternal destiny. After some preliminary discussion, I asked him if he knew where he would be going when he died. He began to smile and shake his head. "No, no, no, I don't talk about that." He spoke half jokingly, but definitely with a firm boundary.

The discussion was over. He was clearly not interested. For whatever reason, he was skeptical about the idea of God and a personal relationship with his Creator. We sometimes forget that people's beliefs have been set for years, and approaching tender, even unfamiliar topics can bring up painful, emotional memories. Past experiences can be triggered and cause an unexpected response. It may not necessarily be our words they are responding to but rather a long forgotten, uncomfortable memory. Perhaps, that was the case with him. I may never know.

At times like this, it's important for us to remember to be gentle and kind. Jesus is always gracious. He invites people but does not force the issue.

Then an interesting thing happened. My neighbor's wife passed away and he had to be put into a nursing home. It was Bill's habit to meet weekly for Bible study with another friend, Dave, who was also a resident in the same facility. Bill introduced Dave to our neighbor and they occasionally visited each other. At one point, our neighbor commented that every time he went to Dave's room, there were other people gathered to visit him. He wanted to know what was going on. Bill used the opportunity to tell him that, like himself, Dave was a Christian and how they frequently got together to study the Bible. Bill went on to talk to him about the Lord and noticed he didn't shut down the conversation. He mentioned that he would like me to stop by sometime for a visit too. Bill said, "Well, you know what Betsy will want to talk about if she comes over, don't you?"

With a smile, he shook his head and indicated it would be ok for me to talk about Jesus. So, about a week later, I stopped by his room and spent some time with him. He seemed ok with me talking about Jesus but made it clear that he had no interest in Him for his own life.

"I've never believed in God," he said. "Where I grew up, no one went to church and I've never felt any need to have God in my life."

Still, he listened as I shared my own testimony of finding the Lord.

Afterward, I said, "You know, you're 97 years old. You don't have much time left. I am hoping I will see you in heaven with me, but that will require you making a decision of faith in Christ."

Then I went on to talk about several answers to prayer that I knew involved the hand of God. All the while, he listened politely and didn't shut me down. I plan to stop by again sometime and meanwhile, I will pray that God is moving in his heart to soften him and give him a reason to turn to Him. I don't believe God is finished with him yet.

Skeptic #2
Nan was a grade school friend whom I hadn't seen in many years. As adults, since we lived within easy distance from one another, we decided to meet in a town between our homes. It would be great to reacquaint and hear about each other's lives.

We met in a restaurant and after a bit of small talk, I said. "Nan, I remember you were raised Lutheran. Are you still following a path of faith?"

From her answer, I knew she had drifted and really didn't have any interest in following Jesus. Then, somehow, we got into a conversation about creation versus evolution. Clearly, her convictions were with the evolution side of the debate. While that could have closed the door for further discussion, I felt led to gently challenge a couple of her beliefs.

"Nan, in Darwin's later writings, he made a simple point which he may have later lamented. He said that there were several things that had to be true or his theory would be discredited. One of these was that if transitional species could not be found, the theory of evolution was invalid. Scientists are hesitant to admit it, but they have not found any transitional life forms. Rationally speaking, doesn't it seem there should be millions of transitional species if evolution is correct? But, in reality, they don't exist."

Nan and I didn't get to the other issues. She showed no interest in the logic of this insight. It was like she was blind to obvious reality. Although, she had no way to refute this apparent truth, she remained skeptical.

From there, we moved to the second law of thermodynamics which, in simple terms, explains that anything left to itself eventually breaks down. "Nan, it can be observed that over time, things left to themselves tend to become more disordered, not more organized. Evolution, of course, teaches that order comes out of disorder even in the face of empirical evidence that compels the opposite conclusion. What are your thoughts about this?"

Convinced of her position for evolution rather than a Creator God, Nan looked me right in the eye and said, "The second law of thermodynamics is wrong. Order does proceed from disorder."

End of conversation. What could I possibly say to such an irrational statement? I realized I was speaking with a skeptic. No sense arguing. Reason, logic, or obvious truth would not penetrate. So, I changed the subject and we enjoyed a casual lunch with no further challenge.

With a twinkle in her eye, Nan impressed me with these words, "Betsy, I don't usually talk about these things. The only reason I am willing to talk with you is because we have history. Although we haven't seen each other in many years, we grew up together. I knew you when we were children, so I trust you." I accepted the compliment.

It's possible I was the first person who had challenged Nan's world view. Our history gave me an opening that might not have existed with others. While our conversation was respectful and cordial, I was disappointed to find her mind so closed to truth. Happily, I did have a chance to share with her who Jesus is to me and the difference He has made in my life. It is not usually threatening for someone to hear a personal testimony as long as no demands are made of them. She listened politely and without comment as I told her how Jesus was my whole life.

When someone has a completely different world view, it is tempting to become angry and frustrated when they don't acknowledge our biblical world view. I have learned we have to allow for difference of opinion. We are seed planters. No need to take offense when people disagree with our position. I have to remember they have their own journey in life. Perhaps, I am the first person of faith they have encountered. I have to consider what is important for them to take away from our dialogue. Even if they don't recall our conversation, they will most likely remember our attitude. By not taking offense, we may leave the door open for further conversation at another time.

When we speak with skeptics, scoffers or mockers, who is really being rejected? I wonder if Jesus feels the same hurt that we feel when His words of life are refused. I think the disciple's response is the best way to look at these moments. Mark 6:11 says, *"Any place that does not receive you or listen to you, as you go out from there, shake the dust off the soles of your feet...."*

We can only do so much. If people don't respond to the opportunity to consider Jesus, we are not called to force the issue. It is often best to let it go and shake off the dust. Otherwise, we run the risk of spreading more heat than light, heat that can cause a destructive fire in a relationship when they are not ready to hear. To violate that boundary can end in disaster. That fire can shut down any potential later conversation after the person has time to ponder things we have said. Some people have never talked to anyone about spiritual issues. It's likely they will think about what they have heard. Perhaps, they will dismiss it all, but there is always a chance God is at work to win them and something in them will be drawn to His love.

Our part is to be praying that God will lead us into occasions where we can share our faith openly and honestly. It is He who draws people to His Son. Jesus said in John 6:44, *"No one can come to Me unless the Father who sent Me draws him...."* God always has a purpose when He leads us to share our faith. It may just be a first step of bringing awareness to a person, one that may resonate and bubble up in their mind after we are gone. After all, Jesus, Himself, only did what the Father initiated. John 12:49, *"For I did not speak on My own initiative, but the Father Himself who sent Me has given Me a commandment as to what to say and what to speak."*

We know that Jesus also met with many skeptics and scoffers. What we endure at these times could only be called "light" verbal persecution compared with the ultimate persecution Jesus endured.

A Scoffer and a Seeker

Sitting by our community pool one afternoon, a neighbor started a conversation with me. To my knowledge she had no interest in God. As we talked, she referred to a celebrity who had recently come to the Lord. "Look at him," she spat out. "He waited until he was quite well off and now he says he's found *Gaaawd*," she sarcastically mocked. She went on to expound on how disgusting she found this. At a loss for words, I endured an uncomfortable few minutes as I listened to her scoff God. I said nothing in reply and soon left the pool.

I was greatly disturbed by my silence. My lack of response left me feeling like a failure. Many other times, I had comfortably shared the Lord with people. Why couldn't I think of anything to say that day? How could God possibly use someone who can't even verbalize her faith, who can't even stand up for her beliefs? My self-condemnation left me distressed and browbeaten.

When I got home, the house was empty as Bill had taken our daughters out for ice cream, so I took the opportunity to talk to God. *Lord,* I prayed, *I feel I've let you down. My mind just went blank this afternoon. I want to be a witness for you. Give me wisdom. What in the world just happened at the pool? I felt so useless and demeaned.*

A quiet thought from the Lord formed in my mind... *I did give you wisdom.*

But Lord, I didn't say anything, I blurted back to Him.

Still puzzled, the next day my Bible reading led me to Proverbs 9:7-8. *"He who corrects a scoffer gets dishonor for himself, and he who reproves a wicked man gets insults for himself. Do not reprove a scoffer lest he hate you, reprove a wise man, and he will love you."*

Wait a minute....was God trying to tell me that the friend who had scoffed the idea of God would be better off left alone? Was He intimating that my lack of response was actually how He wanted me to handle that situation? I was astonished as I considered that thought. I had always believed that I should have an answer for every circumstance but now it seemed God was revealing to me that maybe every off-handed accusation doesn't need an answer. I spent some time pondering that idea. This person was not just a skeptic; she was scoffing and sneering the idea of someone coming to God.

I compared my reading in Proverbs to the Living Bible's paraphrase and had to smile when I got to Proverbs 10:14, 19, *"A wise man holds his tongue. Only a fool blurts out everything he knows, that only leads to sorrow and trouble. Don't talk so much. You keep putting your foot in your mouth. Be sensible and turn off the flow!"* Well, I guess God had my attention! I began to understand that God had given me wisdom for that situation after all. My neighbor was a scoffer. In that circumstance, God had not allowed me to respond out of emotion and therefore had kept me out of trouble. Proverbs 10:19 says, *"... he who restrains his lips is wise."* I could not use that as an excuse to never witness; but for that particular occasion, God had revealed His wisdom to me. He knew my heart's desire to share my faith. I again remembered that Jesus never did anything on His own initiative, but only spoke the things the Father taught Him.

Besides being disturbed over my lack of response, I had also felt offended by my neighbor's comments at the pool. Bill later explained to me that in those situations, we have two options: We can "step over" the offense or we can "trip over" it. When someone says something that offends our faith, we can take the low road by becoming angry and bitter. This can lead to spewing out things we later regret and even lead to a heated argument. Bill called this, "tripping" over an offense. "On the other hand," he explained, "We can choose to take the high road and "step over" the offense by not reacting aggressively. By stepping over an offense, we take the sting out of it and apply grace." Great wisdom!

That same weekend, on Sunday morning in church, God brought about an opportunity for us to share our faith with a couple also from our neighborhood. Delighted to see them visiting our church, we invited them out to lunch after the service. We had prayed for them in the past because they had not yet come into a personal relationship with Jesus. At lunch that day, the Lord gave Bill and me a clear opportunity to share our faith. This couple was 'searching' for answers. They were seekers.

They began the conversation by commenting, "We've watched your lives in the neighborhood for several years, and we have noticed there is something different about you and your family. What makes you tick? It seems like you are able to associate with anyone

64

in the neighborhood but you don't get caught up with the party-ing. How do you do that?"

What a great opening question! That day, God gave us an op-portunity for a sweet witness to our neighbors.

"Thanks for noticing," we said. "We're Christians and because of that, we care about people." We went on to explain to them what a personal relationship with Jesus means and how it had changed our lives. They listened intently. God had set up a divine appoint-ment by sending this couple across our path. He had spoken a lesson to me the day before about scoffers and taking offense and now, He was showing me the other side, that there were people He had prepared to hear, people with listening ears who were eager to know about God. Clearly, these people were not only not skeptics or scoffers, but they were seekers, and we had an opportunity to plant some seeds.

God is the one who had initiated and opened the door. Though His word commands us to be witnesses, He is the one who selects and empowers. *"Faithful is He who calls you, and He also will bring it to pass,"* (I Thess. 5:24). After all, He loves seekers and weeps for the lost.

Here is what have I learned from these various experienc-es. God can be in both the silence and in the release of words. They are His to initiate. He knows the hearts of people. I do not. Sometimes, it is best to say nothing; other times, I am to talk. In either case, my part is to be in tune with His will, to listen for His voice, always remembering that He measures success differently. His idea of success is when I am faithful to perform what He asks. He knows that not everyone will respond to Him. My part is simply to follow His lead.

CHAPTER 11

A WITNESS TO INDIA

As I boarded a plane from Phoenix to Chicago, I quietly breathed my usual traveling prayer, *Lord, give me an opportunity to share about You with someone on this trip.* Settling into my seat, I glanced at the lady next to me and realized she was from a foreign country. "Where are you from?" I asked.

"I'm from India," she smiled back. Her English was perfect. In fact, I learned later that she spoke six languages fluently. I liked her instantly. Her demeanor was one of genuine warmth and acceptance and I sensed God was up to something. I was reminded again of words from Henry Blackaby's workbook, "Experiencing God," where he says we are to watch for where God is working and join Him. I felt that was exactly what was about to happen as our plane soared through the sky.

After asking her name, she replied, "Aashi." I'm always intrigued by how many names there are in the world. Of course, hers definitely sounded foreign to me. Aashi shared some things with me about her country and her life and that she was in America on business. She worked for the U.N. That, in itself, was impressive. I had never known anyone who worked with the United Nations.

Not one to mince words, I jumped right in with a question. "Aashi, do you think there are many Christians in India?"

"Yes, there are some Christians in India," she replied, "but I was raised in the Zoroaster faith. I've studied many religions over the years and now practice the Hindu religion."

Zoroaster! Hindu! *Lord, I know nothing about these religions. Where do I go from here?* At a later time in my life, I studied various world religions in my Master's program in Biblical Studies, but at this time, my knowledge of these two religions was zero and I had no idea how to proceed. In retrospect, however, this was a good thing because it meant I was completely dependent on God to reveal what to say next. I love when the Lord brings revelation and He was about to do just that. In the few seconds I pondered what to say, quietly the Holy Spirit gave me another question for her.

"Aashi, are you familiar with the claims of the Christian faith?" I asked.

"Why, yes, I am. You see, I was raised in a Christian school," she replied, "and I also have a maid who is Pentecostal." With that, I knew this was a divine appointment and that there was a Christian woman in India who was probably praying for Aashi's salvation.

Sensing that she had never heard the real gospel message, I then asked, "May I share with you a booklet that tells about Jesus?" Since she seemed eager to hear, I rummaged through my purse and pulled out a copy of Billy Graham's pamphlet, *Steps to Peace With God.* (See Appendix B) Aashi listened intently as I shared God's love for her, man's sin problem, Jesus death on the cross, and our need to receive Him personally.

As I covered the basics of the Christian experience, I asked her if she saw herself as a sinner. "Oh, yes," she replied. "I know there are things I do wrong."

Although impressed with the Bible verses I showed her, she still had questions. "I've studied many religions," she explained, "aren't they really all the same? They all have good things in them? What makes Christianity so special and exclusive?"

This woman was a thinker. She was well educated and deserved an honest answer. I could tell from our conversation so far that, although she was raised in a Christian school, she had never made a commitment to Christ. One thing I have observed is that just because someone knows "about" Christianity, it doesn't mean they "know" Jesus. Aashi had asked a sincere question about what made Christianity so special, and I wanted to answer with God's wisdom. I sent up a quick prayer for wisdom knowing that wisdom is promised in James 1:5, *"But if any of you lacks wisdom, let him ask of God, who gives to all generously and without reproach, and it will be given to him."*

"Well," I cautiously proceeded, "let me answer that with a question. You have agreed with me that you are a sinner." She nodded yes, so I continued with a question that would target the core issue. "Can you tell me what the Hindu religion offers you as a way to deal with your sins?"

I could sense this was a question she had never thought about. In all of her religious studies she had never considered an answer to her sin problem. Following a contemplative pause, a troubling revelation seemed to collide with her theology as she haltingly answered, "Well... nothing. The Hindu religion has no way to eliminate sin." She sat quietly and pondered the weight of this discovery.

After a few minutes of letting this new idea settle in, I said, "Aashi, that is the difference between Christianity and all the other religions. You see, when Jesus died on the cross, He took all of our sins with Him. God is a just God and His justice required payment for our sins. He knew that there was nothing we could ever personally do that would excuse us. We needed a Savior, one who would give His life as payment for the sins of the world. It would have to be a perfect person. Jesus, God's only Son, was the ideal, faultless sacrifice who chose to pay the price by giving His life on the cross. He alone could pay our debt and satisfy God's requirement.

"The good news is that our debt of sin was cancelled when Jesus went to the cross. In simpler terms, like a traffic ticket, there is a price owed for the offence. The Bible says the penalty for sin is death, but Romans 6:23 goes on to say that *"...the free gift of God is eternal life in Christ Jesus our Lord."* Because Jesus paid the price, He now extends to us the opportunity to receive that gift. Yes, a free gift. When we receive Him as our personal Lord and Savior, all of our sins are forever washed away, having been paid for by Christ on the cross.

"As Jesus hung on the cross, His last words were, 'It is finished.' He meant that He had accomplished everything that was necessary for salvation and the forgiveness of sins. Our debt of sin was paid for and we could be forgiven.

"After Jesus died, He raised from the dead as proof that He is God, and as proof that He had the power to resolve our sin problem. Because of Jesus' finished work on the cross, His death and resurrection, we can have a personal relationship with God. Jesus has bridged the gap between us and God, a gap no one else in any other religion has been able to bridge. It took the cross of Christ for the sin issue to be settled.

"You know," I continued, "someday we will all come face to face with God. He is holy and His eyes are too pure to behold sin. Aashi, what will you say to Him when you come before Him? If He were to ask you why He should let you into heaven, how would you answer?"

Her thoughtful look told me that she knew she was not prepared to face God. She remained silent.

"I know what I would say," I gently spoke. "I would tell Him I have been washed with the blood of Jesus and that my sins were forgiven when I received Jesus into my life."

Soberly and thoughtfully she replied, "This is serious stuff, isn't it?"

"Yes, it is," I responded. "It is really a life or death issue."

The plane began its descent, and I realized we had talked about Jesus for over three hours touching on many aspects of the Christian faith. "You know Aashi, our meeting on this plane was no accident. I believe it was a divine appointment set up by God."

She nodded in agreement, a sober look on her face. After exhorting her to read the book of John in the Bible, I took her address and promised to send her a book for further reading. She indicated she had much to think about. I didn't feel she was ready to receive Christ at that point, but I knew some hearty seeds had been planted. Perhaps, I was one more link in a chain of people who would pass through her life bringing the good news of the gospel. I pray that she would have further conversation with the Christian maid God had strategically placed in her home and that she would read the books I later sent.

As we landed in Chicago, the Lord reminded me of a prayer I had prayed just a week before. We had attended a meeting in our church where a mission minded speaker had asked us to pray that God would impress a country on each of our hearts. As I had prayed, I became discouraged that no country seemed to fill my heart with zeal. I didn't sense a strong desire to visit or pray for any one country. So, I walked away with these words to God, *Well Lord, why don't you just bring the world to me?* And he did! He brought me India on that flight and an opportunity to enlighten a fellow traveler.

CHAPTER 12
A CURIOUS SEAT MATE

On another flight, as Bill and I boarded a plane on the way home from California, a nervous, eccentric woman, whose name I learned was Ellen, sat down next to me in the window seat. Lost in her anxiety, even though a young woman, she commenced to moan and complain about her aches and pains and the various disasters of her life. Sitting next to her, I figured this would be a long, tedious flight for both of us.

We chatted a bit and then she leaned over me to observe Bill in the aisle seat. *What in the world is she doing now?* I wondered. Bill, leaning back in his chair, relaxed with his earphones, was listening to some of his favorite music.

"What kind of music is he lost in?" my seatmate inquired.

"Oh, he enjoys listening to Christian music, mostly praise and worship," I explained.

After a pause, having sorted through her mental catalog of various kinds of music, she was lost. There was no such category in her cache.

With eyebrows scrunched, her next question was as expected. "What is praise and worship music?"

Perfect opening ... God was at work. I wondered if she even knew what a Christian was.

"Well, we are Christians," I replied, "and part of what we do is worship Jesus with music. We enjoy a personal relationship with God through Jesus Christ and we love opportunities to praise Him for whom He is and for all He has done for us."

I could almost see her brain sifting through her life experiences searching for some possible way to relate to my comments. It was obvious she had no idea what I was talking about. A personal relationship with God was not even a blip on her radar, but she seemed open, so I continued to explain how Jesus had died on the cross for our sins, and because of His resurrection, we could be forgiven and enter into a relationship with our Creator.

A dam seemed to open and she began to share with me how distressed she was about her low self worth and what a disaster her marriage was. Mind you, I was a perfect stranger. But, I've noticed that sometimes when God is brought into a conversation, the mention of His name seems to open emotional floodgates in people.

Psalm 139 came to mind, so I decided to encourage her by helping her to see how God viewed her. "Ellen, Psalm 139 is one of my favorite passages in the Bible because it was one God used many years ago to help me gain self esteem. God helped me to see myself from His perspective. Did you know that the Bible is a book of truth and can be trusted like no other book? There are no distortions or perversions. It is a pure and holy book that will enlighten your heart if you will let it. You can trust it as a sacred book telling about a God who loves us. Listen as I read parts of it to you."

With that, I pulled out my Bible from my carry-on tote and began to read Psalm 139:1-6 to her. *"O Lord, You have searched me and known me. You know when I sit down and when I rise up; You understand my thought from afar. You scrutinize my path and my lying down, and are intimately acquainted with all my ways. Even before there is a word on my tongue, Behold, O Lord, You know it all. You have enclosed me behind and before, and laid Your hand upon me. Such knowledge is too wonderful for me; It is too high, I cannot attain to it."*

"Do you see, Ellen, how God is intimately interested in us? We are His creation and He loves us."

She seemed to be following what I was reading so I went on. "Psalm 139:13-17 says, *'For You formed my inward parts; You wove me in my mother's womb. I will give thanks to You, for I am fearfully and wonderfully made; Wonderful are Your works, and my soul knows it very well. My frame was not hidden from You, when I was made in secret, and skillfully wrought in the depths of the earth; Your eyes have seen my unformed substance; and in Your book were all written the days that were ordained for me, when as yet there was not one of them. How precious also are Your thoughts to me, O God! How vast is the sum of them!'"*

"Isn't it amazing to think that God knows us so well? Think about how meticulous He was as He formed us in our mother's womb? It never ceases to amaze me. Every part was seen by Him and marvelously knit together to form us. I'm wondering, Ellen, if you know this God. He knows everything about you, but do you know Him? The only way to really know Him is by inviting Him into your heart. I wonder... have you ever invited Jesus into your life?"

To my surprise, she answered. "Yes, but it didn't take."

I sent up a quick prayer. *What do I do with that statement? "It didn't take".... What did that even mean?* Then, I thought of another question for her.

"Ellen, have you ever read the Bible?" I asked.

"No, I haven't," she sheepishly replied.

I was suddenly aware that there are probably many people out there who at some time in their lives accepted Jesus but who never followed up. They may have believed Jesus was once alive but, perhaps, never acknowledged their sin. Nor have they considered the meaning of Jesus' cross and resurrection which paid for our sin and offers us new life in Him. Having never truly acquainted themselves with the Lord by reading and studying the Bible, they remain adrift, at sea spiritually.

They may be like the seed talked about in Luke 8:5-7. "*The sower went out to sow his seed; and as he sowed, some fell beside the road, and it was trampled underfoot and the birds of the air ate it up. Other seed fell on rocky soil, and as soon as it grew up, it withered away, because it had no moisture. Other seed fell among the thorns; and the thorns grew up with it and choked it out.*"

Luke 8:11-14 goes on to explain the parable. "*Now the parable is this: the seed is the word of God. Those beside the road are those who have heard; then the devil comes and takes away the word from their heart, so that they will not believe and be saved. Those on the rocky soil are those who, when they hear, receive the word with joy; and these have no firm root; they believe for a while, and in time of temptation fall away. The seed which fell among the thorns, these are the ones who have heard, and as they go on their way they are choked with worries and riches and pleasures of this life, and bring no fruit to maturity.*"

It is impossible for me to know if the soil of Ellen's life was beside the road, rocky, or thorny. All I knew was that the seed God had sown in her heart had somehow not sprouted. Her heart did not seem to be prepared soil. Once again, I realized how important it is to water the seed once it has been planted. While this includes exposure to God's Word and fellowship with other Christians, the ultimate purpose is to deepen trust in Jesus.

Many people have made some little step, a nod, or a prayer for help, but have bypassed the central issue, the Lordship of Christ, which begins by faith in Jesus' finished work on the cross for forgiveness of sins. Salvation seems to have two essentials, first dealing with our sin problem at the cross and then inviting Jesus to be Lord of our lives. Without Lordship, I wonder if a person is truly saved. Has he truly yielded his life to Jesus so that Jesus is now the Master or Ruler, the One Who calls the shots? If we still insist on occupying the throne of our own life instead of yielding to Jesus, what is the point of salvation? Why did Jesus even bother with the cross? He wants to be Lord, and that is a decision not to be trifled with but to be taken seriously. It all boils down to faith.

Bill puts it well in regard to his journey towards faith when he says, "I knew I desperately needed a Savior, but I didn't want Him to mess with my life. I decided I would drive the bus even if it took me over a cliff which almost happened until I asked Jesus to take the wheel."

When I heard Ellen had never read the Bible, I suggested she consider taking time for that when she got home by starting with the book of John. A broad smile came to her face when I mentioned John. "Oh," she said with animation, "I am an avid fan of John Lennon." Clearly, she liked the idea of reading a book called John, a name with which she felt a connection.

She then informed me, "John Lennon was my idol and he was a person who was striving toward peace."

Ok, I thought, *what do I do with that?* Immediately, the Lord gave me a verse for her. "I think everyone wants to find peace, Ellen. Did you know that God says peace starts within a person?"

I read to her some verses about peace. Since she was so enthralled with the name, "John," I picked two verses from the book of John.

John 14:27, *"Peace I leave with you; My peace I give to you; not as the world gives do I give to you. Do not let your heart be troubled, nor let it be fearful."*

John 16:33, *"These things I have spoken to you, so that in Me you may have peace. In the world you have tribulation, but take courage; I have overcome the world."*

I then explained, "It might interest you to know that the only real peace in life is from Jesus. In the world, we can have temporary peace that lasts as long as things are going well, but in Jesus we can have an abiding peace not dependent on circumstances."

We then looked at Romans 5:1, *"Therefore, having been justified by faith, we have peace with God through our Lord Jesus Christ."*

"Ellen, do you see that it is when we have faith in God, that is, when we put our trust in Him, that we are promised peace "with" God? When a person accepts Jesus, she is justified. That means her sins are forgiven. Without the burden of sin hanging over her, she can now be at peace with God."

I continued, "Then in Philippians 4:7, we are told, *"And the peace of God, which surpasses all comprehension, will guard your hearts and your minds in Christ Jesus."*

"Once you are at peace "with" God, He then offers you inner peace that passes understanding? At times, we may even wonder why we have peace in the midst of a troubling situation where we normally might be agitated. It is because He has promised us access to such a peace.

"Ellen," I said, "I'd like to read you one more section of Scripture. These are verses that I like to use so people can understand exactly where they stand with God." Then I read I John 5:11-13, *"And the testimony is this, that God has given us eternal life, and this life is in His Son. He who has the Son has the life; he who does not have the Son of God does not have the life. These things I have written to you who believe in the name of the Son of God, so that you may know that you have eternal life."* I hoped from those verses she would see clearly which side of the fence she stood on.

As our flight neared Chicago, I remembered a book I had brought on our trip, one I had just finished reading. The title was *"Set My Heart Free,"* by Rita Carmack. I sensed the Lord nudging me to give the book to Ellen, so I did. I hope she read it as I felt it would be one more step to her understanding of Jesus and what He offers.

As we parted, I sent up a quick prayer that God would bless Ellen and enrich her life. I will probably never know if she truly accepted Jesus. I may have been one of many who planted seeds along the way. Hopefully, one day someone else will have the privilege of leading Ellen securely into God's Kingdom.

I look back and wonder at times like this. Maybe we just "happened" to be on the same flight with Ellen; maybe I just "happened" to sit next to her; maybe Bill just "happened" to be playing praise music; maybe Ellen just "happened" to be curious. You get the picture. In the end, I believe it was God's providence that I met Ellen on that flight. He was at work to let a lost soul know that He loved her. This is the work of the Holy Spirit. It is how He weaves people's lives together for His purpose. God wishes for none to perish but for all to experience repentance, (II Pet. 3:9). What an amazing, kind, gracious God we have the privilege to serve. Our part as witnesses is to just be available and attuned to what He wants to accomplish, not only in us, but through us.

CHAPTER 13

AWAKENED AT NINETY TWO

This next story is about Bill's, mother, Carmen, so Bill and I are writing it together. Carmen had been a faithful wife to her husband, Lou, for the many years of their marriage. However, like Lou, she had not been a woman of faith. Lou, as I mentioned earlier in the chapter on Skeptics and Scoffers, was adamantly opposed to "religion." We don't know why but we have our guesses. It is possible that the loss of a daughter at birth may have so crushed his heart that he never recovered. I have wondered if Lou endured a lifetime of blaming God for taking his daughter. We don't know for sure.

At that time, the doctor advocated that Carmen not have more children, so Bill is an only child. I recall that forty years after the loss, tears still welled up in Lou's eyes at the mention of his lost daughter. It is sad that he never allowed for the comfort and healing the Holy Spirit could have offered him through that time. The wound was still laid open and painful even in his elderly years. So adamant was he against Christ, he had forbidden our family to ever speak of our faith in his presence. Carmen had also submitted to that request and, except on rare occasions, we had respected their desire.

Bill writes: As Betsy said, neither of my parents knew the Lord, yet, as they observed our children and the interaction we had as a family, they frequently made mention as to how special our family was. Still, they totally denied and dismissed that the reason could possibly be the presence of Christ in us.

In their elderly years, my parents had moved to Arizona for health reasons. They had lived there for a number of years before I received the dreaded phone call from my dad indicating the start of his demise. He started out the conversation with this statement. "Bill, I have noticed some funny things going on in my head. I think I am in the beginning stages of Alzheimer's." Such sobering words left me speechless. He went on with evidence that led him to that conclusion. Sadly, he was right. Within two years, Dad passed from this terrible wasting disease and my mother was alone. If you are dealing with an Alzheimer's victim, Betsy's book, "Mother has Alzheimer's," is a helpful resource as her mother also succumbed to this disease.

After dad died, we asked Mom if she would like to move to Michigan to be closer to us, but she declined at that point. She loved the weather, the residence facility and the town where they lived in Arizona. To move close to us would be yet another step away from the life she knew. There would also be a huge emotional cost for her to move here as they had lived in Michigan for almost twenty years, and being California natives, they had hated the winters. Suffering from arthritis, the thought of moving back to a humid, colder climate was difficult. But, with Lou gone, she felt somewhat lost and lonely living by herself in Arizona. There were no relatives close by and most of her friends were deceased.

In time, there was an event that eventually opened her to the move. She had a small stroke. It was serious enough that she needed more help. Weighing her options, she knew moving closer to us was now the prudent thing to do but, in reality, it meant she could no longer take care of herself.

As Betsy and I reopened the idea of her moving here, there were many things that weighed on us as we considered our role as partial caretakers for an aging parent. I looked forward to seeing her more often, but it would also involve a balance of time and responsibility. Mom was fortunate to have the resources and desire to live in a very good facility in our community, one which was faith based and loving. Although it was different than what she was used to, and the weather was still a challenge, she would be near family and still partially independent which was important to her. I think the hardest part for us, though, was contemplating whether she, like my dad, would continue in denial and unwillingness to hear about our faith and God's love for her. Although my father, with his anti-God persuasion, had passed, would my mother still support his position or had she softened?

Betsy's turn: While we agreed the decision was in Carmen's best interest, I had some struggles with the idea of having her living so close too. Selfishly, I wasn't sure how we would get along. While she was a docile person and quiet natured, I had never developed much of a relationship with her. I found her very hard to get to know and even harder to talk to. I felt like I didn't know her any better after forty years than I did when we first met. How would it be having her live in our community? I knew I would have to lean on God to give me the love and compassion she needed. Bill helped me to adjust to the idea as he looked at it as an opportunity to serve her just as we had served my mother in her latter years with Alzheimer's. I knew God had met me at every turn during my mother's demise. Could I trust Him with my mother-in-law?

The decision was made and Carmen's move went smoothly. Between Bill and me, we visited her several times each week and also took her on outings and to our home as often as we could. Interestingly, I quickly noticed a change in my feelings toward Carmen. Seeing her on a regular basis, my heart began to open toward her and I sensed God building a genuine love between us.

I found her disposition to be sweet. God even gave us conversation and I, at times, felt quite chatty as I got to know her as if for the first time. She also gained favor with the nurses at the villa who enjoyed her immensely. Some even claimed she was their favorite. I can understand that because, with her agreeable personality, she cooperated with anything they wanted and she never complained, definitely an asset in her situation. Oh, and she loved chocolate and kept a stash with the excuse that she could offer those to the girls who served her at her residence. Smart lady! And it worked.

One day, an amusing conversation took place between Bill and his mother. She had been eating a lot of chocolate and this had caused her blood pressure to rise. Being the dutiful son, Bill expressed his concern to which she stoically replied, "So, what's the worst thing that could happen, Bill? Might I die?"

What could Bill say? She had a good point. After all she was 92 years of age. He conceded that she could enjoy eating anything she wanted.

More thoughts from Bill: Even though Dad was gone, we continued to abide by the code of silence when it came to issues of faith. I remember one day, as we talked, Mom said that she wanted to be more involved with our lives. It was a simple request, but it was the opening that I had longed for. I softly and as lovingly as I could, told her, "Mom if you continue to shut off the most important part of our lives, you have to realize that you have pushed aside many of the things that define who we are, our values and our faith. We have tried to walk, really tiptoe, around conversation about the Lord and have kept silent regarding the things that you didn't want to hear. But by cutting off this part of us, you have denied the core of our family, our faith, life principles, values and our life experiences which all stem from our relationship with Christ."

After explaining that our lives revolved around God, I said, "We can continue to keep our conversations on shallow topics, but if you want to know us better, you will have to allow for some spiritual dialogue. If you want more of us, then you have to allow us to speak of that part of our lives. For us not to speak about God would have been like telling Dad he could never speak about his life at the county club or golf" (like that would ever happen). "Think about it, Mom."

She later came back and told us that she wanted more. We assured her that we wouldn't pressure her or preach. Gently, so as not to overwhelm her, we began to occasionally share something God was doing in our lives, teachings we had heard, miracles, answers to prayer, healings, principles we were learning to help raise our children, the ones whom she adored and loved being around. Our time together improved significantly.

Betsy's turn: Carmen listened politely but never entered into the conversation. While this was frustrating, I am sure it was all foreign to her and without any personal frame of reference, what could she contribute? She had never been a curious person so there were not even questions on her part but at least she was listening.

Because Carmen was also seriously hard of hearing, I prayed as to how we could really reach her and give her understanding of the gospel message. When we talked about any subject, since she was often silent, I wasn't sure she even heard half of what we said. About this time, I sensed God calling me to write her a letter to explain the gospel and to appeal to her to consider the claims of Jesus. God had built a deep love in my heart for her, and I truly wanted to see her in heaven with us. I composed a loving letter with an appeal to her heart to consider the Lord's offer of salvation. I gave her my personal testimony and shared with her the positive impact Jesus has had in our lives. I hoped that the letter would make a difference at least in her understanding of the benefits Jesus offers.

Carmen never responded to the letter but I wasn't discouraged because I knew some seeds had been planted. We continued to love her, take her on outings, have her over to our house, and visit her in her apartment. Time went by.

One day, a friend of ours heard that Carmen was living in Michigan now and she asked if she could visit her to get to know her. Loretta was an evangelist so we felt God was up to something. You may remember Loretta. She is the same friend God used to pray for healing for my burnt arm. We introduced Carmen to Loretta and they began regular visits. Then one day, Carmen said she wanted Bill to tell Loretta to stop coming for visits. I suspect Loretta was getting too personal and Carmen was not used to personal conversation. Wisely, Bill replied that if she didn't want Loretta to visit, she should tell her so herself.

Being a shy person, Carmen never relayed her feelings to Loretta and Loretta continued to visit. Eventually, they formed a friendship and Carmen even looked forward to her visits.

Loretta was a person who could turn any conversation to Jesus. They could be talking about a secular book Carmen was reading and somehow, Loretta would bring a principle of Jesus into the plot.

Then, the day we had all been waiting and praying for occurred. Here's how Loretta told it when I asked her to write out what happened. For us, this was an epic moment.

November 29, 2002

"It is 3:00 p.m. I just got home from a visit at the Villa with Carmen. When I arrived there, I knocked on her door and she invited me in. As usual, I sat on the footstool next to her chair. Since Carmen was hard of hearing, I needed to sit close to carry on a conversation. As she laid a book that she had been reading on the end table, I asked her what it was about. She explained it was about a man trying to find his way into Heaven. (Hmmm…sounds like God's up to something)

After some small talk, I picked up her book and looked at the inside cover. It said this man had been dead for forty six years and still had not gotten to heaven. He was trying to find out why.

"This must be a novel and not true," I said.

She smiled and agreed.

"He must not know how to get to Heaven. Do you know how to get to Heaven, Carmen?"

"Yes, by believing in God," she replied. After a pause, she added, "Isn't that right?"

"Yes, Carmen, you must believe but you must receive God's Son, too."

Then I pointed at the door, "When I arrived today, I knocked at your door and you invited me in. Otherwise, I would not be welcome, right?"

"Yes, that's right," she replied.

"Carmen, the Bible says that Jesus stands at the door of our heart and knocks. If we will invite him in, He will come. Have you ever done that?"

"No, I haven't," she replied.

I looked at my watch, and noticing it was close to 3:00 p.m., I didn't feel we would have time that day to pursue spiritual matters further as she had plans to play cards with some others at 3:00 o'clock. As I prepared to leave, however, she stopped me with, "Well, aren't you going to pray for me before your leave?"

I sat back down. "Sure, Carmen, what would you like me to pray for?"

"Aren't you going to ask me to invite Jesus into my heart?"

With joy and amazement, I asked, "Would you like to?"

"Yes," she said, so I took her hands in mine and prayed.

"Father, we come to you in Jesus name. Thank you for Carmen and that you love her. I ask you to enable her to open her heart and invite Jesus in and that you would help her understand that salvation is in Jesus."

I don't remember what all I prayed but when I stopped I told her she could invite Jesus into her heart.

I rejoiced as she prayed a simple, child-like prayer, "Jesus, come into my heart."

Then I said, "and forgive my sins," and she repeated that. I led her in a couple other statements and then I thanked God for her and prayed for healing from hurts that may have happened in her life.

When I finished, I looked at her and said, "Jesus said if you invite him in, he would come. So what just happened?"

"He came into my heart," she said.

"That's right. You have just received an early Christmas gift."

Then I picked up her book and there was a piece of paper in it. I took the paper and held it up. "If this paper were a check for a million dollars and I put it in this book and said you could have it if you took the whole book, what would you have to do to get it?"

She said, 'I'd have to ask you for the book."

"That's right," I said, "and God said salvation, eternal life, is in Jesus. Jesus is like the book in this illustration. When you receive Him, you also get eternal life. If you have Him in your heart, you are going to heaven."

She smiled, and while placing the book back on the stand, I said, "Now you know how to get to heaven, right?"

She said, "Yes."

I then told her the story about an Arab man who visited our home and how he understood we must accept God's Son in order to be accepted by Him. I brought the illustration down to a practical level by explaining that if the Arab had not accepted my son, he would not have been welcome in my home. Likewise, God said we must accept His Son, Jesus, in order to be accepted by God. I think she understood.

With a smile, I said, "Well, I didn't come here to preach."

With a grin of feigned surprise, she said, "You didn't?"

"No," I replied.

"You're doing a good job of it," she said. She was smiling.

As I was leaving, I reminded her, "Don't forget, something important happened here today."

She replied with, "Thank you."

I pray that Jesus will commune with Carmen and her salvation will become a wondrous gift to her and that she will share it with someone.

Carmen lived three more years after she received Christ. Throughout that time, she remained stoic and never really talked to us about her decision. Some people, by nature, just are not as vocal about their faith. She was never one to show emotion but I felt her salvation experience was real. The nursing home had church services each Sunday and we noted she began to attend some of the meetings. We were encouraged.

Can you see in this story how God persevered with Carmen over the years? Our part was to persist in prayer for her salvation. Then we planted a few seeds here and there. Loretta eventually had the joy of bringing Carmen into the Kingdom. God used each of us along the way. Every step was important. *"Already he who reaps is receiving wages and is gathering fruit for life eternal; so that he who sows and he who reaps may rejoice together. For in this case the saying is true, 'One sows and another reaps,'"* (Jn. 4:36-37).

Truly, in this case, we and Loretta rejoiced together with the angels, and today, they are both in God's presence praising Jesus before His throne of grace as Loretta passed into eternity a few years later.

Although Carmen was not a verbal person, she was a painter and expressed herself through her art. Years before she had given us a beautiful painting on cork of a cross in front of a California Mission that she had visited while on a vacation. Although the painting did not have any spiritual meaning to her at the time, we had always treasured it and hoped someday it would be meaningful to her in a new way. Perhaps, it was God who had nudged her to paint it so many years ago. For years, we had enjoyed it on a wall in our family room.

Carmen had given us a number of paintings over her lifetime, so it resonated with us when, one day, she asked if we would give Loretta one of them from her as she celebrated her birthday. She so appreciated their friendship and wanted to do something to express her love for her. Although one of our favorites, we immediately knew that the painting of the cross on cork was the one Loretta should have. After all, it was Loretta who had led Carmen to the cross for salvation. Loretta was overcome with gratitude when Carmen presented it to her and she displayed it prominently in her home.

When Loretta passed, we were thankful that she had previously indicated to her family that, upon her passing, they were to return the painting to our family. We appreciated this sweet gesture and the painting has once again been placed in our home. It is a special reminder of God's grace and compassion to our beloved Carmen as well as Loretta's faithfulness in presenting the gospel to her.

CHAPTER 14

BILL MEETS THE LORD

It seems appropriate that Bill should tell his own faith story which took place many years before his mother's.

I was raised in California by parents who had decided early in their marriage that religion would not be part of their lives. Because of that, my experience with church was sparse throughout my childhood and conversation about God did not exist. In my late teens, I attended college for two years and then went off to the Coast Guard for two more years. During that time, I admit I was more interested in the party lifestyle than in anything spiritual. In reality, looking back, I would say I was an empty vessel trying to fill my life with as many worldly distractions as possible.

After military service, I went to work as a salesman for Kirsch Company where the state of Kansas was my first territory. Still living a bachelor lifestyle and able to live anywhere in Kansas, I chose to move to Lawrence with, you guessed it, the hope of meeting girls from the University of Kansas. Betsy was attending KU at the time and had been dating a friend of mine who also lived in my apartment building. When Betsy and I met, I asked her if she would be willing to set me up with some of her sorority sisters so we could double date. She agreed to do that but soon we both realized that we enjoyed each other's company and, in time, her boyfriend drifted out of the picture.

Betsy had been raised in church and although not a born-again believer yet, church attendance was her normal routine. So, I began attending church with her.

By then, her father, Ralph, who had come to the Lord when Betsy was in high school, was involved in supporting Campus Crusade for Christ. This Christian organization met on campus and Ralph invited me to meet the leader, Jim Hiskey. My interest was piqued so I agreed to go. Jim was slightly older than me, a smiling, outgoing man who clearly enjoyed people. After our meeting, he asked if he could take me to breakfast sometime. I said, yes, not realizing that he would be sharing something with me that could turn my life "right side up". However, it took seven years for me to take what he told me to heart and to seriously accept the offer that he made that morning.

After we ordered our breakfast that day, Jim used his napkin to share several biblical principles that put forth a simple presentation of the gospel of Christ and His love for me. These principles were later printed by Campus Crusade in a pamphlet called "The Four Spiritual Laws". The four steps were simple and, as I heard them in my heart, I knew they were true. I was a sinner, a broken man and I knew something was missing from my life.

God pierced my heart when Jim read Romans 10:9-10, *"If you confess with your mouth Jesus as Lord, and believe in your heart that God raised Him from the dead, you will be saved; for with the heart a person believes, resulting in righteousness, and with the mouth he confesses, resulting in salvation."*

I remember clearly that I was immediately convicted. However, even with the awareness that I was a sinner in need of a Savior, sadly, I still said, "No". In the stubbornness of my heart, I was not ready to give my life to Jesus. Although I liked the idea of Jesus dying for my sins, the thought of Lordship, giving some unseen being the reigns to my life was a whole different story. I rejected His offer. What I strongly said in my heart that day was that I was going to drive the bus, even though I sensed there was a cliff coming up in my future.

Saying goodbye, I left Jim in the parking lot, all the while knowing that I was wrong to say, "No," but afraid to let go of the steering wheel of my life. What I realized years later was that what I was hanging onto was actually pulling me down. I was like a drowning man hanging on to an anchor. My way of life, even though corrupt, was all that I knew and it seemed better to hang onto what I knew than to something I didn't know. Later, I realized that is what faith is all about, letting go of what you can see, and grasping that which you cannot see. Hebrews 11:1 describes faith this way: *"Now faith is the assurance of things hoped for, the conviction of things not seen."* At the time, that was a hard concept to grasp and seemed so unnatural.

I wish that I could say that a week later, or even a year later, I decided to yield my life, but it was seven years later, and by then, I was at the cliff. My wheels were over the edge and the bus was rocking. That said, I still held on to the steering wheel, unwilling to give it over to the One who had died on the cross to save me.

One morning, I received a call from a regional manager, a man I knew because my father, who had been an executive with Kirsch, had hired him years earlier. He called out of the blue, or so I thought at the time, and told me that he needed a salesman in California. Knowing I was in trouble with work, he wanted me to come west and settle in the area where I had been born and raised. Because of his loyalty to our family, he was very frank with me, even brutal at times, yet lovingly patient. In all honesty, I should have been fired from my job, but somehow, I was promoted.

He told me, "Bill, I have fought to not have you fired. I know you are having trouble in sales so I have a proposal for you. I would like you to move out here to California and allow me to mentor you in business. I see potential in you and right now, you need a guiding hand."

Although, to my knowledge, he was not a Christian man, he had just hit the nail on the head. With humility and thanks, I agreed to come. Many things needed to change. I was awestruck that even though I deserved to be fired, I was not only promoted but given the best sales territory in the United States...California.

After getting off the phone, I smiled at Betsy and said with a twinkle in my eye, "If you could move anywhere in the United States, where would you like to live?"

Without hesitation, she enthusiastically answered, "California!"

"Well," I said, "Pack your bags. That's where we're going."

Needless to say, she was elated.

With my life falling apart in many ways, I had been holding on by a thread. Besides work issues, our marriage was also in trouble. At times, I had considered leaving, even taking off in my van and becoming a hermit in the mountains like so many of my Hippie generation. But now, distracted with a move to think about, I was unaware that God was about to do an amazing work not only in me but also in our marriage. I have often thought about how a mother cat, seeing her young in a place of danger, will move toward them, pick them up by the scruff of the neck and move them to a place of protection. Looking back, I believe that was what God was about to do with us even though we did not yet know Him personally. All this time, I was still holding tightly to the steering wheel of my life, or maybe the anchor that was drowning me, but God had different plans.

Betsy was pregnant and about to deliver our second daughter when the news of the move came. Within six weeks after giving birth, we had sold our house, had a garage sale, sold our boat and were ready to move with our baby, Laurie, and two year old, Kim.

While Betsy readied things for a move, I traveled to California to find us a house. This meant Betsy would not see where we would be living until we moved in. Soon after I found a house, we packed our belongings in a moving van and left Oklahoma for California.

Fortunately, she loved the new house which was nestled cozily in a neighborhood located in the rolling hills. After seeing the home prices in California, I realized why the slogan of many heading west is, "California or BUST". Although stretching our budget, this would prove to be a new start in both of our lives.

While we had been going to church for years, it was more for social reasons. Faith wasn't really a part of it for me. It was simply a good thing to do, and really, I still didn't want to give up being the lord of my life. But church was an important part of Betsy's life and had now become routine for me as well. So, when we arrived in California, we immediately looked for a church.

Not seeking the Lord or knowing where to go, we checked the phone book for our denomination. Off we headed with our two young daughters to a church situated in a lovely area near a beautiful senior retirement village. That should have been the first clue that it might not be a fit. Because of the age of our children, our first question was, "Where are your nursery and child care?"

We were met with blank stares. That may have been because the "youngsters" in this congregation were in their sixties. Seriously, there were no children. Laughing, we left to seek a younger and more family centered church. Since we were used to a small church, we supposed that would be what we would look for but our next try led us to a mega-church of several thousand people. Compared to what we were used to, this one was huge. We wondered if we could possibly fit in. This church was very different from what we had come from.

On the first day there, we met people who would go on to become lifetime friends. It seemed everyone talked about the Lord and they even read and studied their Bibles, things I was not in the habit of doing. The people we met were also loving, accepting, and interested in knowing us. Their acceptance quickly opened our hearts and we were drawn back for more each week. Clearly, it was where the Lord wanted us. By Providence, we were led to this particular church. The Lord was in the process of leading us out of a dark place and into His light, not only regarding work, but also regarding a church and eventually a relationship with Him.

Along the path that God used to lead me to the cross were several meaningful events. Until now, I had tried to make myself acceptable to God and I well knew the frustration of feeling like I always came up short. One year, as I had looked at my new year's resolutions, I realized that I couldn't even follow my own goals and the changes that I had planned for my own life let alone follow the standards that God had for me. God had me in a perfect position of futility, a launching pad for His plan. Some years later, I discovered a verse in Romans that described my situation. *"For the creation was subjected to futility, not willingly, but because of Him who subjected it, in hope that the creation itself also will be set free from its slavery to corruption into the freedom of the glory of the children of God,"* (Rom. 8:20-21).

While I was still teetering on the edge of Christianity, God brought a man into my life who had a great impact on me. Ron Miller was a barber who befriended me at church. He and his wife, Carol, are jewels in the kingdom of God. Ron had made the decision for Christ several years before and was sold out to Him. He was determined to have me join him. The Holy Spirit used him mightily to gently lead me to understand the depth of Christ's love. It wasn't teaching so much as showing me God's love. I have often said that Ron loved me into the kingdom by consistently demonstrating God's love.

Besides Ron's influence, a series of God ordained events also took place. As a salesman of curtain rods, I was making a call one day to a lady who made draperies in her home. She was a friendly widow who began talking with me about her beliefs, very adamant that her beliefs were the only truth. She talked a lot about her church instead of Jesus and a big part of her religion revolved around working to earn God's favor. Although she was a pleasant person, I didn't quite know what to think about what she was saying. As I listened to her, a thought kept ringing in my heart, *You need the truth, but this is not the truth!*

As I finished the call and started to drive away from her shop, I was quite confused about what she had said. As I pondered the conversation, I felt the Lord saying again, *This is not the truth!* Her beliefs certainly didn't line up with what little I knew from the teachings of our new church. There, I was learning that a person is saved by grace through faith, not of works, that it is a free gift from God, (Eph. 2:8, 9). Confused, I pulled off the road and sat for a minute just thinking. While it wasn't out loud, a question formed in my mind, *"What is the truth?"*

Since we were now going to a church where people brought their Bibles each Sunday, I happened to have my new Bible in the car that day when another thought came to me, *Read the Gospel of John.* I had no idea where that thought came from and I had no idea where the book of John was located. After finding it in the index, I started reading from the beginning of the book. I was immediately pulled into John's writing and read the whole book, all twenty-one chapters. In that time, I realized God was telling me what the "Truth" is. In John 14:6 Jesus said, *"I am the way, and the truth, and the life; no one comes to the Father but through Me."*

Again, in John 10:10-11, *"The thief comes only to steal and kill and destroy; I came that they may have life, and have it abundantly. I am the good shepherd; the good shepherd lays down His life for the sheep."*

John 3:16 -17, *"For God so loved the world, that He gave His only begotten Son, that whoever believes in Him shall not perish, but have eternal life. For God did not send the Son into the world to judge the world, but that the world might be saved through Him."*

Still sitting in my car, incredibly, the Holy Spirit had led me to the very thing I had asked for. He was filling the emptiness of my heart. He had shown me the Truth. I began to realize that the Truth is a person, Jesus Christ. But He wasn't finished. I remembered that John also wrote three other books of the Bible, actually letters, so I turned to the index again, having no idea where they were. Upon locating them, I read those small letters of I, II, and III John. Well over an hour later, putting my Bible down, I realized I was hearing, for the first time, what was on God's heart for my life.

It was all so interesting. I had read so many things. My heart was full, but when I read the fifth chapter of I John, two verses lit up like a neon light, ones that Betsy has used many times in sharing Christ with people. I knew instantly that it was the truth God had wanted me to hear. In verses 12-13, John said, *"He who has the Son has the life; he who does not have the Son of God does not have the life. These things I have written to you who believe in the name of the Son of God, so that you may know that you have eternal life."*

The question that had come to my mind all those years, although I had never actually voiced it, was, *How will I know, how can anybody know?* And now God was telling me that I could know. I could know because He told me that I could know and it was His Word that told me so.

This was not the message my customer had shared with me. Later, I learned that she belonged to a cult, one based on works for salvation. But the message from the Bible was based on faith in what Jesus Christ had done for us, what His Father had sent Him to do. What God showed me that day was a 'rhema' word, a personal word to lead me to Truth. It hit me like a sledge hammer. I didn't have to do things to make myself acceptable to God. Believing what He had done at the cross was all that was necessary to make me acceptable to Him. Putting my trust in Him alone, *"He who has the Son has the life…"*

I remembered Jim's message during that breakfast years before and I now knew in my heart that Jesus was the answer. I remembered my resistance and the message from Romans that Jesus' desired to be my Lord. Romans 10:9-10, *"…that if you confess with your mouth Jesus as Lord, and believe in your heart that God raised Him from the dead, you will be saved; for with the heart a person believes, resulting in righteousness, and with the mouth he confesses, resulting in salvation."*

God wanted me to come to Jesus, not simply as a Savior, which He is, but as my Lord, the One who takes the wheel and sits in the driver's seat of my life. He is the One who led me away from the cliff, the One who offered the free gift of eternal life and who wanted to lead me every day.

Soon after that, I slipped out of bed one night, fell to my knees and asked Jesus to be not only my Savior but also my Lord. Those few words that God had spoken to me about truth were the turning point and Ron's love was the human demonstration of God's *agape* love. Now, I have the Son and I know I have the life He offers so freely at His expense, the cross.

I give all of the credit to the Lord, but I give thanks to those He used in the process. My boss, Phil, who believed that I could be more than I believed I could be. He mentored me, corrected me and drove me to become what God had created me to be. Even though not a believer himself, God used Phil in my life for good. Through Phil's influence, I went from one of the worst salesmen in the company to one of the best. Additionally, God used the influence of Jim, who boldly shared the gospel with me, and Ron, who loved me into the kingdom of God. Each, in his own way, imparted to me the heart to mentor other men, to help them discover just what God has for them.

I have studied the Scriptures for over forty-five years and discovered many deep truths that bring life and hope to those who will dare to trust in Christ and His Word. But I will never forget that it all began with one man, Jim, who dared to share with me the love of God and the gospel message. I'm also grateful to the many others who have since taught, loved, encouraged, exhorted, and corrected me and, of course, to my wife who has stood by my side through the journey.

CHAPTER 15
TWO YOUNG CULT MEMBERS

E ver since Bill's encounter with the customer from a cult who
had tried to persuade him to her religion, like most people,
he has avoided confrontation with those who come to the door
espousing their doctrine. However, that all changed with an interesting encounter he had one afternoon.

Bill: It was a warm summer afternoon and I was working in my
home office. I happened to glance out the window and noticed two
young men dressed in coats and ties coming up the street toward
our house. Immediately, I identified them as either Mormons or
Jehovah Witnesses. They were armed with their Bibles and other
literature in hopes of converting our neighborhood to their belief
system. Like many people, I had an immediate reaction to go in
the other room, turn off the lights and hide. As they neared, I happened to recognize the two men as they had been to our home several times before wanting to share their doctrine, but this time my
response was going to be different. God had revealed something
to me that changed my attitude toward people in cults.

I had recently been watching Focus on the Family's video series
on Christian worldview called "The Truth Project". In that series,
God used Del Tackett, the teacher, to challenge my point of view

on cults with something I had never considered. I was incredibly touched by a statement Del made concerning John 8:32, "*...and you will know the truth, and the truth will make you free.*" At first glance, this familiar verse may not offer a new revelation. In its context, the verse was about Jesus encouraging the Jewish believers to continue in His word because then they would know the truth that would free them. It was a surprise then when Del offered a stunning conclusion from this verse. He simply stated that, "If the truth sets us free, then it is lies that hold us captive."

As I pondered this, I knew in my case this was certainly true. I grew up believing I was stupid. In school, I seemed to have trouble in every subject and eventually stopped trying. I was held captive by what I later found out was a lie. As an adult, I learned that I had a motor problem in the connection between my eyes and my brain which made reading really hard, almost impossible. It wasn't my brain, after all, that was defective as I had thought. I had believed a lie. In truth, it was simply a glitch in the way my eyes tried to coordinate, a problem that was overcome fairly easily once identified. The consequence of believing the lie that I was just stupid, however, had held me captive for many years.

As I considered this new revelation regarding people caught up in the lies of cults, it gave me a new way to look at them. I thought back to the many cult members I had talked to, served in the Coast Guard with, and worked with in the business world. Until that day, I had never realized they were captives to lies. Captives, not enemies.

A captive is one who is enslaved, restrained, held prisoner or dominated by something. Surely, a captive is not an enemy but rather someone who needs to be released, someone who is trapped and needs to be freed from a form of oppression. Colossians 2:8 says, "*See to it that no one takes you captive through philosophy and empty deception, according to the tradition of men, according to the elementary principles of the world, rather than according to Christ.*" Even leaders of cults, who purposefully sway people away from Christ, although they are clearly enemies of the gospel, are captives themselves.

As I watched the familiar men coming up my driveway, I was seeing them in a new light. *These young men were not the enemy. They were "captives" of a false belief system. They believed a lie.* They were probably not even aware that they were misrepresenting faith in Christ. For the first time, seeing them as "captives," I felt compassion for them, not fear of them.

Knowing that their organization begins to indoctrinate members almost from birth, I knew they were filled with false teaching. Their teaching veers from the truth of being saved by grace through faith in Christ and Christ alone. They not only embrace a works theology but that theology is the center of their worldview. Even verses like Ephesians 2:8-9, which clearly contradicts that belief, are somehow missed. *"For by grace you have been saved through faith; and that not of yourselves, it is the gift of God; not as a result of works, so that no one may boast."*

My decision that day was not to hide but to interact with them, not as enemies, but as young men who believed the lies they had been fed. Quickly jumping up from my desk, I ran out to the driveway and waved at them. Probably gleeful to see a friendly, accepting face, they cheerfully waved back as they headed toward me. My guess was they were thinking they had found an easy target, perhaps someone who would take the bait. Little did they realize that I, too, was hoping for an opening to share a different message. As they approached, I felt love well up in my heart, a love that could only have come from God.

A familiar verse went through my mind, one that had also been used in the Truth Project. Colossians 4:2-6, *"Devote yourselves to prayer, keeping alert in it with an attitude of thanksgiving; praying at the same time for us as well, that God will open up to us a door for the word, so that we may speak forth the mystery of Christ, for which I have also been imprisoned; that I may make it clear in the way I ought to speak. Conduct yourselves with wisdom toward outsiders, making the most of the opportunity. Let your speech always be with grace, as though seasoned with salt, so that you will know how you should respond to each person."*

Such good advice, something I needed to remember, to "conduct myself with wisdom and grace" to those outside the faith. I didn't want my response to be canned or insensitive, but personal and caring. Hopefully, God was giving me a door for His Word.

After we greeted each other, my first comments were to commend them for their dedication to their mission experience. I had to admit that, although they had been misled, they were sincere and devoted to their cause. As nice young men, well trained and polite, they were eager to talk. I was also excited to chat with them and watch how God would turn our conversation to the gospel of Christ.

Quickly, a question formed in my mind. "You know, I have a question that I have always wanted to ask someone from your group."

Instantly, I had their attention. Thrilled to have someone interested in their message, they were eager at the chance to respond. I wasn't trying to trip them up or prove their beliefs to be false at that point. I wanted to show genuine interest in them. I honestly wanted to hear their convictions and beliefs. It is one thing to hear or read "about" other faiths and another thing to have a real person verbalize their personal convictions. I felt I could find out best by directing a question to them that was a familiar one to me, one I frequently used in conversation with unbelievers. Depending on their response, I would ask a follow-up question.

"My question to you is a simple one," I began. "When you leave here and step into the street, if a car would run you down and you would die, where do you think you would spend eternity?"

It was an honest question, not a challenge, so I was surprised when both young men's responses were identical. Their heads went down and a very sad expression filled their eyes. The question had hit a nerve and was obviously disturbing to them.

After a moment, the leader began his response by saying, "We know that we are sinners and that is why we are out knocking on people's doors. For us, this is a way to work to offset our sins."

I was struck by their honesty, but also by the obvious pain I detected on their faces. I let their response sit for a couple of moments and then asked, "May I read something to you from the Bible?"

I sensed an openness in this tender moment. Since my car was parked in the driveway, I stepped over to it and pulled out my Bible. Turning to I John 1:8-9, I handed my Bible to one of the boys and asked if he would mind reading it out loud.

He took my Bible and when he located the section, he began reading. *"If we say that we have no sin, we are deceiving ourselves and the truth is not in us. If we confess our sins, He is faithful and righteous to forgive us our sins and to cleanse us from all unrighteousness."*

Clearly, they already knew they were sinners. Not wanting to leave them in despair, I then asked them to look through that section again and point out where the verses talked about works. They both looked more closely expecting to find something.

First one, and then the other, looked up and both slowly acknowledged, "It's not there."

They were on the road to discovery and I wanted the Bible to continue to reveal truth to them. It was important that they see for themselves what scripture says without me telling them.

I continued, "What do you see, then, is required for forgiveness of sins from verse 9?"

It was obvious to both of them that confession, not works, is mentioned as the requirement for forgiveness of sins. I could tell they were pondering this revelation. They had no comeback to the words of Scripture.

After that, I took them further into 1 John and had them read 5:13, *"These things I have written to you who believe in the name of the Son of God, so that you may know that you have eternal life."*

Then I asked the obvious question. "Tell me, boys, as you see, this verse says that we can 'know' that we have eternal life. So, my question to you is this, do you know for sure that you have eternal life?"

Again, they struggled, which was wonderful. I sensed the Lord was moving in their hearts, drawing them to Himself, so I directed them to the two previous verses. With that I had them read I John 5:11-12, *"And the testimony is this, that God has given us eternal life, and this life is in His Son. He who has the Son has the life; he who does not have the Son of God does not have the life."* Again, they were seeing that works were not mentioned, only belief in Jesus.

This brought me to my second question, "If the Lord asked you, 'Why should I allow you into heaven,' how would you answer?" As expected, they began to tell me of their works, learning doctrine, and their commitment to the mission they were on. I brought them back to Ephesians 2:8-9 where it is clear that it is about faith and not about works. I had them read the text for themselves, *"For by grace you have been saved through faith; and that not of yourselves, it is the gift of God; not as a result of works, so that no one may boast."*

The younger of the two became edgy at that point and seemed somewhat anxious to get away. The leader, however, stopped and with all sincerity asked, "Can you tell me what I should read?"

As they prepared to leave, I answered. "I think a good place for you to start reading would be in I John where I pointed out some pivotal verses already. Read the whole book, then go to the gospel of John. Ask God to reveal His truth to you." With that, we said our goodbyes.

It was a sweet time with no confrontation, a time to plant some seeds. The Lord had opened their hearts as they simply read His word. Two young men who were faithful to their mission but not to the truth of the Bible. Two young men who had become captives to lies. Captives, not enemies.

I invited them back, but never saw again. It is freeing to know that it was not my responsibility to save them or to convict them of their sins. That is the job of the Holy Spirit. John 16:8, in speaking of the Holy Spirit, says, *"And He, when He comes, will convict the world concerning sin and righteousness and judgment."* My job was to simply offer them truth, spoken in love.

CHAPTER 16

REVELATION FROM ACROSS THE ROOM

(Jack's story as told by Bill Tacchella)

Have you ever been driving and run into a fog that was so thick that it was like a blanket shutting you off from seeing anything? As a California native, I grew up experiencing what we knew as Tule Fog. It is named after the native Tule grass because of the way it settles down to the ground. In this type of fog you can barely see your nose let alone the hood of your car or the road ahead. When it is thick, the only way to drive is to roll the window down, stick your head out and hope to see the side of the road and avoid hitting mailboxes. You can't safely go forward, you can't turn around and go back, and you are afraid somebody is going to run into you. Basically, you are driving blind. You simply can't see anything, although you know everything is really still there.

I remember going into a store one day in Pasadena, California on a day when everything around me was hidden by the Tule fog. An hour later, as I walked from the store, the fog had lifted, and to my amazement, not more than two hundred feet away was a beautiful mountain with lush trees. It had always been there but I had been blinded by the fog. The beauty of the mountain was only revealed as the fog lifted.

A similar type of revelation came to my friend, Jack, the day he began to clearly see what his life had become. As the fog lifted, he saw his life in a panorama and it stunned him to realize how empty and without purpose it was.

While Jack had a decent job working on a street crew in our small mid-western town, living life without purpose and with little hope for change began to gnaw at him. Yes, he had friends and family, and although he'd had excitement in his life, like being buried alive in a street repair cave-in, he usually found himself in a repetitive cycle day after day. Getting up in the morning, going to work, then to a local social club where he drank beer. Usually staying until closing, he went home, slept, and returned to work the next morning. After work, back to the club, night after night in a place where too many people find themselves without joy or direction in life.

Unknown to Jack, God was about to interrupt this endless cycle through an encounter with Tammy, a member of our church at the time. It was not uncommon to find Tammy sitting in our local McDonald's restaurant chatting with one or more strangers, or friends, who were drawn to her table. Tammy also had a way of seeking out lonely people, sitting with them, befriending, and encouraging them, often talking about faith issues and then praying for them. With strong gifts of compassion and evangelism, and a heart to reach people for the Lord, she would sweetly share Jesus' love. As a Hospice volunteer she had used her gifts ministering to many people in their final days.

Some evenings, Tammy went to the social club where Jack spent his evenings. Although not one to drink alcohol herself, she knew this was a place where she might have opportunities to share her faith and God's love with those like Jack who were regulars. One night, Tammy was sitting at a table at the back of the room where she was waiting to meet an elderly lady friend. She saw Jack, whom she already knew, seated in his usual place at the bar. That night, she decided to ask him if he would like to sit with them, not knowing this would become the first of many times that Jack would join the two of them.

Tammy's friend had lost her husband and was lonely. One evening, as the jukebox played a song that had been a favorite of hers, she tearfully reminisced. It was a nostalgic moment so, Jack, always the gentleman, tried to soften the moment by asking her to dance.

After the dance, returning to their table at the back of the room, for the first time, Jack began to observe the rest of the room from this different location. From a distance, his gaze fell on the customers that sat in the bar area where he usually sat. His perception from this viewpoint stunned him. Sometimes, perspective can make a remarkable difference, and that night, it certainly did for Jack.

Looking back at that night he has said, "Usually, I was only aware of the bar stools to my left and right and the bartender in front of me, a pretty narrow view with not much perspective. That night, seated further away, what I saw shocked me."

From this new angle, looking back at the bar, he suddenly saw what his life was like on a daily basis. He now noticed the customers leaning on the bar and how they appeared lonely and a bit lost. It was a gut wrenching revelation to suddenly realize that his own life had also become one of desperation and sadness. It was a painful insight. Later he confessed, "In that moment, the fog lifted."

As Jack pondered what he was seeing, Tammy was telling her story, one of trial but also of faith and purpose. She shared how she had met Christ and how much a local church had helped her. She warmly invited Jack to come to her church on Sunday morning and to visit the Sunday school. Perhaps he would see and experience what she had found.

Jack showed interest but he continued to visit the club where, on another evening, Tammy asked him a very simple question. "Jack, do you know where you are going to spend eternity?"

He pondered that for a bit and finally said, "Well, I don't know. I don't think I am good enough for heaven, but then I don't think that I am bad enough for hell!"

Her follow-up question further opened his eyes and brought him up short. "Jack, there are only two choices. Which one will be yours?"

The next Sunday as I entered our Sunday school class, there was Jack. I had seen him before with the city workers at lunch or coffee, but we hadn't talked much. That day, I happened to be teaching Sunday school. I have no recall of the subject, and I bet Jack doesn't remember either as he sat looking around and listening. It was all so new to him yet he found himself enjoying the discussion.

A really pleasant guy, Jack looked right at home in the class. The participants loved having him there and welcomed him warmly. Later, after the worship service, as I talked with him, he looked at me with a smile on his face and said with incredible emotion, "Where has this been all my life?"

After a few days, he went to the pastor's office to inquire more about God. In a short time, Jack gave his heart to the Lord. The gospel, which translates "Good News," was indeed good news to Jack. His life began to change immediately as a dramatic transformation was set in motion.

I started to meet with Jack occasionally and had the privilege of getting to know him and encourage him in his faith. He also joined several **B**ible studies and was taking his new faith very seriously. As he grasped concepts from the Bible, he grew rapidly by combining knowledge with understanding. The sincere growth that I saw come quickly to Jack was rare for a new believer. Jack began to discover that God not only wanted to bring a new, redeemed life to him, but He wanted to use Jack and give him purpose. He realized he could serve God in many ways as he trusted Him to use him.

One of the most amazing things that came through His new faith walk was an opportunity offered by a lady he knew. She started a conversation with him one day by asking if it was true that he had just become a Christian. Jack replied, "Yes, I have given my heart to Jesus." She then asked if he would visit her son who had cancer and didn't have too much time left. She explained that her son was in a hospital an hour away.

You might imagine that even a seasoned pastor would have backed up a bit at a request to minister to a dying stranger, but not Jack. He confidently said, "Sure."

As he told me the story later, I asked him how he had felt so confident in accepting the invitation. His answer convicted me. "Well," Jack said, "The Bible tells me that when I received Christ that He came into my heart, so I figured if He is there, He will tell me what to say."

For a young believer, that was a rare insight. So, off Jack went to the hospital to visit this young man in the Critical Care Unit.

Later I asked Jack, "So how did it go?"

"Ok, I guess," he cheerily responded. "I don't remember much of what I said, but I do recall suggesting that when he was released from the hospital and went home the next week, that he should go to his pastor, get right with the Lord and get baptized."

Jack related that the young man had told him that he had made a commitment to Christ several years earlier but had not followed up very well. In fact, at one point, he had denied having faith. Jack asked if he had been baptized to which he said he had not.

Later, I asked Jack what had happened when the guy returned home and he casually said, "I talked to him after he got home and he had gone to his pastor, gotten right with God, and was baptized. He said he had peace with God. Shortly after that, I found out he passed away and went home to be with the Lord."

Jack, with his uncomplicated faith, had trusted God to work in him and through him, as God promises. The result was that he helped a man in need. He had no training, but he had faith. Jack was a man being transformed by God, like a caterpillar transformed into a new beautiful creation. It was truly a miracle. *"But we all, with unveiled face, beholding as in a mirror the glory of the Lord, are being transformed into the same image from glory to glory, just as from the Lord, the Spirit,"* (II Cor. 3:18).

That experience was the start for Jack. Much more happened as God continued to change his life and open up more opportunities. Clearly, all of the changes didn't come in one day, but asking Christ to be his Lord and Savior was a great start. While we are saved in a moment by God's grace, He continues to change and transform us throughout our life here on earth. It seems that most permanent outward changes begin with an inward revelation from the Lord. A decision is usually involved that leads to an inward change of heart. What then follows is a change in outward behavior.

Shortly after giving his life to the Lord, Jack was sitting at that same club one night and the thought came, "I think I'll just have a Pepsi tonight." Then surprisingly a couple of nights later, he again thought, "Why not just stop the beer and switch to Pepsi all the time." It wasn't a legalistic decision to stop drinking. God had wooed him with new friendships, Bible studies, and Christian events that just became more fulfilling to the point he no longer felt a need to drink every night. Being in Christ had brought new freedom to his life and greater joy.

Also, soon after accepting Christ's gift of salvation, the church had their annual outside baptism and Jack took the plunge with great enthusiasm, sharing the story of God's remarkable work of redemption in his life.

I have seen the indwelling Christ not only change him into a man with a new heart but also give him purpose, hope and ministry.

The influence and difference this tender and humble man has made in the lives of others, mine included, is profound. God wants to use those whose lives have been touched and changed by the power of the resurrection.

Jack has gone on to become a friend, a brother, and co-worker in Christ. He still enjoys hunting, hot rods, and many old friends but also serves as a church deacon and in other leadership positions which fit his love for others and his willingness to help, to pray for and to serve.

Jack is rock solid proof of the loving power of God to pick up a man, deliver him from a wasted life, and repurpose him for His own use. It took a simple step of faith on Jack's part and a willingness to walk in that faith to make him a genuine man of God. If you think about it and look for it, God is willing to lift the Tule fog in all of our lives so that we can see the opportunities that He has set before us. It is always God's desire to lovingly bring revelation of Himself to us. We simply need to ask, seek or knock. *"Ask, and it will be given to you; seek, and you will find; knock, and it will be opened to you,"* (Mt. 7:7).

CHAPTER 17

A QUESTIONING HEART

Lori was a prominent society lady in our town. I had known her for years but not as a close friend. We had played bridge together and she had been very welcoming when we first moved to Michigan. But our relationship never went beyond acquaintance.

As I prayed one morning, her name came to mind. When that happens, God is usually up to something, so I prayed for her and asked the Lord if He wanted anything else. Sensing he wanted me to talk to her about the Lord, I asked Him to set up an opportunity. Not feeling led to call her, I asked the Lord if He would arrange a meeting in His way and His time. Knowing God is creative, I looked forward to watching Him bring it about. Not wanting to rush ahead of His will, I waited expectantly for this new adventure to unfold. I had no idea how He would work out His strategy.

Little did I know that God would use one of Bill's mentoring sessions with a young lady in our church to begin unfolding His plan. Though I hadn't met Donna, as is my custom when Bill mentors a young lady, I sat in on the session. So many girls are missing a healthy relationship with their father, it is a blessing that Bill is willing to talk with them so they are able to gain perspective from a godly man. As the evening progressed, Donna began to tell us about some conversations she had recently had with her grand-mother. We listened as she explained how she had recently shared her faith with her grandmother who had then expressed interest.

"I want to tell her more about Jesus," she explained, "but I am a new Christian, and I don't know much about the Bible. Maybe I could arrange a luncheon for the three of us, Betsy, and you could answer some of her questions."

Honored with the opportunity, I said, "Well that sounds very nice Donna. I would enjoy meeting your grandmother. By the way, what is her name?"

You guessed it. God had arranged for Lori's granddaughter, Donna, to start attending our church and meet with us for counsel. Then He had spoken to me about getting together with Lori. Upon my request that He bring it about, He planted the idea in Donna's mind to suggest a lunch date. Clearly, God was all over this meeting.

When the day arrived for the three of us to meet, I watched expectantly to see what God had in mind. While we had a warm and lively discussion over lunch, our conversation did not flow to anything especially spiritual. However, having enjoyed each other's company, we followed up with plans for another lunch date.

Ok, Lord, maybe this was just the "get to know you" session. God's timing isn't always the same as mine. He never seems to be in a hurry. I, however, eagerly awaited our second get together.

Before we met the second time, I asked the Lord to stir Lori's heart to bring up spiritual matters. Although I usually look for a chance to bring Christ into a conversation, this time I sensed God wanted me to hold back and let her lead.

Interestingly, after chatting for about an hour, Lori seamlessly moved the subject to an opening. She explained that she had been watching a Christian television show recently and something about it seemed to touch her heart. I immediately knew God was at work. Being familiar with the particular show she was viewing,

I was delighted to hear her positive response. I knew this preacher was trustworthy and would speak truth into her life.

Lori did have many questions about faith that day and was glad for the chance to discuss them with someone who would listen and give her straight answers. I was pleased with the opportunity to also give her a clear presentation of the gospel. I knew the Lord had intentionally placed Lori in my life. She was there by design and for a purpose and I looked at it as an exciting adventure. Although she didn't come to the Lord that day, many questions were addressed. Later, I heard that the TV preacher had led her to Christ. I was only happy to be a small part of her journey toward eternity.

God wants to be personally involved in our lives, and when He begins to reveal His plans for us, they often lead to an occasion for adventure. I think God enjoys opportunities to be creative with us and it is so faith building to cooperate with Him in His exploits.

CHAPTER 18

GROCERY STORE OPPORTUNITY

Keri worked in one of our local grocery stores. We had struck up a conversation one day as I was shopping the produce aisle. With blond hair and a perpetual smile on her face, I instantly liked her. At that time our son, Mike, was a baby and Keri, who loved babies, always enjoyed visiting a few minutes with us to hear how he was doing. She was easy to talk to and I soon looked forward to seeing her each week as we shopped for our groceries. A sweet relationship formed as we talked about our families and our lives.

Although our visits had to be short, we soon began sharing on a more personal level. One day, Keri shared a private trial with me, something difficult that she was going through. I felt it was time to venture forth and tell her about Jesus and how He could be trusted with our deepest problems. I wanted her to know how Jesus could bring direction, strength and comfort in her situation. She listened attentively and expressed her appreciation for my time and input regarding her painful circumstance. I got the impression she might not have people in her life to talk to on a personal level so it was a blessing for me to be able to share in her struggle and pray for her.

As time went on, the Lord began to nudge me to look for an opening to give her an opportunity to pray to receive Jesus into her life. On another grocery outing, that moment came. As she shared another struggle with me, I sensed it was time to ask her if she had ever received Christ as her personal Lord and Savior. I wanted her to know that God loves her and is a present help in times of need. Her immediate answer was, "No, I have never invited Him into my life but I would like to."

Without any forethought or planning for this moment, when I noticed no one else was in the aisle with us, I asked her if she would like to pray right then to receive Christ. When she answered, "Yes," we quickly bowed our heads and prayed. I think God kept people away for those few minutes because not one person ventured into that normally busy aisle. What a joy to know my grocery store friend was now my sister in Christ.

I was so thankful for the privilege of being used to lead her to the One who could fill her up and come alongside her in the midst of her troubles. It is amazing how, if we take the time to notice those around us and care about their needs, the Lord tends to show up. He cares deeply about people and I believe He smiles when we choose to be His hands and voice. We have the privilege of offering people the hope that He offers. With Keri, God opened an opportunity for me to unlock a door for her to know God, and with that encounter, her life was changed for all eternity.

CHAPTER 19

COFFEE SHOP EXCHANGE

Betty was a new neighbor. For the first couple of years, since she worked, we were just casual acquaintances, occasionally engaging in a chat when we ran into each other. When she was later laid off at work and had time to pursue a friendship, one morning, we went out to coffee together. I had wondered where she stood with the Lord, whether she had faith or would she even be interested in spiritual things. Finding a seat at the coffee shop, we chatted about our lives for awhile and then I felt led to turn a corner in our conversation and invite her to church. I could tell there was interest by her affirmative answer. With that, I wondered if she would also be receptive to talking about God so I continued with the gospel message and found she was very open and seemed to track with everything I said. I thought why not ask her if she had ever invited Christ into her heart. When she answered that she had not, I knew God had set up our meeting so I asked if she would like to and without hesitation, she answered, "Yes". So, right there in the coffee shop, we bowed our heads and I led her in a simple prayer which she repeated after me. Again, I noted that God seemed to clear out the coffee shop for those few moments while we were praying so that she would not be uncomfortable.

Later, I invited her to a Bible study I led in my home and she eagerly joined right in.

Now, I know that this story seems kind of cut and dry, right to the point. Of course, there was probably more conversation than I have recorded but the point is that sometimes, we don't have to make lots of plans as to how we will talk to someone about Jesus. At times, it just naturally evolves. When meeting with people, I am always aware that God may want me to say something. I rarely plan ahead as to what I am going to say. It is so much fun for me to just show up expecting the Holy Spirit to come alongside and prompt me in conversation.

Like most people, there are times it would be easier to say, "I can't do this because I don't know enough; I don't know what I should say; I am too shy, or I am not perfect." What I have learned, though, is that while it is true that I am not adequate, it is also true that God is. I love the verses from II Corinthians 3:5-6, *"Not that we are adequate in ourselves to consider anything as coming from ourselves, but our adequacy is from God who also made us adequate...."*

How many opportunities would I have missed if I had chosen to sit back and say nothing about Jesus? I have no doubt that, over the years, I have missed many chances to share my faith with others. I am called to be a witness and while there is no condemnation from God if I choose not to be, it is also true that I have probably missed blessings He has wanted to pour out to me. As believers, we are all called to be a witness. We are not alone in this calling. He goes with us and empowers us for this ministry.

In sharing Christ with people, I sometimes begin the conversation with two telling questions. First, I ask, "If you were to die tonight, do you know for sure that you would go to heaven?" With that question, I learn whether a person has any idea as to their salvation. Interestingly, it should be noted, that I have found many Christians still do not have an affirmative answer. How sad to have accepted Christ and not know whether your salvation is secure. I have likened it to a child going off to school one morning and arriving home in the afternoon to find the house empty and their family has moved away. How anxious and apprehensive that child would feel. Surely, our loving heavenly Father would not leave us, His children, in such an insecure, frightening circumstance.

Verses that explains this well are Ephesians 1:13-14, *"In Him, you also, after listening to the message of truth, the gospel of your salvation--having also believed, you were sealed in Him with the Holy Spirit of promise, who is given as a pledge of our inheritance, with a view to the redemption of God's own possession, to the praise of His glory."* Ephesians 4:30, *"Do not grieve the Holy Spirit of God, by whom you were sealed for the day of redemption."*

God loves us and when He says we are sealed with the Holy Spirit, we can be confident that we are secure in Him. Psalm 94:14 is also a comforting assurance, *"For the Lord will not abandon His people, nor will He forsake His inheritance."*

With the answer to the first question, I then follow up with another question. "If you were to meet God tonight and He asked you, "'Why should I let you into My heaven?' how would you answer?"

This second question quickly reveals what the person is depending on for salvation. Most often, the answer I hear is, "I have tried to be a good person." Sometimes they will say, "I keep the Ten Commandments," or "I have lived a moral life." Sadly, none of these answers will insure a path to eternal life.

When people give these kinds of answers, I like to tease them a bit before telling them about the only path to God. I'll say, "Oh, did you know that Galatians 3:10 says, *'All who rely on observing the law are under a curse...'* (NIV), "or did you know that II Corinthians 3 says the law brings condemnation and death? So, are you still sure you want to rely on keeping the law to get to heaven?"

When I use this logic, as you can imagine, I have their full attention. Interestingly, they usually are at a loss, then, as to how to acquire entrance to heaven. It is with great joy that I have the privilege of explaining that the only entry we have to God's Kingdom is through the wonderful blood of Jesus which he shed for our sins. By paying for our sins through His finished work on the cross, we can have access to God and eternity. It is nothing we have done or can do. It is all about Jesus.

CHAPTER 20
LUNCH WITH LINDA

Two years had passed since I had seen Linda. We were just acquaintances with one common interest, attending our daughters' high school swim meets. Weekly, she and her husband joined Bill and I along with several other couples as we traveled together in an RV to distant swim events. It was a fun, relaxed group. Our conversation never went too deep but we felt comfortable with one another and shared a team spirit and camaraderie.

Our routine was to take turns providing dinner for the group to be eaten in the RV at various school parking lots. Arriving early at the meets gave us ample time to enjoy a nice meal together before going to the pool. Meals were kept warm in the RV oven as we drove to the designated school. I recall one time it was my turn to provide dinner, so I made lasagna, one of my favorite meals and easy to prepare. It kept warm in the RV oven, but as we made a hard turn around a corner into the parking lot, apparently the oven door had not been latched properly because it flew open and out bounced my lasagna...all over the floor. What a mess! *"Oh no,"* I groaned. I felt terrible. My contribution for dinner was ruined. I tried to be mature and just help clean it up, but I'm sure my disappointment was evident. I put on my best smiling face as others expressed their regret that dinner was a bust.

There's always an optimist in the crowd and he quickly came to the rescue with a cheery, "I guess we'll make a run to Kentucky Fried Chicken." *Ok, I can deal with that.* All was not lost. I felt better and we again enjoyed dinner together and the swim meet afterwards.

Now, years had passed and I hadn't seen or thought about Linda since our girls had graduated from high school. Although I had enjoyed her friendly personality on our journeys to swim meets, we had not kept up a friendship when they were over. I guess we were both involved in our own lives.

That's why it was curious when, one morning as I was reading my Bible and praying, Linda's name came to mind. Being the analytical type, I wondered why I was thinking of her after all this time. Then, another thought drifted across my mind… *Invite Linda to lunch.*

At first, this seemed like an odd thought. How absurd to think of inviting her to lunch. We barely knew each other, and too much time had passed since we had last met. The thought of calling her felt awkward. Plus, I had not even seen her around town. Clearly, I felt uncomfortable with the idea. What would I say? Would she even remember me? I dismissed the idea as too bazaar, never giving it another thought and went on with my day's activities. Surely, God wouldn't be asking me to do something so strange, but I should have known better.

The next day, as I sat down to pray, you might guess what wafted across my mind again. *Invite Linda to lunch.* My heart jumped. *Oh no, really?* This time I began to question the Lord. *Is this really You, Lord?* I was hoping to hear a resounding *No, of course not, I would never ask such an absurd thing of you,* but instead, an affirming *"Yes"* floated into my mind. I knew immediately that it was the Lord.

Still, I pondered this strange request for several days but it just wouldn't leave my thoughts; so, finally, I decided to make an appeal. *Lord, if this is from you, would you arrange for me to run into Linda somewhere in town in the next week? If this happens, then I'll ask her to lunch trusting that you must have a purpose, although I can't imagine what it would be since I haven't seen her in years and hardly even know her.* I shook my head and rolled my eyes in a "what next?" sort of way.

It wasn't so much getting together with Linda that bothered me but more of what was God expecting from this meeting? It felt intimidating to step out in faith with no direction as to what the purpose was going to be. I like to have at least a little information ahead of time, but this didn't seem to be God's agenda on this occasion.

With my prayer settled, I watched with guarded anticipation to see what would happen next, all the while hoping it would all just go away. The whole idea still felt intimidating to the point of being ludicrous.

Several days later, I made my weekly trip to the grocery store. As I meandered up and down the aisles, focused on shopping, Linda was the farthest thing from my mind. However, as I turned down the next aisle, guess who was coming my way? *No, it can't be!* I felt my heart skip a beat. I was taken off guard. Fear rose up. *What should I do?* I hadn't really expected to see her, at least not so soon. *Maybe I should just turn my cart around and pretend I didn't see her. That's it...I'll just avoid her.*

But then, I recalled the appeal. Although squirming on the inside, I almost had to suppress a chuckle as I realized God was leading me right to her. Taking a deep breath, I directed my cart straight down the aisle. "Well, Hi Linda. It's nice to see you." I was glad she remembered me...or was I? Of course, Linda was oblivious to the quandary I was feeling so she was her usual friendly self.

We chatted a few minutes but I said nothing about asking her to lunch because it still seemed too awkward. I decided to return home before making the call. I needed to process what just happened, how God had obviously brought Linda across my path.

The next morning I picked up the phone, and with a sweaty hand and heart palpitating, I dialed her number. "Linda, hey, it was fun running into you at the grocery store. It's been years since we've seen each other."

I'm one to get right to the point so I continued without hesitation, "I wondered if you might want to get together for lunch sometime." I spoke as casually as I could muster hoping she didn't think I was crazy.

"I'm delighted to hear from you, Betsy. Yes, I'd love to do lunch. I have to tell you, though, that I'm working now and would only have about an hour. If that works for you, let's plan on it."

After a mental sigh of relief, feeling encouraged, I responded. "I think that would work. Why don't you just come over to my house, and I'll fix something simple." *Whew...that went better than I thought it would. Linda sounded delighted with the invitation. Maybe I was making too much out of this.*

The date was set, but I had no idea what I was supposed to talk about with her. We had never spoken about spiritual matters. Yet, surely that must be God's purpose for this meeting. *Well Lord*, I whispered, *I'll be watching for your plan to unfold.*

The day of the luncheon arrived. After warmly greeting each other, I invited Linda to come sit at the table where I already had lunch arranged and waiting since I knew we would only have an hour. We chatted for the first ten minutes about our families and the weather. While we talked, I shot up an anxious prayer, *Lord, we only have fifty minutes left. When are you going to do something?*

No sooner had I breathed out this prayer than Linda took a deep breath and looked at me with troubled eyes. "You know, Betsy, I've been talking with a friend of mine lately, and a question has been stirring in my mind."

"Really?" I asked with peaked interest. "What would that be, Linda?"

"Well, I'm very concerned because I'm not sure when I die that I'll go to heaven. Betsy, I know you're a Christian. Do you have any insight as to how a person can know for sure what his eternal destiny will be?"

At this point, I'm sure my mouth must have dropped open in amazement. Linda was asking me the most important question a person can ask. The Lord had been giving me all those nudges in preparation. Now I knew I had indeed heard His voice. This was truly a divine appointment that He had set up with purpose. God had seen Linda's seeking heart and was allowing me the privilege of being a catalyst to point her to Him. In His love and mercy for Linda, He had arranged this luncheon to allow her a chance to hear about Him and His plan for her life.

Instead of this being an uncomfortable meeting like I had expected, I learned that day that God's voice can be trusted and that He indeed does have a plan when He brings someone to mind to call or get together with. I was delighted with this wonderful opportunity. All my fear vanished and for the next half hour, I shared the gospel message and my personal testimony with Linda.

As we finished up, I thought it would be helpful to give her an affirming section of Scripture. "Linda, it might interest you to know that it is possible to have assurance that when you die, you will go to heaven. It is actually something we can know with certainty. Many years ago I confessed my sin to God and accepted Jesus into my heart as my Lord and Savior. Then someone shared with me a very impactful verse that has warmed my heart ever since. Would you like to hear it?"

"Yes, of course, tell me what it is," she asked with piqued interest.

Linda was like a sponge, thirsty and eager to hear about God. What a joy to share this verse with her. "In the Bible, I John 5:11-13 says, *"And the testimony is this, that God has given us eternal life, and this life is in His Son. He who has the Son has the life; he who does not have the Son of God does not have the life. These things I have written to you who believe in the name of the Son of God, so that you may know that you have eternal life."*

"Linda, from these verses, it is possible to know with confidence whether you have eternal life. It is simply a matter of inviting Jesus into your heart as Lord."

At that point, I felt it would be meaningful to share with her how I had come to invite her to lunch. "You know Linda, it's no accident that you are here today having lunch with me. I believe this is a divine appointment set up by God."

With wide eyes, clearly soaking it all in, Linda agreed that indeed there was something supernatural going on. God had used forty minutes of time to clearly reveal the path to eternal life to a searching soul. Although Linda did not receive Christ on that occasion, some good seed was sown, and she was challenged with some truth to consider for her life. I later wrote down more verses and shared further with her before she and her family moved away. Perhaps others have also sowed seeds in her life. I hope so.

Indeed, I had heard God's voice in my quiet time, and I was glad God prompted me to cooperate with Him and participate in the kingdom work of witnessing that He had set apart for me.

One of the greatest hindrances to witnessing is fear. I experienced a generous dose of apprehension in regard to Linda. Looking back, I realize, of course, that it was all unnecessary and I noticed my fears dissipated as soon as God revealed His plan that day. I learned that when God calls me to share Christ with someone, He can be trusted. I'm not in it alone. He is right by my side. I think God loves to include His children in His escapades. They are, in part, what makes life such a fun adventure. God is not one to violate our will but what if I had said no to the opportunity He gave me with Linda? I would not have known the joy He intended. I would have missed the delight of partnering with God to accomplish His will. This incident is probably not the last time fear may try to creep in when God is asking me to witness, but I can say that today it is not as paralyzing as it used to be. I have found it to be both a pleasure and a privilege to be allowed to be part of His work.

No wonder the Bible has close to three hundred verses addressing fear of which Isaiah 41:10 is one. *"Do not fear, for I am with you; Do not anxiously look about you, for I am your God. I will strengthen you, surely I will help you, Surely I will uphold you with My righteous right hand."* It all seems to come down to trust.

CHAPTER 21

DIVINE APPOINTMENT AT SEA WORLD

Vacationing in Florida one summer, our motel offered free tickets to Sea World to anyone who would attend a sales pitch for a condominium. We planned to go to Sea World but had never participated in this sort of promotion. Even though we had been warned about the high pressure of these sales events, for some reason we felt drawn to participate this time.

"Bill, why are we doing this?" I asked. "We never do this kind of thing. I wonder if God has a plan in mind." Both Bill and I sensed God directing us to go to the presentation though we had no intention of purchasing a condo.

Our young salesperson, Cindy, quickly realized we lacked interest in the sales pitch although she did give an articulate presentation. Soon, we began trading information about our lives. Walking to the condo, she commented on our son, Mike, who was early grade school age at the time. "I am impressed with Mike's good behavior while we have been visiting," she observed while smiling at Mike. "What do you do to make him so good?"

Thanking her for the compliment, we immediately sensed we knew why God had sent us to this place. "Cindy, the reason Mike behaves well is because he has the Lord in his life," I explained. "We are Christians and we have had the joy of raising all of our children according to biblical principles."

How Cindy responded to that statement would determine whether we would proceed to share our faith with her. From experience, we knew it was important when we brought up our faith to wait for a response and let that determine how to proceed. If the person seemed agitated or uninterested, we quickly changed the subject but if they showed interest, we continued. In a way, it is like putting out bait on a fishing rod and then waiting to see if the fish grabs it. We didn't have to wait long with Cindy. Her interest was piqued with her next question.

"Are you born again Christians?" she asked.

"Yes, we are," we happily responded.

She continued, "My boyfriend says he is born again and just last night he talked to me about it. I was brought up Jewish so I am not sure I understand what it means to be born again. Can you explain it to me?"

Positive affirmation. We knew that God was drawing Cindy to Himself. Timing is important. Her boyfriend "just happened" to talk to her the night before and here we were the next day. A coincidence? Probably not. In John 6:44, Jesus says, *"No one can come to Me unless the Father who sent Me draws him; and I will raise him up on the last day."* God had already been drawing her as she talked with her boyfriend. Now, we were another step as God continued to woo her. With her obvious interest in hearing about Jesus, we shared Billy Graham's pamphlet, *"Steps to Peace With God,"* which explains the gospel message in easy to understand terms. (See Appendix B)

Realizing she was Jewish, we also told her about Jesus' fulfillment of prophesy. "Jesus is the Messiah the Jewish people were, and still are, waiting for, Cindy," Bill explained. "He is spoken of often in the Old Testament. Many things about Jesus' life are found in the Jewish Torah."

We explained a few verses to her so she would understand. For instance, verses like Isaiah 7:14 predicted that Jesus would be born to a virgin and that His name would be Immanuel.

"Therefore the Lord Himself will give you a sign: Behold, a virgin will be with child and bear a son, and she will call His name Immanuel." In Matthew 1:23, this Old Testament prophecy about Jesus is mentioned again, and we are told Immanuel means, "God with us."

Isaiah 9:6 is another prophetic verse that describes Jesus' role on earth. *"For a child will be born to us, a son will be given to us; And the government will rest on His shoulders; And His name will be called Wonderful Counselor, Mighty God, Eternal Father, Prince of Peace."*

In John 14:27, Jesus said *"Peace I leave with you; My peace I give to you; not as the world gives do I give to you. Do not let your heart be troubled, nor let it be fearful."* Truly, Jesus is the Prince of Peace spoken of in Isaiah. Many verses in the New Testament testify of Jesus being the one who offers peace. II Thessalonians 3:16 is another one, *"Now may the Lord of peace Himself continually grant you peace in every circumstance...."* Only Jesus is capable of giving people the peace they so long for. In John 14:27 He says, *"Peace I leave with you; My peace I give to you; not as the world gives do I give to you. Do not let your heart be troubled, nor let it be fearful."* Many other verses also substantiate Jesus as the peace giver such as Romans 5:1, Colossians 1:20 and 3:15. These all point back to Isaiah where Jesus is called the "Prince of Peace".

"You might also be interested to know, Cindy, that Psalm 22 describes Jesus' death on the cross." Verse 14 says, *"I am poured out like water, And all my bones are out of joint; My heart is like wax; It is melted within me."* Verse 16 says, *"... They pierced my hands and my feet."*

We showed her that verse18 speaks of casting lots for His garments, *"They divide my garments among them, and for my clothing they cast lots."* This is later recorded concerning Jesus in Luke 23:34, *"But*

Jesus was saying, 'Father, forgive them; for they do not know what they are doing.' And they cast lots, dividing up His garments among themselves."

After talking at length with Cindy about prophecy in the Jewish Torah (our Old Testament), I felt prompted to say, "Cindy, I believe talking with you about Jesus right now is a divine appointment. It is no accident that we are here." With wide eyes, she agreed. We didn't see Cindy come to the Lord that day, but God opened the door for a clear presentation of the gospel to a young Jewish girl who was sincerely seeking the Messiah. On that day, we thought we had gone to hear a presentation, but it turned out we were there to give one, one that offered a seeker the most precious gift that God could extend, His Son as payment for her sins.

Many Christians think they have failed if they don't bring a person to Christ. They experience great disappointment if people don't pray the prayer of salvation. Be encouraged. Remember, as I have said before, God never called us to be successful, only faithful. In His eyes, faithfulness IS success. We listen to God's direction and follow. Jesus, Himself, said, *"My sheep hear My voice, and I know them, and they follow Me,"* (John 10:27). We felt euphoric knowing that God had used us in Cindy's life. Our conversation was one more stepping stone for her toward Jesus. We were planting seeds. Hopefully, someone else was there to later harvest the crop. We must be aware that the seeds we sow in people's lives land on all kinds of ground. We would love for all the seed to land on good ground and take root, but God has said that won't happen.

The type of ground seed falls on represents the state of the person's heart. Because of the various conditions of hearts, many people we witness to will not accept Jesus or continue on with Him. Yet, the Lord has called us to be faithful in witnessing. We shouldn't let negative responses stop us from telling others of His wonderful grace. Jesus said He would make us fishers of men as we follow Him. He leads the way and tells us where to go, and we follow. It sounds simple, but often we find we lead the way and ask Him to follow. We must remember that God accomplishes His work when He leads.

A good definition of evangelism that not only defines it but also reminds us where the responsibility lies comes from Bill Bright, founder of Campus Crusade for Christ, International. He says, "Successful witnessing is taking the initiative to share Christ in the power of the Holy Spirit and leaving the results to God." (Bill Bright, *Witnessing Without Fear,* (Thomas Nelson, Inc., Nashville, TN, 1993).

CHAPTER 22

FOREIGN EXCHANGE STUDENT

One school year, we agreed to house a foreign exchange student from the Ukraine. Bill, Mike and I discussed taking in a student and we all wholeheartedly agreed that it would be a fun adventure. Bill and I had traveled in Europe a few months after the fall of the Berlin wall and were intrigued by several former communist countries, not only their history, but in the delightful people we met along the way. Communism is a very different value system than ours, and the thought of having someone from the Ukraine, someone whose family had lived through the nuclear meltdown in Kiev, sounded interesting.

We had entertained other foreigners in the past and found the experience to be quite rewarding. One lady from Switzerland, Helena, had lived with us for five months. It had been a wonderful experience, rich in learning about another culture as well as an opportunity to serve and share our American ideals. Other foreigners we had entertained in our home over the years had also been remembered as positive experiences. We now looked forward to yet another pleasant, growing and stretching season with Arnold. In retrospect, we did grow and stretch but maybe not exactly how we had imagined.

With Mike going into his senior year in high school and the only one of our three children still at home, he was excited to have a friend his age live with us for the school year. He was looking forward to introducing Arnold to his friends and including him in his various church and school activities.

When Arnold came to live with us, the school year was already under way. He had been living with another family in our town, but when they had decided not to have an exchange student after all, this left the exchange program director in dire need of a family to take him in. We found out later that we had not been told the whole truth as to why the original family wanted him out of their house. In retrospect, we felt that we were blindsided.

At first, Arnold seemed to be a nice fit with our family. He was outgoing, a good conversationalist, polite, agreeable and very interested in America. Because of his insatiable curiosity, we loved talking with him about our country and answering his many questions. Everything seemed to be fine as we warmly welcomed him into our home and our lives.

The exchange program that Arnold was part of was designed for students from low income countries, students who otherwise would never have had a chance to visit America. Because of our government's altruistic attitude, they paid for almost everything for students in this program and the student paid nothing to come here.

Upon his arrival, Arnold carried only a paper bag with a couple of items of clothing. Since our government provided $100 per month for him to buy clothes and school supplies, we immediately headed for the mall to fit him with some appropriate clothes. Our part in the program was to provide a home, meals and a number of outings. We knew going in that we would not be reimbursed so it was not a problem. We were happy to afford this opportunity for a foreign student.

At one point, Arnold's mother questioned why Americans were willing to take in strangers and pay for everything so they could have an American experience. The question had never crossed our minds. We told Arnold to tell his mother that was just what Americans did and for our family, being Christians, it was a joy to serve others. She never did understand that mindset. Arnold explained to us that in the Ukraine, it is every man for himself. You only look after yourself and to help others would be a foreign concept.

During his time with us, Arnold and I often had long conversations about the Lord. Being an inquisitive person by nature, he was full of questions about God and very interested in hearing about our faith. We were pleased with this, of course. It seemed we didn't have to look for opportunities to discuss our faith because Arnold, himself, eagerly moved conversation to God.

In time, however, we noted that, while his interest was piqued, Arnold's personal world view did not incorporate the idea of a God who loved him, wanted a relationship with him and offered to be the Lord of his life. Although interested in discussing faith, it was not something he saw as affecting him personally. While many seeds of faith were planted by our family and in church services he attended with us, his secular world view was deeply entrenched. At the time, nothing about God seemed to really penetrate. Yet, because of his curiosity about Christianity, it seemed like God was drawing him. *"No one can come to Me unless the Father who sent Me draws him...,"* (Jn. 6:44). Surely, God had placed Arnold in our home for a purpose.

While things with Arnold seemed to start out well, soon there was a shift in his behavior. First, he explained to Bill that his grandmother got up very early and fixed him a large breakfast every morning. In a voice that sounded like it came from a communist dictator, he demanded meat for breakfast. Bill offered him cereal. He also told us his grandmother fixed many other large meals for him each day. We soon understood that grandma's sole purpose in life was to serve Arnold. He was in for a rude awakening with us and later realized he would have to adapt to our eating habits.

That was minor compared to what came next. Arnold became demanding in other areas and would not listen to us. He defied our authority and became unpleasantly independent. He declared that he had no intention of returning home to the Ukraine when the school year was over. Fixated on staying in America, he spent hours on the computer trying to find a school that would give him a full ride scholarship. Even with our encouragement that this wasn't going to happen, nothing would convince him otherwise.

Many of our discussions turned to this topic. We tried to help him realize that he had to return to the Ukraine, that he could not legally stay here. "Arnold, you are under contract with our government to finish your school year here and then return home. You cannot stay here. It is against our laws."

Undaunted, his reply was always, "I'm going to find a school that will give me a college education and I'll find a way to stay." He also looked at the military.

"Arnold, that is unrealistic at this point," I countered. "You will need to return to the Ukraine and then try to look for a college here. You are wasting your stay here with this obsession. You are missing out on many aspects of the exchange program with your unrealistic goal."

Arnold did not hear our point of view. He even expressed that he felt America owed him a college education, that he was entitled to this favor. Needless to say, we were shocked by his relentless, self-centered attitude. One of the reasons this particular program sent young people to America from other countries was to help them understand democracy, freedom, and a different way of life. It seemed Arnold was taking this to a new level.

Another goal of the exchange program was to demonstrate the unique idea of philanthropy and volunteerism to these young people who had been raised under communism. That is, that Americans love to give and share their abundance. Clearly, this idea did not compute with Arnold's world view.

Since volunteerism, a foreign word to Arnold, was knit into the exchange program, there were a number of opportunities for him to help out with community projects without compensation. He never understood why people would want to help each other if they weren't being paid for it.

"In our country, we look after ourselves. No one helps anyone else," he spouted.

For one volunteer opportunity, our community came together to build a playground in a local park. The whole city showed up to help. All the teens in the exchange program were expected to participate to learn for themselves the joy of serving others. Before the big day, we had several conversations with Arnold trying to facilitate his understanding of the benefits involved in this chance to serve. We talked to him about the good feeling that comes as you cooperate with others toward a common goal. We mentioned the sense of unity and the enjoyment of watching children play on the equipment knowing you had been a part of it. He still could not grasp that anyone would show up to work for free. In his country, that was unheard of. "People just look after themselves," he lamented. "Why should I help someone else if there is no benefit for me?"

Serving others was definitely an alien concept to him. However, we made sure Arnold arrived on time for his job. Not that he really had a choice, but he finally agreed to go when he heard there would be a free lunch. I am not sure he ever grasped the satisfaction of working with a team to do something good for the community, but he definitely got his fill of food that day.

Arnold's presence was turning into a trial in our home. He alienated our son and others in the community and eventually, we discovered that he was using our computer for immoral activity, even inviting friends in when we were out. He also snuck out of the house several times at night. We found out later he was meeting with girls. The final straw came when he locked Mike out of the house. One afternoon, Arnold and his friends were engaged in immoral computer activity and refused to let Mike in. I was out of town at the time, but when Bill arrived home and learned what had happened, he immediately called the program director and asked that Arnold be removed from our home. Since there was no one else to house him, the director took him into her home, but even she soon came to the end of her patience with him. Because his exchange program was under our government's State Department, she contacted them and had Arnold sent home early. Sadly, Arnold was reaping what he had sown. He was a very self-absorbed young man whose behavior had caught up with him.

After he left, he began emailing us, acting as if nothing had happened. We eventually asked that he not contact us in the future. That would be the last we heard from him...we thought. We assumed he had gone home and continued his immoral life style.

But, that's not the end of the story. Fast forward ten years. Internet had become popular and the Facebook phenomenon had captured most Americans, if not the world. Mike, while perusing Facebook one day, found Arnold's page. He informed Bill that Arnold, still in the Ukraine, was married and had a little girl. Curious, Bill looked up him and his wife, and what a surprise! He discovered that she worked for an organization called "Living Water." Hmmm...that had kind of a Christian ring to it. Scanning down her page, he noted that she had listed worship music as her favorite music and the Bible as her favorite book. With piqued interest, Bill began to wonder if it was possible that Arnold had married a Christian. It seemed such an unlikely prospect.

Mike decided to "friend" Arnold and began to message him on Facebook. Upon hearing his story, Mike related some astounding news to Bill who then wrote Arnold an email. What he received in reply blew us away. Arnold had become a Christian, and according to him, his whole life had changed.

He explained that after returning to the Ukraine, he met a girl and fell in love. For months, they debated their world views: Her Christian position versus his secular stance, a life apart from God. Finally, her mother suggested he attend a church service with them. Arnold agreed to go. God had not forgotten Arnold because, during the service, he said he finally really "heard" the gospel message as though for the first time and it penetrated his heart. Jesus' love permeated the room and he could no longer resist. Feeling almost air-borne, he rushed to the altar to give his life to the Lord. Jesus truly swept him off his feet. He was smitten as he understood how much Jesus loved him and cared about his future.

That day, Arnold was radically saved and his life has not been the same since. In that moment, Jesus revealed Himself and Arnold knew instantly that Jesus was who he had been looking for all his life, that all of his immature and sometimes immoral behavior was because he had been searching for something that would satisfy and fulfill him. With great relief and joy, he realized it had been Jesus who had been wooing him all along. He even remembered how we had spoken to him about Jesus. He explained that while he had sensed God tugging at his heart at that time, he had not yet been ready to submit his life to God.

The day he finally accepted the Lord, he realized that nothing from his past experiences had ever truly satisfied or completed him but had only left him more frustrated and hungry for something real. Today, Arnold and his wife follow the Lord together and are in ministry. His every conversation includes mention of Jesus. Praise God!

God taught me a powerful lesson through hearing Arnold's testimony. It was the "rest of the story". It is simply this…never give up on people. God never does. I admit I had given up on Arnold. I really did not want to see him again or have anything to do with him. He had burned a lot of bridges during his stay with us. While we had forgiven his offenses, we did not trust him to be part of our family. Although I occasionally prayed for him in the ensuing years and wondered how his life had turned out, I really didn't think God would ever get hold of him. Returning to what I considered a godless country, I never imagined he would find Christ in the Ukraine. In fact, when I had heard at one point from the exchange program director that he was going into the police academy in Ukraine, I sometimes wondered if he might come back and shoot us someday. (Grin) But now, amazingly, he is my brother in Christ.

Life in the Ukraine has not been easy for Arnold, his wife and little girl in recent years. They were living in Crimea when the Russians took over that part of the Ukraine in 2014. They fled their home and moved up to Kiev, but fighting kept advancing until they finally left Ukraine and settled in Poland. All this time, they have sought the Lord and waited for His direction. Arnold and his family are in the palm of His hand.

CHAPTER 23

ENCOUNTER AT THE CREATION MUSEUM

(Lea's story as told by Cinda Miller)

Cinda, a dear friend of mine, tells this story about an exchange student she had. I knew it was one to be shared. While Cinda's experience was different than ours with Arnold, it also continues to bring such thankfulness to my heart. I'll let her tell you her story:

Cinda: Lea was a sweet German girl we met in the spring of 2013 when she came to our home for three weeks as an exchange student. My family and I quickly observed that she knew very little about the Lord, and what she did know really had no personal meaning or reality to her. While we did not go out of our way to talk about God more than we normally do, we also did not hide our beliefs.

Each morning, before I took my children to school, we all took turns saying a prayer. I explained to Lea what we did and, to my surprise, she asked, "May I pray too?"

I said, "Absolutely". I was delighted to have her join us because I knew this was something that she did not do at home. Lea also attended church with us, heard our conversations about God and mealtime prayers.

When Lea went home, it was very hard as she had melted our hearts and truly become a part of our family during those three weeks. Even though she expressed that she wanted to come back for another visit, I knew there was a chance we would never see her again. Because of that, I began to regret that I had not asked her if she wanted to invite Jesus into her heart. Even so, I also felt God saying not to worry, that everything would be ok.

Happily, after a few months, Lea sent a message that she wanted to come visit us again over Christmas break. While surprised that she could come back so soon, we were also very excited. I heard the Lord whisper in my ear, *This is it. This is the time for Lea to be saved.*

In the meantime, my husband, Loren, and I had been discussing going to visit relatives for a few days during the holiday break. We decided that we would go after Christmas and also stop by the Creation Museum in Kentucky. This wonderful museum teaches about how God made the world and His crown of creation, mankind. It also gives a lot of evidence to support creation and contradict evolution. When Loren mentioned going to the museum, I knew that it was not only for us to enjoy but also exactly where God wanted us to take Lea.

Lea arrived on December 18th and it was like she was home and had never left. I loved it. Our family was complete again. We made cookies, played games, and visited my parents. Lea shot a gun for the first time; we cleaned house, washed dishes, laughed, cried, exchanged gifts, sang together, read the Bible, and enjoyed family sharing. Most of all, we grew to know and love each other even more.

After Christmas, we visited our relatives and then headed to the Creation Museum. Lea's interest was piqued as to what a Creation Museum would be about. As we walked through the various sites, she carefully looked at each display and asked lots of questions. At one point, she stopped, and with a pensive look on her face said, "This is so different. I've never heard creation explained like this before. What the Bible says makes sense."

Lea strolled slowly through the museum as she looked and read as much as she could. I engaged her in conversation along the way and explained about sin and what it did to mankind. There was a part about sin where they had awful pictures and sounds which really upset her. Her response was a simple, "I don't like this part."

I used the opportunity to help her understand. "Lea, we aren't supposed to like it. Those were to portray the darkness of sin."

As we walked along, the museum narrator talked about the Old Testament blood sacrifices that people had to make to cover their sin. He also mentioned the flood and Noah's ark, each step leading up to Jesus. At one point, I asked my family to slow down because Lea was going at such a leisurely pace pausing at each display to ponder all the new information she was gleaning. I didn't want her to miss a thing God was revealing to her.

Along the way, a short movie explained what Jesus did on the cross. I observed Lea watching very closely, concentrating on every word. It was obvious God had her attention. After the film was over, pamphlets about receiving Christ were made available. Lea took all the information that was offered.

I felt now was the time to ask Lea some questions. "Lea, did you understand what the movie was about? Did it make sense to you that Jesus was the sacrifice for our sins and is the only way to heaven?

"Yes," she answered, "but I still have many questions. This is all so new to me. I have never heard any of this before. My school never taught this. I have heard about Jesus but never like this. Yet, it seems so real to me."

I knew that God was stirring her heart.

The next morning, back home, to my surprise, Lea was the first one up. I heard her in the kitchen and sensed God was speaking to me. *Go out there. This is it.* In the kitchen, we chatted a little bit and then I asked her, "What has been your favorite part of your visit with us this time?"

"Oh, the Creation Museum," she said enthusiastically, "because I have never heard or understood that before."

"So Lea," I ventured, "How do you feel about Jesus?"

She smiled and asked me, "Are we going to talk about this right now?"

With a smile, I answered, "Yes we are, Lea. I want to ask you a question. At this point in your life, do you know where you would go if you died today?"

"I think so," she responded. I could tell her answer was more of a hope than an assurance.

"You know, Lea, that really isn't a good enough answer. You need to know for sure. Would you like to invite Jesus into your heart so that you will have assurance of eternal life?"

Without hesitation, she answered, "YES!"

I was overjoyed. This was an answer to my prayer. God had been stirring her heart to receive Him as her personal Lord and Savior and now the time had arrived to cement her future destiny. Together in my kitchen, my sweet Lea and I prayed and she asked Jesus into her heart to forgive her sins and to be her God. We cried together, tears of delight, and I shouted for joy.

One by one, as the other kids got up. I couldn't wait to tell them the good news. "Guess what happened!"

Eyes rolling, they teased facetiously, "We know mom. We heard you shouting."

For the next few days Lea and I would cry very easily. We were both so touched and in awe of her salvation. The time for her to go home was very close and it was harder than the first time. An extra bond had been forever formed.

On the day that we took her to the airport, there was a terrible snowstorm. Lea's fear was that we would drop her off and leave and then her flight would be cancelled and she wouldn't know what to do. She was also afraid for us driving home in a snowstorm. To ease her mind, we instructed her on what to do if her flight was cancelled.

"Lea, also remember you can talk to God just like you talk to us. Ask Him about everything. Tell Him everything. Ask Him what to do and who to ask in the airport for help. He is and always will be with you."

We said our sad goodbye's accompanied with many hugs and tears then headed for home. The storm had not abated which made for a treacherous drive. Although dangerous, God gave us traveling mercies and we made it home ok. Thankfully, we saw online that Lea's flight had only been delayed a few minutes. Relieved, we knew she was on her way safely.

The next morning Lea and I chatted on Facebook. She told me the most beautiful story of what happened as she flew away. "Cinda, I was so worried for you and then I remembered what you had said, *Talk to God about everything. Ask Him anything and tell Him anything.* I prayed to God for you and asked Him to keep you all safe. After I prayed, there was a bright light shining outside in the sky. The light was shining right in my eyes and was so brilliant. Then, I remembered what I had learned about the rainbow from the Creation Museum and I knew that the light was God telling me not to worry, that you would be safe."

I cried when I read her message. "Lea, that was amazing. You are already hearing God's voice."

She replied, "Mom! Now you're making me cry." It was a special moment.

There are no words to express the feelings that I had about this experience. I know that Lea's visit was God ordained and I am honored that He chose us to be a part of it. I am thrilled that He chose us to have a sweet German girl from halfway around the world come to be part of our family and to be introduced to Jesus.

It is wonderful to know that she will be a part of our forever family in Heaven. God is so good. I am so grateful that we were open to His leading and listened to Him. My encouragement to you is to look for every opportunity from Him. We never know the amazing things He will do. I hope that one day you will have the opportunity to meet Lea! If not here, surely in heaven.

CHAPTER 24

THE REBEL

"Sandra is the most difficult child we have at this school," the principal chided. "We don't know what to do with her. If something doesn't change in her life this year, we don't know what will happen to her. We have tried counseling, a big sister program…nothing seems to work. We wish someone could reach her."

Maybe the school just saw a rebellious child, but my heart melted because when I met her, God immediately gave me His heart of love for her. I knew instantly God was opening a door for me when I found myself volunteering to meet with her. She needed a chance.

Let me back up to where it started. I had been doing some substitute teaching in the middle school. That day, I was assigned a 5th grade girls gym class…not my favorite kind of class to teach, but I decided to say yes. As I began the class, I asked the girls to divide up into groups for an activity I had planned. While most of them obediently formed groups, several of the girls chose to challenge my authority by defiantly resisting. "No, we don't want to be in a group."

Ok, Lord, what do I do now? I prayed. Immediately, a thought came to me. *Appeal to their conscience.* I remembered how Paul, in II

Corinthians 4:2 said that he appealed to every man's conscience, so I followed, hoping for results.

Noticing one girl standing by herself because she didn't have anyone in her group, I approached the uncooperative girls. With a smile and an upbeat attitude, I made my appeal. "Hey, girls, I was wondering if you could do me a favor. Do you see that girl over there? She's all alone, and it would really help me out if you would all go over there and join her. I'm sure you know how it feels to be alone without a group. Do you think you could do that?"

They looked at one another and then to their leader and as a group, they arose and joined the lonely girl.

For some reason, my heart went out to these unruly pre-teens, especially one in particular named Sandra who seemed to be the ring leader. That day worked out well and the rebellious girls were accommodating for the rest of the class.

A few days later, I noticed Sandra was in another class with me. Was God up to something? To confirm whether He was, I asked Him several weeks later if He would arrange for me to be in a class with her once again. God was definitely doing something because my very next sub job was in her class. I felt an excitement and anticipation as I entered the classroom, but as I looked around, Sandra wasn't there. I later learned that she had consistently been such a problem that she now spent most days in detention. Sometimes, she was even expelled. I prayed for another opportunity.

That day came. A sub forgot to show up, and at the last minute, I was called in. This time, Sandra, who was still in detention, was in the room to get her books. It was recess so no one else was there. After spending a few minutes talking to her, I found I liked her and felt an immediate connection…so much so, that after she left the room, I broke down and cried for her. Truly, there was a very sweet side to Sandra that had been pushed away for reasons I might never know.

Again, I asked God what part I should have in her life and would He arrange it. As I walked down the hall to the lunchroom that day, the principal joined me. As we began to chat, the subject she immediately brought up was Sandra. This was too much of a "coincidence." I hadn't even mentioned Sandra's name.

"We just don't know what to do with her," she explained. "If something doesn't change in her life this year, I don't know what will happen to her. We have tried everything and nothing seems to work with that child. If only someone could reach her."

Whether I could reach her or not, one thing I knew as we walked down that hall, God was calling me to volunteer to spend time with her. Without time to even think it through, the words popped out of my mouth that I would like to volunteer. The principal was thrilled. She gave me the school counselor's name and phone number. When I called her, she said she would phone Sandra's father to make arrangements. As we hung up from our conversation, the counselor affirmed me by saying, "I wish I could clone you."

Sandra's father gave permission for me to meet with his daughter and expressed that I could do whatever I wanted with her. I sensed his frustration about her continual negative choices. Next, Sandra was asked if she would agree to meet with me, and happily, she did. The adventure was about to start. Time to start praying!

On our first meeting, I took Sandra to McDonalds and we just talked for about an hour. She didn't want to leave so we talked some more. Afterwards, when I took her home, I stayed a minute to meet her parents. Her father was a large man who suffered from emphysema. His breathing was labored but he seemed a congenial sort. Her mother was much quieter and quite reticent. She was watching TV, and I had the impression that was where she spent much of her time. It appeared her soul had been shut down for many years.

The house was dark, oppressive, and filthy. It felt chaotic. Dishes were piled high in the sink and on the counter. Dried food indicated they had been there for some time. Just walking across the room added its own challenge with piles of clothes, cigarette butts, and food ground into the carpet. Besides the dirt and grime, smoke was thick throughout the house. It appeared, however, that the house was not the only thing neglected. Sandra seemed to receive no personal attention or affirmation. Couple that with poor nutrition and lack of sleep from being out at all hours, it was no wonder she felt ill much of the time with stomach problems and headaches. And, like her mother, Sandra seemed to be out of touch with her emotions, except for outbursts of anger in school. Perhaps they had both disassociated from life in order to cope. I began to understand some of the issues Sandra had in school. I wondered if she had just "shut down" in the same way her mother had modeled. When something arose that she couldn't deal with, instead of talking it out, she just shut down or lashed out.

Sandra took me into her room and seemed proud to show me this part of the house. By comparison, it was neat. Her bed was made, and she proudly showed me her modest doll collection, a bright edge to her life in their pretty, colorful dresses, all with sweet smiles on their faces. Possibly, they were a way of escape from her dreary life or maybe a glimmer of hope that life would someday be better. Perhaps, I saw the "real" Sandra reflected through her room and her dolls.

On our next meeting, I brought her to my house to bake cookies and play games. I found Sandra to be a sweet and gentle girl, as kind and thoughtful as she could be. None of the boisterous, rebellious animosity was present in our time together as it was in the school setting.

Our outings continued where we took her water skiing twice with a neighborhood girl who was homeschooled, quite a contrast to Sandra's life. She appeared to enjoy our outings which were definitely different from her normal routine. Sandra and I were off to a good start. Later, her counselor told me that Sandra's eyes lit up when she spoke of me. We seemed to hit it off.

As time went on, we met weekly, and each time, I told her how much God loved her and that He had plans for her life. Once, at McDonald's, I prayed with her. Out of the corner of my eye, I glimpsed to see she was just staring at me. My guess is that no one had ever prayed for her before. Maybe she had never even seen anyone pray until then. It really came as no surprise that Sandra was not only un-churched but had never attended church. Besides that, she also had no interest in going to church.

I began to sense that God wanted me to pray with her often and to share my love for the Bible. On a sunny April day, we took a hike at a local campground. We both enjoyed tromping through the wooded paths, breathing in the fresh air, and enjoying the camaraderie of being together. Stopping at a bench in the woods, I asked if I could pray for her. We held hands as I prayed blessings into her life and again shared with her how special she was to God. Sandra sat quietly without response. Surely, she was taking in the love God and I extended to her.

One day, I invited her to my house with the intent of show-ing her how to sew. We had a pleasant afternoon as I helped her guide material through the machine. While doing an activity such as this, conversation was easy. Maybe I shouldn't have been sur-prised at her reaction when I asked her about her birthday, but I was. With her head lowered, she offered that her family didn't celebrate birthdays and that she had never had a birthday party. I was taken aback.

I thought back to all the birthdays I had celebrated with my own children and how many sweet memories we had built over the years. My heart sank as I realized Sandra had never been re-membered with a party or gifts, not one time in her twelve years. So, I made a decision right then. We were going to celebrate her birthday that year. She would be turning thirteen, becoming a teenager. I couldn't wait.

Bill and I, along with Mike, decided to take her out to a nice restaurant. I knew she wouldn't have anything nice to wear, so I took her shopping. We picked out a cute outfit, white slacks and a colorful sweater along with some shoes to match. Sandra looked adorable. Sheepishly smiling, as she saw herself in a mirror, perhaps for the first time in her life, she felt like a princess. We bought her gifts, and at the restaurant had a cake with candles. It was a sweet evening to remember, one I will always cherish. I hope she still recalls the love shown to her on her thirteenth birthday as together we welcomed her into her teen years.

Since I knew Sandra was interested in dolls and had a doll collection, I wondered if she would like to make a doll herself. Knowing of a lady in town that helped with that sort of endeavor, I called and made arrangements. It became a wonderful project for us to work on as we fashioned the doll and dressed her in a cute little outfit.

As the months passed, I began to be impressed by the Lord that it was time to share the full gospel message with Sandra and give her an opportunity to accept Jesus as her personal Lord and Savior. She had begun to occasionally stand me up when we had after school plans, and although I knew she was under a lot of pressure in her life, it was disappointing when we didn't have our time together. Whatever time we had left, I wanted it to count.

The next week, I called her and arranged for us to meet after school. I knew God was working on her heart, but I longed for her to make a decision for Christ. As we sat in McDonald's for a drink that day, she gave me an opening and I launched in with the gospel. We discussed sin, wrong doing and rebellion. *"All have sinned and come short of the glory of God"* (Rom. 3:23), I explained. I told her about Jesus blood covering sin and why I knew I was going to heaven. When I asked her if she liked hearing about God, with a shy grin, she said, "Yes." So, I continued and asked her if she would like to go to heaven to be with God when she died. Again, she answered, "Yes."

I decided to be bold, so I persisted, "You know, Sandra, you will never resolve your conflict with authority until you submit to God. You need Jesus. You need to know, though, that He loves you when you are good, but He also loves you when you make poor choices."

Sandra listened intently and made eye contact as I shared Jesus with her, but when I asked her the key question, "Would you like to receive Jesus into your heart?," she said "No."

I have not figured out what her holdback was. I told her she could come as she was, that God totally accepted her and didn't expect her to change before coming to Him. Her "No," still rings in my ears.

Over time, I continued to share Jesus with Sandra. I told her more of who Jesus is as we read about His miracles, His power, and His healings. We read Scripture together as I explained God's desire for her to obey her parents out of Colossians and Ephesians. Some days, I did not want to take her home and even thought of pursuing having her come live with us. I loved her with the love of God.

One day, we decided to take her parents out for a meal to get to know them better and to report how we felt Sandra was doing in our relationship. They gladly accepted, but it was an odd meeting. Midway through the lunch, her mother jumped up, ran to the car, and locked herself in. She looked so distressed that I followed her out having no idea what was going on. She let me in the car but she was like a wall and would not talk to me. I'm not a counselor but I did try to get her to open up as gently as I could. She would not. I think, however, that I received more insight into what Sandra lived with on a daily basis. Again, shutting down must have been a learned response.

I also began to understand how Sandra looked at various incidences in her life as she related difficult events to me. Once in school, she explained, she had been lost in the hall and had a confrontation with an authority figure. It turns out she had been hurrying to the bathroom. The authority thought she was being insubordinate as she bypassed the procedure for leaving a classroom. Another time, she defied authority by refusing to put on a swim suit for gym at the pool. In reality, she said she was embarrassed by her poorly fitting swimsuit. Still another time, a teacher wanted her to come in after school. She didn't show up and was sent to the office the next morning. It turned out she told me she had been afraid to walk home alone which she would have had to do if she went in after school. Sandra skipped picture day because she felt she had nothing to wear, and she had a migraine. I began to wonder how many children with perceived authority issues are really so stressed in life that they react in ways that appear disobedient.

Time went on and now, Sandra was starting high school. While I tried to make time for her each week, increasingly, she didn't show up. When she did, she seemed distracted. Finally, our meetings came to a standstill. It was then that I learned she was pregnant...a freshman in high school and pregnant. Fourteen years old and carrying a baby. I remembered back to the days I had told Sandra how smart she was and how much potential she had. I spoke into her life about how she was intelligent enough to go to college if she wanted to, that she could do whatever she put her mind to. Sadly, in the end, other things became more important or maybe her need for the attention of a man took its toll.

Basically, Sandra eased me out of her life. I continued to pray for her and still do. I don't believe God is through with her yet. Every year after that, I sent her a birthday card with a gift card in it. I wanted her to know I would never forget her.

Occasionally, I ran into her at Walmart and we would chat a minute. Thankfully, she did not abort her baby and eventually married the father. Today she has two teenagers of her own, a son and a daughter and has been a faithful employee at her job. Then one day, out of the blue, I received an invitation from Sandra to a tote bag party...one of those parties where you custom order a tote or purse. Although, I don't usually go to this type of party, I gladly accepted the invitation and bought a lovely tote that I didn't need. But I was thrilled to see Sandra and support her new business.

While at the party, I noted that Sandra's house was spotlessly neat and clean. It pleased me to observe that she also seemed to be closely attending to her daughter, now a teenager herself. I noted with interest that her daughter was not even allowed to use the internet. Sandra wanted her to learn to occupy herself in better ways. She seemed like a good mother. When I met her daughter that day, she indicated she would like to visit my home, so I immediately invited them both over for tea. We had a lovely afternoon and my heart again swelled with love for Sandra. It was so good to spend time with her again and to see how sweet her daughter was.

I asked if she had received my birthday cards and gifts over the years. She looked puzzled and said, "No," she had only received one. That meant that over a period of about fifteen years, she had only seen one card. I had sent them to her parent's home, but she was pretty sure her brother had intercepted them and confiscated the gift cards. I was sad to hear that, but at least, she now knew I had tried to keep up with her.

I wrote Sandra a note after the party and the tea to tell her how much I had enjoyed seeing her after all these years. I expressed my hope that we could spend more time together. She seemed eager to renew our friendship, too, and wrote a sweet, affirming note back to me.

Shortly after that, she invited me to another sales party. That time I graciously turned her down. It was not my intent to just see her at parties, and I definitely had no need for more totes. Perhaps, she felt rejected. Her psyche is so tender and easily hurt. I may never know, but that was the last I heard from her. She wouldn't return calls and never responded to another card I sent.

Some people are hard to figure out. Wounds from the past can leave deep scars that show up in odd ways in the present. I have not, nor will I give up on my hope that God will someday reach Sandra. My prayer continues to be that He will touch her life and draw her to Himself. I am hoping to see her again in the future.

When God puts someone on your heart, He has a plan. Our part is to just cooperate. I believe God has heard every prayer I have prayed on her behalf. My hope is in Him. Not everyone we pray for or spend time with will come to know Jesus but as long as He brings them to mind, we can continue to be faithful and obedient. Jeremiah, in the Old Testament, spent his life trying to influence people to repent and turn to God. In his case, no one ever did repent. But Jeremiah had done what God asked of him and that was enough. In the same way, you may have someone in your life that you have prayed for and witnessed to many times with no results. I think many of us have had that experience. Don't give up. Remember my story of Arnold and how hopeless that situation looked, like a failed witness, but ten years later, His life was radically changed by Jesus. Today he is on fire for the Lord. Everything in God's timing...

CHAPTER 25

SPECIAL ED INCIDENTS

Chris

During my years as a substitute teacher, I had some other interesting encounters with students. My bachelor's degree is in Elementary Education, so I was eligible to sub in any grade at that time. Much of my sub experience was in the middle school with students in their early teen years. I think the reason they kept asking me back was because I tried to deal with discipline problems in the classroom instead of sending them to the principal's office.

It was stunning to observe how much school had changed in the years since I had been a full time teacher. Respect for authority seemed to have left the classroom, jumped out the window. While I know that students have always tried to test subs, some classes were clearly used to getting away with poor behavior.

One warm May day, near the end of the school year, I was asked to sub in a Special Ed class for a few days. In those classrooms, there is usually a teacher's aide (T.A.) along with the teacher. That day, I subbed for the teacher and was happy the aide was present to help me keep the class consistent with what they were used to. On the first day, a young teen named Chris was especially defiant and sassy to the aide and refused to do his work. That afternoon, the T.A. spoke to the principal who said if it happened again the next day, she was to send him to the office.

I did not want to resort to that outcome without having a personal chat with Chris first to see if we could solve the problem in the classroom. As I approached his desk the next day, I wondered what could be going on in this vulnerable teen's life to cause such erratic behavior.

It has been my observation that many teens who come from difficult or dysfunctional homes will carry their pain into the classroom and act out. Without knowledge of what was going on in a student's life outside of school, it was easy to assume they were just bad kids. While that may be true of some, the majority are conflicted and the place it erupts is at school. My heart told me Chris was not a bad kid but probably had some kind of trauma going on that was hard to handle.

In a quiet and gentle way, I moved toward Chris's desk and softly spoke to him. "Chris, I've noticed you are having some trouble focusing on your work and have been lashing out in anger against the teacher's aide. What do you think the problem is?"

Lowering his head, with a defeated look on his face, he said, "I can't read."

My heart went out to him. For the next hour, I sat next to him and worked with him on his reading. I found he was able to read but falteringly and with hesitation. When questioned about recall of what he had read, his answers were actually quite good and very logical, better than I might have answered.

"Chris, I bet you have thought of yourself as dumb," I gently queried. With his head lowered, he nodded a yes. "Well, I'm here to tell you, you are no dummy. I think you are definitely smart and capable of doing a lot. Tell me what you do after school."

"Oh, I usually go fishing," he answered, perking up.

"You know, I bet if you find a book in the library and read half an hour every day after school, your reading will improve. Maybe a book on fishing would be interesting to you."

Reflection: While this was not a specific verbal witness of Jesus, I believe we are seed planters, and there are times when the first seeds that are planted are those of human kindness. Here was a boy who was severely frustrated in life, one whose identity had been robbed at a tender age. He thought he was no good and stupid. By approaching him with tenderness, perhaps for the first time anyone had, and believing in him, seeds of hope were planted. We are called to be Jesus hands and feet to show people the love and kindness of our Savior. I don't know what happened to Chris in the future, but I do know that God loved him enough to send him a word of encouragement on a day when it was very much needed.

Jamie

In the same class, a girl named Jamie pulled a chair up next to my desk to do her work. A smiling, vivacious teen, she seemed to enjoy chatting with me.

"I'm bilingual," she explained, "and I can write and speak fluently in English and Spanish. When I grow up, I hope to be a translator. I have already traveled to Spain, Guatemala, and Mexico."

I was impressed and wondered why she was in a Special Ed class. Being bilingual is quite an accomplishment, one I have never mastered, for sure.

Intrigued, I asked, "Would you like to go out for a coke after school?"

"Yes, I'd like that," she responded.

We met after school and she brought a friend along. During our conversation, I learned some interesting things about her life, how her father had died and because her step father had abused her, she had been taken out of state for awhile. She had no relationship with her mother.

Saddened by the outrageous things that had happened in her short life, I brought God into the conversation and told her how important He was in my life and how I believed He also had good plans for her life.

"Have you ever read the Bible, Jamie?"

"Yes, I used to," she responded, "but it got lost in our move."

Since she had told me during the conversation that her birthday was coming up, I made a mental note and decided to buy her a Bible. I delivered it to her at school on her birthday. She was amazed and touched that I remembered her on her birthday.

I had no further contact with Jamie but I hope she has been reading her Bible.

Reflection: My time with Jamie was short. Sometimes, God sends people across our path for a short season. He had a purpose in mind. A seed was planted. Jamie now had a Bible. I pray that God moved in her heart and encouraged her to read it. Whether she did or not, I will never know. I was only asked to be the delivery girl.

Tim

My third memorable encounter in Special Ed was with a boy named Tim. After lunch, another boy named Danny accused Tim of calling his mother names. Danny had started the problem by hitting Tim. As I talked to the two boys in the hall, I asked them, "How do you think we can handle this problem, boys?"

With much anger, Tim replied, "I think we should fight it out!"

"Well, that's one way to approach it, but I think there's a better way. Would you like to hear it?"

I had noticed Tim was chewing on a cross necklace as we talked, so I asked, "Tim, I notice you are wearing a cross. Does that mean something to you?"

He looked at his cross and nodded.

"You know, that cross stands for Jesus, and His way of solving problems like this is forgiveness," I said. "Do you two think you could just ask each other for forgiveness, Danny for hitting and Tim for name calling?"

Amazingly, they took me seriously, turned to each other and asked for forgiveness.

One problem solved, but it was not long before another issue arose with Tim. The next hour Tim became very hyper and couldn't seem to settle down to do his work. Things quickly escalated to behavior that was sassy, disobedient and unruly. Soon, he went into a rage.

"Tim, you will need to sit down or you'll have to go to the office," I tersely explained. Yes, there are times when the office visit is necessary.

Paying no attention to my directive, I had no choice but to send him to the office (a first for me). His behavior was out of control, incorrigible. Tim got two days of detention then returned to my classroom. During his absence, someone informed me that prior to that time, Tim's house had burned down, and he now lived with his grandparents. My heart melted. What a sad turn of events for a boy already struggling with life. Like I said, there were times students misbehaved and I would have no idea what was going on in their lives that might have triggered it. Tim was dealing with a lot of grief from the fire.

When he returned to class, I asked him about the fire. His comment stunned me.

"I wish I had burned in the fire and died," he spat out.

"Why would you want that to happen?" I asked.

"Because nobody likes me."

"What makes you think that?" I replied.

"Because they call me skuzzball and other names and make fun of me."

I could see the tears welling up as he tried to hold them back. How could I help this poor child who had been dealt such a hard life? It was then that God gave me His heart and words. "I like you,

Tim, and I think you are very special. God made you and He loves you, too, and has a special plan for your life.

"How can that be?" he spurted. "I was formed by a sperm."

Without choking at such an unexpected response, I replied, "Yes, but remember, it was God who made you in the womb and He loves you."

I hoped Tim would consider what I told him. I left him to do his schoolwork, then later as he left class, I whispered to him, "I'll tell you what…when you see me in the halls, you can know that I'm your friend. I like you and think you are special."

Reflection: I don't know how Tim's life has turned out but I do know that God had me in that classroom at that time to remind a young, floundering boy that He was special to God. I hope, as an adult, he remembers that thought. We are just called to be a witness, to show love, to help lift one another up.

I am thankful God allowed my path to cross with these needy children and gave me opportunities to remind them how loved they are by Him.

CHAPTER 26
A WORD OF ENCOURAGEMENT

Someone once lamented to me, "Betsy, reading all your stories of sharing your faith is really making me feel guilty. I want to talk to people about Jesus but it doesn't seem to happen for me. I know God wants me to witness but there don't seem to be opportunities. I have even prayed that God would give me opportunities but when they don't seem to happen, I feel I must be doing something wrong or maybe God isn't happy with me."

I thought about her comment and realized that there have been many times when I have also felt that I came up short when I have heard other people's glowing stories of witnessing. It is easy to compare and feel like you aren't up to par. There have even been times when I have wondered if God intended to use me at all. Comparing ourselves with other people can be a deadly occupation that usually leads to guilt and may even stall forward movement.

I answered her by saying, "You realize that my stories cover a span of almost fifty years of serving the Lord. There have been whole years go by when I have not spoken to anyone about Jesus. I know the feeling you are talking about. I have experienced it, too, in those dry spells and wondered if I was doing something wrong.

My mind reasons like this: *If I were in God's will, surely, I would be aware of people He wants me to talk to about Jesus.*

Over the years, I have come to some conclusions about this sticky subject. God has each of us on a personalized, unique, individual plan in our walk with Him. There are seasons for our gifts and callings. Our part is to be diligent in prayer and aware of people around us. If we have asked God to give us opportunities, then all we can do is watch for them and be prepared to give an answer to anyone who shows interest in our faith. If this doesn't happen, then we can assume, it is not on God's "to do" list for us that day.

The commands in the Bible for us to witness have more to do with an overall lifetime. We can't make something happen and then hope God will bless us any more than we can dictate to God how He should use us. Our part is to be attuned to Him and walk through the doors when He opens them, knowing that we will be met with everything from ripe fruit ready to pick, to no interest at all.

Occasions to share our faith should feel somewhat natural, and yes, it can also feel a little scary. We don't want to be rejected. Remembering that it is God who initiates is helpful. I usually have a sense when He is nudging me to say something. Then it is up to me to start the conversation. This is where my faith is tested. Will I open my mouth? I have to remember what God said through Moses in Deuteronomy 31:8, *"The Lord is the one who goes ahead of you; He will be with you. He will not fail you or forsake you. Do not fear or be dismayed."* If I believe that God has gone ahead of me and will be with me, it somehow gives me the strength to move forward.

Jesus commanded us to go into the world and preach the gospel. In a general sense, God calls all believers to witness what Jesus has done in their lives. Every Christian who is walking with Christ has a testimony of forgiveness, freedom and a changed life. Paul went a step further when he prayed specifically in Colossians 4:3-6, that God would open for him a door for the word, so that he and the disciples might speak forth the mystery of Christ. He prayed that he would be clear as to what to speak. He exhorted believers to let their speech be with grace, seasoned with salt so that they would know how to answer every man. That's a great prayer!

Paul knew the significance of his witness. He was aware that he was to share what he had observed and experienced. He leaned on God to reveal to him what to say, what stories to tell about his relationship with Jesus. He knew that he had to listen to the voice of the Holy Spirit. In Romans 15:18, Paul said, *"For I will not presume to speak of anything except what Christ has accomplished through me...."*

The prerequisite for witnessing is that we, by faith, have entered into a relationship with God through Jesus Christ. How can we witness what the Lord has done in us and through us unless we have first made our own faith contract with God? God must transfer us out of the kingdom of darkness into His kingdom of light, forgive our sins, lead us to repentance and impute His righteousness into us. Then, as we observe Him working changes in our lives, we are positioned to witness and now have something to share with others.

As we continue to walk in faith, we begin to grow. *"...If you abide in my word, then you are truly disciples of Mine,"* (Jn. 8:31). By spending time in the Bible, we begin to learn God's ways. As we walk in obedience, God changes and matures our character. Listening for God's voice, we gain a new awareness of God and enjoy experiences that we know are from Him. This gives us a testimony to confidently witness concerning the goodness of God in our lives. By the power of the Holy Spirit, we can share Scriptures and our experiences with others and thereby witness.

A witness is one who simply tells what he has seen and heard. If you were driving down the road and observed an accident, your report to the police would be what you saw, what you encountered. For a Christian, that means we share what we have watched Christ do in our lives.

Part of witnessing is trusting God to lead us to the people He has prepared to hear our message. At times, you may find yourself in a situation where you sense God nudging you to tell someone what He has done in your life. If you have spent time in the Bible and in prayer, you will more likely be tuned in to opportunities He brings your way. If you are filled with the Holy Spirit, He will give you the confidence to witness. Jesus said in John 15:5, *"...apart from Me you can do nothing."* Remember, results are up to God.

II Peter 1:8 goes on to promise that as we persevere in the things of faith, they render us neither useless nor unfruitful. God does His part and we do ours. We can trust Him to produce fruit in us and through us as we proceed in faith.

There are some who might say, "Well, that's fine for you to talk to people about your faith, but I don't feel I could ever do that. I feel powerless to share my faith verbally. I will just live a Christian life before people and let my life speak." Once, a Christian sister even admonished me for asking someone if they were born again. "You just don't ask people that kind of question, Betsy," she chided. Actually, I had just enjoyed a wonderful conversation with a lady who needed to hear about Jesus. While God does ask us to live a holy life before others, there is more. Every incident of witnessing that we read about in Scripture also involved verbal interaction. Paul said in II Corinthians 4:13, *"...I believed, therefore I spoke...."*

Many times, we feel we just aren't adequate to share our faith. Actually, that is true. It's not about our adequacy at all. It's about the adequacy of Jesus who dwells within us. Christ alone is adequate. It is not about our ability, our cleverness of speech, or how great we present an argument. It is about the Holy Spirit doing His work and us leaving the result to Him. *"Not that we are adequate in ourselves to consider anything as coming from ourselves, but our adequacy is from God,"* (II Cor. 3:5).

"But you shall receive power when the Holy Spirit has come upon you, and you shall be My witnesses both in Jerusalem and in all Judea and Samaria, and even to the remotest part of the earth," (Acts 1:8).

The key to the manifestation of God's power for witnessing comes through an awareness of God's voice and the nudging of the Holy Spirit. Sometimes, no opportunity presents itself, and other times, witnessing occurs spontaneously and even appears planned. We cannot box God, but we will never experience His power until we take a step of faith and speak when He calls us. If God leads us to a particular person, we can ask Him to open the door for us to witness. Joshua 1:3 says, *"Every place on which the sole of your foot treads, I have given it to you, just as I spoke to Moses."* As we step out in faith when God calls us to go, we can be sure He has gone ahead of us and that His power is available. The question is, are we available?

When God spoke to people in the Scriptures, His words always carried with them the power to do the job. Philip had this experience when the angel of the Lord told him, *"...Get up and go south to the road that descends from Jerusalem to Gaza. (This is a desert road.)"* Upon following these directions, Philip came upon an Ethiopian eunuch sitting in his chariot reading Isaiah. *"Then the Spirit said to Philip, 'Go up and join this chariot,'"* (Acts 8:26-40).

Philip could have said, "Oh, no, I don't even know this fellow. What will I say to him? I feel so powerless. My heart is pounding. This can't be God asking me to witness. I know... I will sit and read this Christian book, and he will see me and know by my life that I am a Christian."

Nonsense! God had spoken to Philip and he knew that the power to accomplish His purpose would be available. Philip began his conversation with the Ethiopian with a simple question, *"...Do you understand what you are reading,"* (Acts 8:30)? The eunuch responded that he didn't and invited Philip to join him in the chariot. Philip recognized the man had given him permission to share his faith.

When an opportunity opens up, we should take it as far as the listener will allow. The eunuch indicated he was receptive when he invited Philip to sit with him. He didn't cut off the conversation. Eager to hear, the eunuch pursued discussion. However, if a person does cut off dialogue, we should graciously change the subject. I wonder how often potential fruit has been bruised or picked green because overly zealous Christians have insisted on pushing their beliefs down people's throats. We need to remember that the Lord is a gentleman. Perhaps, He even cringes sometimes as He watches us try to cram the gospel into people.

We should also note that Philip preached Jesus to the man. He was able to do this because, having spent time reading and studying the Word, he was familiar with the Scriptures. Sometimes, I have heard people proudly say they have witnessed when really, all they have done is mention what church they go to. Witnessing means that we tell someone about Jesus and what He has done in our life. It is not a religious thing to do, but rather about our personal relationship with God. It is wonderful to tell people about our church, but that in itself is not witnessing.

In Philip's experience, he led the eunuch to commitment to the Lord. When the Lord leads us in that direction in witnessing, it is good to give people the opportunity to invite Jesus into their heart. Some are ready and others are not. For some, God may choose to present an opportunity at a later time. Our part, then, is to be patient and persevere in prayer.

In Acts 4:7, the rulers and high priests approached Peter and some of the disciples. Irate because the disciples had just brought five thousand people to the Lord and healed a man, they asked, "*...By what power, or in what name, have you done this?*" Can't you hear their scoffing, angry tone? Notice in verse eight, it states Peter was "*...filled with the Holy Spirit....*" From that, we know that he drew power to witness and heal from the Holy Spirit living within him. The same Holy Spirit had authorized him to speak in Jesus' name.

Boldly and confidently, Peter explained that, by the name of Jesus, people had received salvation and healing. So disturbed were the leaders, they forbade them to speak or teach in the name of Jesus again. The disciples responded with a beautiful, confident decree of their own in verse 20, "... *we cannot stop speaking about what we have seen and heard.*" In other words, they had no intention of discontinuing their witness to hungry souls.

They prayed, never asking for release from persecutions and threats, but that they might speak God's word "*with all confidence.*" In verse 32, "*...they were all filled with the Holy Spirit, and began to speak the word of God with boldness.*"

God had called them to this ministry and supplied the power to do it. Their job was to preach in the name of Jesus. Are we called to any less as we witness? Are we not also to speak in the name of Jesus as the Lord gives us openings and fills us with the boldness of the Holy Spirit? Let's take up the challenge to listen for God's voice and follow His lead to witness to those He puts in our path.

It is good to know that if we tune in to God, He will direct our thoughts and steps to the people He wants us to witness to. At times, God stops us and at other times, He presents an opportunity. Paul had an experience in Acts 16:6-10 where the Holy Spirit stopped him. Accompanied by some of his disciples, Paul traveled through Phrygia and Galatia because the Holy Spirit forbade them to speak the word in Asia. Then again, when they tried to go into Bithynia, the Spirit of Jesus wouldn't permit that either.

Finally, God spoke to Paul through a vision and directed him to Macedonia. Paul concluded that God had called him to preach the gospel there. He had received a personal word from God. It ended as an occasion to win Lydia to the Lord. As a result of her conversion, she eventually carried the good news back to Asia, the place God forbade Paul to go. God had a plan and Paul's obedience brought about fruitfulness.

Following that experience, in the same region, religious people persecuted, beat, and imprisoned Paul for his faith. As he endured this ordeal, the knowledge that God had led him there sustained him.

Bob Wattles, an excellent Bible teacher, once said to me, "Never forget in the dark times what God has spoken in the light." If He speaks a word, we can know it has power. When suffering comes, that word has the potential to sustain us. Paul had heard from God and knew he was exactly where God wanted him to be. He was in the center of God's will, even willing to suffer for his faith.

At this point in America, we do not endure that type of persecution but what if we did? Would we be willing to speak out in faith if we knew we would pay a price and perhaps even go to prison? The day may come when that question will need to be answered. Now is the time to prepare.

Brother Yun, a former Chinese prisoner for his faith in Christ, offers a nugget to ponder in his book, "Back to Jerusalem". *"One day Jesus saw some fishermen by the Lake of Gennesaret who had pulled their nets up and were washing them, (Luke 5). Washing our fishing nets from time to time is necessary if we constantly use them to catch fish, but today many churches have become professional net washers. Instead of catching souls for the kingdom of God, they spend all their time talking about fishing, studying various fishing strategies and techniques, listening to the lectures of fishing experts, and singing songs about fishing. Yet they rarely, or never, actually go fishing!"* (Brother Yun, Peter Xu Yongze, Enoch Wang with Paul Hattaway, *Back to Jerusalem,* (Piquant Authentic Media, 2003), 132.)

Let's take up the challenge, listen for God's call, obediently step out in faith and experience the sheer joy of cooperating with God in witnessing to lost souls.

CHAPTER 27
A TRAP TO AVOID

I know of a man who felt compelled to witness to someone every day. If he started to get ready for bed and realized he had not witnessed that day, he got dressed and went out until he had done his "duty." I might add...self-imposed duty. At times, his family suffered from his neglect due to his obsession with witnessing. Is this what God wants? Does feeling driven please Him? Was this compulsion really from the Lord in the first place? While I can't judge for sure, it would seem to me this man had opened wide the door of "legalism".

We attended a church once that held the law over people. There was a family who wanted to join the church. The wife was saved but the husband was not. Sadly, he was a man who smoked and in this church, there was a rule that smokers could not join. As they spoke with the pastor about their desire to become members, instead of inquiring as to the man's salvation and giving him the opportunity to come to the Lord, the pastor let him know that because he smoked, he could not join. Apparently, smoking took precedence over salvation to that pastor. The couple left the church and never returned. An opportunity lost. This is misguided "religion" at its worst.

When we witness from a stance of law and even put ourselves under the law, we are in danger of also inviting our converts into a life of law instead of grace. Paul said in Acts 15:19, *"It is my judgment, therefore, that we should not make it difficult for the Gentiles who are turning to God,"* (NIV). What did he mean by that? In the next verse, he made it clear as to what rules the disciples should place on new believers in their day and culture. They narrowed it down to four. He told them: 1) to abstain from eating animals that had been sacrificed to idols, 2) to refrain from fornication (any sex outside of marriage), 3) to abstain from eating any strangled animal because it still has blood, and 4) they were not to eat blood.

I'm good with that list. How about you? Actually, in our day, three of those probably don't even apply. However, many churches have added their own list of "don'ts," and church leaders sometimes hold those over people as criteria for entering the kingdom of God. The list goes something like this. Do not smoke; do not drink; do not go to movies; do not wear make-up; don't listen to certain music; be at church every time the doors are open and on and on.

What is the problem with legalism? It looks at the outer man and ignores the state of his heart. I Samuel 16:7 speaks to this when it says, *"...for God sees not as man sees, for man looks at the outward appearance, but the Lord looks at the heart."* It is possible the man I mentioned would have accepted Christ if the pastor had taken a different approach but he focused on an outward issue instead of the inner issue of the man's heart condition. Jesus accepts any sinner into His kingdom and it is then His job to bring the person to repentance and clean him up. After all, it was while we were yet sinners that Jesus died for us (Rom. 5:8). Putting people under the law strangles any possibility of grace. It can't be both ways. No one comes to Christ through law keeping. In fact, in II Corinthians 3, we read that though the law is glorious, it is also a ministry of condemnation and death.

While the Law is spoken of in Psalm 19 as perfect, sure, right, pure, clean and true, it still lacks the power to change a heart. Only God can do that. Happily, the Law was fulfilled in Christ. Matthew 5:17 Jesus said, *"Do not think that I came to abolish the Law or the Prophets; I did not come to abolish but to fulfill."* That means if a person has Christ in their heart, they have the fulfilled Law living in them. After salvation in Christ, the Holy Spirit guides us into right living. We are led by the Spirit; we walk by the Spirit; we live by the Spirit. Galatians 5:18, *"But if you are led by the Spirit, you are not under the Law."* Now, that is good news!

Galatians 3:21 says, *"Even we have believed in Christ Jesus, so that we may be justified by faith in Christ and not by the works of the Law; since by the works of the Law no flesh will be justified."*

Then, you may wonder, why was the law given? Galatians 3:24-25 answers for us. *"Therefore the Law has become our tutor to lead us to Christ, so that we may be justified by faith. But now that faith has come, we are no longer under a tutor."* The Law is meant to lead us to Christ once we realize that we can't possibly keep it.

We could then ask this question: Are there any laws we, as Christ followers, are required to pursue? The answer is yes, there is one. It is not a requirement for salvation, but it is a command after we accept the Lord into our lives. Have you guessed what it is?

The singular and only law we are commanded to keep, after our salvation is secure, is called the Royal Law (James 2:8) or the Law of Liberty (James 1:25). It is also called the Law of Love spoken of in Luke 10:27, *"And he answered, 'You shall love the Lord your God with all your heart, and with all your soul, and with all your strength, and with all your mind; and your neighbor as yourself.'"*

It is really quite a simple concept. Love God and love people. It is a higher law, one that supersedes the Ten Commandments. How is that, you may ask? Think of it this way. When you love God, you will have no other gods before Him; you will not have an idol before you; you will not take His name in vain. Those things would not be loving, so you will choose not to do them.

In the same way, when you love your neighbor, you will choose not to commit adultery, not to steal, not to commit murder, bear false witness or covet. Those things would not be loving, so you will choose not to do them. Do you see how love trumps the Law? When we act out of love, we automatically make better choices. This is a much better and more satisfying way to live, a way not based on "Don't," but on "Do." Do love.

Can we consistently show love in our own power? No, we cannot. We are incapable and will fall short but the good news and bonus in all of this is that the Holy Spirit is the One who empowers us to live out of love. Without Him living in us, none of this would be possible. We walk by faith. Hebrews 11:6, *"And without faith it is impossible to please Him, for he who comes to God must believe that He is and that He is a rewarder of those who seek Him."* To sum up: When we, by faith, invite Jesus into our heart, Jesus comes in by way of the Holy Spirit. The Holy Spirit, who then dwells in us, is the One who leads us to love. It is a beautiful process confirmed by the One who loves us more than we can imagine.

CHAPTER 28

THE BUDDHIST TEMPLE

It was our first trip to Asia. We were on our way to China with a brief stop in Taiwan to spend time with Frank, an indigenous Taiwanese business associate of Bill's. Frank planned to manufacture products in a factory he owned in China that would be used in Bill's newly launched business in Michigan.

Over the years, Bill and Frank had developed a rapport having worked together while Bill was employed at Kirsch Company. Long business phone conversations often included enquiry about each other's family. Frank had visited Michigan several times and we had enjoyed entertaining him in our home. Bill and I both looked forward to his visits.

Now, we were his guests in Taiwan and looked forward to enjoying the kind hospitality of Frank and his wife. It was a beautiful, sunny day in May, and Frank wanted to show us around his city of Taipei before heading to China the next day. He introduced us to his wife, a lovely, quiet spoken lady who kindly showed us places of interest in Taipei while Frank attended to business. Although she was a gracious woman, it was a little awkward since she did not speak English, but we made do with an afternoon of sight-seeing. Although a genial woman, I am sure it was a bit uncomfortable for her as well.

That evening, when Frank invited us to come to his home, we were delighted. We were especially pleased because we had been told it is unusual for Taiwanese people to invite foreign guests to their homes. We felt honored by the invitation. As we entered his residence, we were introduced to Frank's parents and two sons who lived with them.

Frank was a successful businessman who worked with several countries including America and Japan. Because of that, I was surprised his home was in the inner city of Taipei rather than on a luxurious estate. The main entrance was down a tight alley where everything looked old, and his home, a one floor apartment, was quite unassuming. Although modest, it was tastefully decorated. I was surprised to note that their bedroom consisted of two woven bamboo mats on the floor. That's it...they slept on the floor. Perhaps their Buddhist faith had encouraged their humble choices. In America, people of their wealth would most likely live in a multi-million dollar mansion, but all of their rooms were small and unpretentious...until we reached the last room, the meditation room, as they called it.

This was the room where they worshipped. It was empty except for a beautifully adorned, heavy mahogany table which extended the width of one wall. Atop the table were various religious artifacts, candles, incense, and a rosary. There were also photos of family ancestors. Frank explained that they were part of a sect of Buddhism that worshipped ancestors. He pointed out that, eventually, when his parents passed away, they would add their photos to the collection and they, too, would be worshipped. Candles were burned during their services as an expression of honor and respect for those who had gone before them.

I found all of this interesting, if not fascinating, to observe. It was so foreign to my Christian faith. In my pragmatic way of thinking, it wouldn't cross my mind to worship my ancestors. After all, while they were to be respected, they were merely fallible humans like me and certainly did not hold any supernatural power that would help me in my present or future life. I listened to Frank's explanation of his choice of worship and realized his religion was very real to him and an important part of his life. Buddhism was his spiritual identity, taken as seriously as my Christian faith was to me. Yet, I couldn't help but feel the emptiness of it, the futility.

Frank had previously explained to Bill that part of the Buddhist faith was the idea of never becoming upset about anything that happens in life. Growing toward perfection involved a state of mind that was always at peace. Because of that, Frank tried to deal with any business or personal issue with a calm attitude. Certainly, this was a noble idea to be cultivated, yet I have wondered how it was possible without Christ. I suppose anyone can make choices as to how they will respond in situations, but for me, I would ultimately fail at such a venture, and each time I failed, I would probably condemn myself. I am thankful for two promises in the Bible about God's peace, promises that Jesus will supply me with peace so that I don't have to conjure it up myself from my limited resources. Truly, God given peace is a wonderful gift.

1. Jesus said,*"Peace I leave with you; My peace I give to you; not as the world gives do I give to you. Do not let your heart be troubled, nor let it be fearful,"* (Jn. 14:27).
2. *"And the peace of God, which surpasses all comprehension, will guard your hearts and your minds in Christ Jesus,"* (Phil. 4:7).

During our visit, Frank asked if we would like to visit a Buddhist temple. Being a curious person, I jumped at the chance. As we walked up the broad steps to the temple, we soon entered a covered courtyard where I noticed a small table with a box of long, smoking sticks. Each worshipper stopped to pick one up. Frank cordially invited me to take one but I graciously declined. It was not my God that they were worshipping. I was merely an observer of Buddhist customs. The sticks were lit on one end, not exuding a flame but just smoke and the smell of incense. It was a very strong perfume smell that, to me, was not pleasant or soothing, but rather caustic to my sensitive nose.

Worshippers seemed not to notice the odor as they advanced and knelt before a huge glassed in case which covered an enormous wall and was filled with a wide variety of statues and figurines. Some of the larger statues were bronze Buddha's while others were made of wood. Not all were of Buddha. In the front of the case was an assortment of dolls. Yes, they looked like the dolls our children play with. Some even reminded me of something a child might win at a carnival. They were dressed in colorful Asian attire with nylon hair and painted faces. Some were large and some were small. It seemed strange to my western way of thinking that these man-made dolls and statues of wood and stone were what they worshipped. That concept was hard to grasp.

As I observed the people sincerely calling out to their gods, I felt I was in the presence of darkness. What they were doing seemed so futile, so useless. These were people who probably knew nothing about Christ and His redemptive offer of salvation apart from works. In their uninformed minds, their only hope lay in the bondage of appeasing their many gods. Some of the people brought fruit and others offered flowers before these inanimate, lifeless gods. I wondered what their hope was. Did they feel their offerings would pacify their god for the moment? Were they afraid of their gods? I could only guess.

That's when I noticed something interesting happening. Several of the women sat on the floor in front of the case full of idols. They each had two small pieces of wood in the shape of a half-moon which they shook together in their hands and threw out on the floor. It was somewhat similar to how we use dice in a game of Parcheesi or Monopoly. Upon observing how the wood pieces landed, they would then pick them up, pause, and throw them again. I had no idea what they were doing, so I asked Frank if he could explain.

Cheerfully, he enlightened me. "Oh, they are asking their god a question, and depending on how the dice land, they have their answer. If two half moons go a certain direction, the god has answered yes. If they go another direction, that means no. If they go opposite directions, that means wait for an answer." To Frank, this was all perfectly normal, acceptable religious behavior.

Knowledge of what the Buddhist women were engaged in caused a question to form in my mind. "Frank, I'm looking at all these statues and dolls encased behind a glass window and understanding that to these people, they are gods to be worshipped. But there's something I don't understand. All these figurines and dolls were made by people, right? They are not alive. Since they aren't living, how do people think their gods will be able to bring them help and answer their questions?"

Like Paul in the book of Acts, I was observing that these Taiwanese people at this temple were lost and ensnared by a false, pagan religion. Indeed, they were slaves to counterfeit gods. I felt the Lord nudge me to say something to Frank about Jesus. While I knew he was entrenched in his Buddhist faith, I also knew that he had a brother living in America who had become a Christian and accepted Jesus as his Lord and Savior. In conversations with him, I was aware that Frank knew of Jesus.

Before he could answer my question about what seemed to me to be lifeless gods, I went on, "You know, Frank, I think that is one of the differences between my faith and yours. The God I serve is a living God, who is a real person, not an idol. Jesus is a man who lived on this earth, died for my sins and was raised from the dead. He still lives today because He was resurrected, and He wants to have relationship with people. When I approach Him in prayer, I know that He is alive and listening. I know I am talking with a real person."

I was truly perplexed by Frank's mystical religion of Buddhism. How could an inanimate god made with human hands possibly interact with the people who worshipped it? I was reminded of Paul's conversation in Acts 17:16 with the Athenians, *"Now while Paul was waiting for them at Athens, his spirit was being provoked within him as he was observing the city full of idols."* Yes, I also felt my spirit being provoked and hoped what I said about Jesus was meaningful to Frank. Bill and I had such respect and love for him. We so wanted him to know Christ, to enjoy a relationship with Him and find the true way to God.

I was also reminded of Paul again in Acts 19:26, *"... saying that gods made with hands are no gods at all,"* and in Galatians 4:8, *"However, at that time, when you did not know God, you were slaves to those which by nature are no gods."*

While I was pondering what to say next, Frank broke in with an answer to my original question, an answer that seemed perfectly logical to him but stunned me. I had asked how these inanimate, lifeless gods, who were designed and built by men, could answer questions and direct people's lives.

With excitement, Frank answered, "Oh, Betsy, yes, these gods are made by people, but you need to know that behind each god, there is a spirit."

To say that a chill ran down my spine would be an understatement. Of course... there was a spirit behind each of their gods, and I knew who they were. I had just never come face to face with the demonic world before. I was reminded of 1Corinthians 10:20-21. *"No, but I say that the things which the Gentiles sacrifice, they sacrifice to demons and not to God; and I do not want you to become sharers in demons. You cannot drink the cup of the Lord and the cup of demons; you cannot partake of the table of the Lord and the table of demons."*

Frank, at that time, while polite in listening about my faith, showed no interest in knowing Jesus for himself. Since it is not wise to push people when they are not ready to hear, that is all that was said that day. God is a gentleman and it is prudent to follow His lead when talking with people about the Lord. I pray that God will draw Frank to Himself, that He will reveal Himself so that one day Frank will give his heart to the One who loves him and longs for a personal relationship with him. I pray he will come to know that Jesus is the way, the truth and the life, the one and only way to God.

Bill and I once knew an evangelist, Walt Bleeker, who shared with us a wonderful and enlightening story that helped us understand the heart of God in a better way and gave us a gentler way to share Christ. He told us that farmers, when they go into their apple orchards to test the ripeness of fruit on the trees, will place their hand on an apple, gently twisting and lightly pulling at it. If the fruit is ripe, it will fall into their hand. This way, they know it is ready. However, if the fruit resists separating from the tree, they would understand that it was not yet ready for harvest.

They did this knowing that gentleness was important so as to not bruise the fruit. When fruit is bruised, it often gets damaged or spoils and never becomes fully developed the way that it would if left for harvest at its peak of ripeness.

We love this story because we don't want to bruise people while sharing our faith, After all, it is God who is doing the work, not us, and when they are ready, they will come to Him, literally fall into His hand, just as a ripe apple would. It is comforting to realize that concept and to trust Him for the harvest. We are simply the workers. We plant seeds, we water, and we may or may not be part of the harvest in His timing, at His choosing.

Although it has been years since we have seen Frank, we know that the Lord loves him and desires him to yield his life to Him. *"The Lord is not slow about His promise, as some count slowness, but is patient toward you, not wishing for any to perish but for all to come to repentance,"* (II Pet. 3:9).

CHAPTER 29

BELLA, MY YOUNG CHINESE FRIEND

One of the most exciting events of our trip to Asia occurred while in a restaurant in China. We were about to place our order when the restaurant manager approached our table and spoke to Frank in Mandarin which Frank then translated. "He wants to know if you are Americans," he explained.

"Yes, we are," we smiled back.

Actually, from what we had observed, we were the only Americans in this Chinese town. Bill and I are both taller than most Chinese. Bill, at 6 foot 2 inches, was about a foot taller than nearly everyone. Besides our height, I'm sure my "blond" hair stood out amidst a sea of people with silky black hair. I think we each stuck out like a tree in the midst of a lawn. Many people gawked at us as we walked the streets. I had to smile as I told Bill, "This must be what it is like to be a movie star."

Frank continued to translate as the manager said, "My daughter is learning English. Would it be okay if she came to your table for a short chat to practice her English? I know she would enjoy meeting some people from the United States."

"Of course, we would be happy to meet her," I replied. "Send her over."

Soon, a delightful, darling eight year old girl with a winsome smile and dancing brown eyes came bouncing over to our table. We learned her name was Shirley. Although this was not her real name, Asian people often take an American pseudonym because their names can be foreign sounding to westerners and hard to pronounce. It is just easier to use a fictitious name. Of course, some Chinese are unaware of popular American names so they tend to pick old movie stars, perhaps a name like Shirley Temple that catches their fancy. She later changed her name but I will refer to her as Bella.

Speaking confidently with us, we were smitten by Bella's vivacious personality and sanguine temperament. She was so adorable. We were also amazed by her command of the English language as we engaged in conversation. Even at eight years old, we could tell she was very smart. After a fifteen minute chat, while we awaited our food, we exchanged addresses and I promised to send her some American stamps for a collection she told us about.

Later, as we finished our meal and left the restaurant, I was still smiling at our brief encounter with this sweet little girl. Frank interrupted my thoughts when he asked, "You know who that little girl is, don't you?"

"No, who is she?" we inquired, having no idea who she could be other than the daughter of the restaurant manager. Frank was tickled to let us in on who Bella was in her country.

"Well, she is on television here in China," he related with a twinkle in his eye.

"Really, what does she do on TV?"

"She has her own program where she teaches English to several other Chinese children each week. She's the teacher and has two or three students who are learning English."

Impressive, I thought. *I just met a Chinese TV star.*

Upon returning to America, I followed up on my promise to send Bella some stamps, and with that, we started what has become a lifetime friendship. For several years, we wrote longhand letters until computers and email became popular. Then we began writing regularly through email. All through her high school years, we chatted about the differences in our cultures and our everyday lives, Bella being a very curious young lady.

Academics are taken very seriously in China, so I frequently heard about her studies, but I wondered if her school also offered after school activities, so I asked, "Do you have any extra-curricular activities through your school, Bella?" After all, I thought, in America, sports and after school activities are often as important as academics, sometimes more important, or so it seems.

"No, school is just for academic work," she explained, "but on weekends, I do attend dance lessons, foreign language classes, badminton, and other private lessons. English is a very important subject in China as it is the bridge we have to the rest of the world, so it is important to learn that language. During the week, however, I'm in school from early morning until dinner time. Then, from the time I get home until I go to bed, I study. We don't do sports through the school or during the week. Studying is extremely important here because at the end of eighth grade we must all take a test which will determine whether we can go on to prepare for college. If we don't pass this one exam, we can never attend a university. There is a lot of pressure with such a weighty exam that literally determines our future."

Hmmm... very different from America, I thought.

Bella was a brilliant student through high school and turned out to be one of the top students in all of China. As a high school junior, she took the American SAT in English which, of course, was her second language, and scored 740 out of 800 on the verbal section and a perfect 800 in math. I have never met an American, whose first language is English, who scored that well!

I asked her how she studied for these tests. One of her answers was that she had memorized three thousand (yes, 3,000) English vocabulary words. As I said, academics are very important in China.

Then, in an email, with all sincerity and even trepidation, she asked me, "Betsy, do you think these scores are good enough to get me into an American university?"

I almost choked with laughter as I read that question. My obvious thought was, *Uh, yes, Bella, with those scores, I think you could get into ANY university you desire in America. Take your pick.*

She ended up leaving high school halfway through her senior year to begin college in Singapore on a full scholarship. Later, she studied for several years at two of America's most prestigious universities as well. Upon finishing graduate studies, she interned at a job in New York City and later moved to Singapore to work in a very lucrative profession.

From the beginning of our relationship, I let Bella know that I was a Christian. This was a new and unexplored topic for her academic mind but, I think, also for her heart. Jesus was drawing her to Himself right from the beginning. Her natural inquisitiveness led to many interesting emails and a very special relationship developed between us. Coming from China, an atheistic nation, where neither her parents nor her friends practiced any religion, Bella's interest was piqued when I spoke of God. Naturally, I wanted Christ to be as central to our relationship as possible.

Through the years, Bella and I had animated conversations about Jesus. She was a thinker, so our correspondence on faith topics took many twists and turns. I found all of it delightful as we wrestled together through deep spiritual issues. For instance, at the beginning, I had to determine if she had been involved in any other faith. It is common knowledge that, although atheism is prevalent in China, Buddhism is also popular.

So, I inquired, "Bella, the reason I asked if you had any religion in your life was because, if, for instance, you told me you were a Buddhist, then I would know that you had many gods and that perhaps you would just incorporate Jesus as one more god in a pantheon of gods. When a person truly comes to Christ, however, it is necessary to renounce all other gods because He is the One and Only true God. Christianity is monotheistic, but you will find that Jesus is more than enough. He is able meet any need you have."

Bella assured me that she and her family had not believed in any god at all. They were atheists, but she, herself, was definitely becoming more intrigued with the idea of Christianity after talking with me about having faith in the one true God. Over time, I went on to tell her in detail the message of salvation and hat Jesus is not like many other gods who are from the imaginations of man. "Jesus is a 'historical' person about whom much has been written in history, our best source being the Bible," I told her. "There, we learn about Jesus from many people who knew Him personally, most of whom staked their lives on the truth of what He said, even to the point of being martyred. There were eye witnesses to His life, death and resurrection, Bella. They recognized His Deity and worshipped Him. They gave their lives to Him and for Him. So my first question to you is this: Are you willing to accept that the Bible is truth?"

"Yes," she explained. "From reading in a Bible and having you explain faith to me, I do believe the Bible speaks truth."

I went on to explain that Christianity is a wonderful religion based on love. "To be honest," I told her, "I don't think of Christianity as a religion at all because it is really a two way love relationship with God. It is not like other religions of the world because every other religion tells people to 'do' something to be acceptable to their god. Other religions are based on good works to please a god, but Christianity is based completely on what God has done for us, not what we can do for Him. It is a personal relationship with God through faith in Jesus Christ.

"Bella, here is what God did for us. He sent His Son, Jesus, to die on the cross for our sins. We are separated from God because we are all sinners. Sin began with Adam and Eve when they disobeyed God and ate from the one tree from which God had commanded them to abstain. From that point on, all people have sinned. Therefore, all need a Savior.

"The good news is that Jesus took our sins upon Himself and was crucified on the cross to pay for all of them. Then He resurrected, that is raised from the dead. This was proof that God even has power over death. The resurrection of Christ is pivotal in Christianity because it proves Jesus is Deity. No other religious leader has died for people's sins, and no other religious leader has ever risen from the dead. Only Jesus has done that. The good news is that because Jesus rose from the dead, He is alive today. So, in truth, Christians serve a living Lord.

"In Christianity, what God asks is that we believe in Jesus and accept Him as our Lord. You might ask, what does that mean? In simple terms, it means that we have been on the throne of our life, living our lives apart from God, without heeding His voice or acknowledging Him. We now repent of walking without God, make a 180 degree turn and begin walking toward Him. We allow Him His rightful place on the throne of our lives. This means God is now the focus of who we are and what we do. He is the one who has taken control, and we give Him permission to direct our lives. The Bible says, *"If you confess with your mouth Jesus as <u>Lord</u> and believe in your heart that God raised Him from the dead, you shall be saved,"* (Rom. 10:9). Many people want Jesus as Savior, but He wants to be Lord. The word Lord in Greek means 'supreme in authority, controller, and by implication, Master.' When we accept Jesus as Lord, He then becomes our Savior.

"From the Romans verse, you might wonder what you are saved from. Well, Jesus loves us so much that He died to save us from God's wrath against unrighteousness and an eternity apart from

Him which would be described as hell. When God created us, He had a goal of giving us an abundant life here on earth and a joyful eternity with Him in heaven, but sin caused a detour in that path. Jesus, therefore, died to give us an opportunity to get back on track with God and His plan.

"Jesus paid the price for our sins and, by accepting Him, He guarantees we will be forgiven and will spend eternity in His presence. The Bible says that, *"God so loved the world that He gave His only begotten Son, that whoever believes in Him shall not perish but have eternal life,"* (Jn. 3:16).

"Bella, God loves everyone in the world with a profound love, and He has a plan for each of our lives. But until we accept Jesus as Lord, we don't know His personal plan, one that is individually unique to whom He created us to be. The Bible says there is only one mediator between God and mankind, and that is Jesus (I Tim. 2:5).

"People, on their own, try to find all kinds of ways to please God. They think if they obey the Ten Commandments or do a number of good deeds or live a moral life that they will be good enough to earn heaven and God's favor. But that is not God's redemptive plan. Jesus has already done everything we need to get to heaven. If you think about it, how many good works would it even take to please God? Trying to earn heaven would be a vicious, unending, stressful cycle, like running in circles and never finding an end. Remember, if you plan to get to heaven by good works, perfection is the only acceptable way. Perfect in every area at all times; and of course, that is impossible.

"Thankfully, Jesus, the sinless one, shed blood on the cross covered all our sins. He paid the price by dying in our place. He alone completed the work of salvation. We only need to accept His free gift of salvation. The Bible says, *"For all have sinned and fall short of the glory of God,"* (Rom. 3:23). Therefore, no one is good enough or ever will be good enough without Jesus' righteousness.

That's why we need a Savior. The Bible goes on to say, *"The wages of sin is death, but the free gift of God is eternal life through Jesus Christ our Lord,"* (Rom. 6:23). Wages are what a person earns. What we earn through sin is death. A gift, however, is what is freely given with no strings attached. Eternal life is free through Jesus. He is the only way to the Father.

"We can add nothing to what God has done to pay for our sins and to pay for our way to heaven. He has done it all. Our good works, baptism, prayers, trying hard, being moral, following rules...none of those will get us into heaven. We can add nothing to what Jesus has already done to obtain our salvation. There is only one thing that will please God in the day of accountability and that is whether a person's sins have been covered by the blood of Jesus.

"I hope that you will think these things over and consider the claims that Jesus made. He said He is God, that He forgives sin. He has all the power and authority of the universe in His hands. Jesus performed, and still performs, miracles and healings. He has given us a wonderful plan and guideline for living here on earth, the Bible. He provides love, peace and joy for His children. God is awesome, Bella. He is our creator. He loves us so much."

In an email response, Bella said, "One of my American friends has also been telling me about the eternal peace and love I'll enjoy if I put my faith into God. Oh, yes, Betsy, if the love of God, of Jesus is really that great, great enough to reconcile any differences and to heal any ills, I'll be glad to worship Jesus without doubt. I'm not questioning the existence of the magic power of Jesus. I'm just wondering if it's a little too late if I start to worship him right now?"

As you can imagine, I immediately wrote back that it was definitely not too late. I was also intrigued that God had now placed another believer in her path. Isn't it just like God to incorporate several people to plant seeds into the heart of a seeker?

It wasn't long before Bella chose to invite Jesus into her life. Later, she wrote, "If there's something that can soothe away the fears of death, it is a miracle. And what Christianity has done for people is exactly a wonder, an incredible and undeserved wonder."

Although, like most of us, she had times of struggle along her faith journey, ultimately, Jesus made sense to her. She accepted Him as her Lord and Savior while still in high school. All of this took place through email.

She expressed, "You know, Betsy, I'm so glad to hear that I'm precious to God. There's nothing else that a Christian cherishes more than the love of God. No doubt the fact that despite the distance between us, despite the distinct cultural and national background, we get to meet, to know and to understand each other and more importantly the fact that you introduced God and Christianity to me and solved so many questions that I raised about Christianity, is amazing and is definitely something God has planned in our lives. For me, knowing you is especially precious, because it's like my life is opened to a new window from which I keep receiving the words of God and heed them. I'm so lucky compared to those who are denied the chance to know God. Though currently, I only have a passing acquaintance with Christianity, I'm sure that if I keep boasting a mind that true-heartedly accepts Jesus as my Savior, keep craving for more words of Him, then one day like you, I'll also be able to pass on to more people, Chinese or foreign, God's words, the greatest truth of this world."

Years later, when Bella became rooted in Christ, to my joy, she began telling others about Jesus. Isn't that God's plan? She wrote, "To my exhilaration, one of my closest friends finally received Christ recently, although she herself wasn't quite convinced at first. But I think that sometimes it is good to exercise that little faith in God and you will find yourself greatly rewarded. One of my other friends also accepted Him a bit dubiously a few months ago, but later on, she grew very fast in her relationship with Him. She found out that she was released from the troubles, the anxieties and the fears that used to nag her in the past, and she may now be rest assured that as long as she did her best and lived a godly life, God will take care of the rest for her."

You can imagine how thrilled I was when Bella had grown in her faith to the point that she began telling me how God was using her. She even began writing Bible verses to me. I treasured the thought that she was moving on in her own faith as she now reminded me of Jesus' words when she wrote:

Jesus said: "...*I am the Light of the world; he who follows Me will not walk in the darkness, but will have the Light of life,*" (Jn. 8:12).

"*You are the light of the world. A city set on a hill cannot be hidden; nor does anyone light a lamp and put it under a basket, but on the lampstand, and it gives light to all who are in the house. Let your light shine before men in such a way that they may see your good works, and glorify your Father who is in heaven,*" (Matt. 5:14-16).

Bella went on to say that "being a real Christian is about being one of those energizer batteries that never dies. When Christ is in me, I illuminate because He shines within me, and when people see this, they will see Him and be attracted to Christ naturally. And I think you are one of those light houses that attract people walking in the darkness. I still remember how you taught me patiently all the way until I finally received Him and became more and more devoted to Him. Thank you, Betsy, you are such a blessing to me, and I believe, to many others."

Bella's words deeply touched my heart. To be part of someone's salvation is an immense privilege. I wrote back, "Bella, do you remember how I talked to you about Jesus over the years? I took a soft approach for a long time and just occasionally mentioned something the Lord was doing in our lives. As you showed interest, I shared more. Another of your acquaintances was also talking to you. Do you realize that God orchestrated the whole thing? What an amazing God we serve! Then one day, you decided to accept Jesus. And now people in your world are seeing Jesus through you."

When Bella later came to the United States, we were thrilled to again meet in person after so many years of correspondence. We had begun our relationship when she was only eight years old and now she was in college. She had grown in her faith over the years and had been faithful to share Jesus with others.

Later, after college when she again lived in Singapore, her fiancé's mother had cancer. It was Bella who led her to Jesus before she died. Bella also brought her fiancé (now her husband) and his father to the Lord. She says it is so sweet to be able to pray with her husband as a fellow believer.

When Bella was preparing for marriage, her own father became acutely ill and had to be hospitalized for many months. Sadly, because of that, her parents were unable to attend her wedding. Bella had shared Christ with her father several times over the years, but being a staunch atheist, he never showed any interest. But now, critically ill, in a visit home, Bella again shared the message of Christ with her father. To her amazement and joy, her father accepted Jesus as Lord before he passed away. What peace this brought to her, knowing her father's eternal destiny was sealed and that, indeed, she would see him again someday.

To me, the story of my relationship with Bella and her coming to Christ is one of the most remarkable journeys God has allowed me to walk through. God knows I love adventure. What could be better adventure than this... that two people living on opposite sides of the world, on different continents, in two radically different cultures would meet in a restaurant, form a relationship and become sisters in Christ? There was no coincidence in this meeting. God had it planned all along, and I give Him all the praise and glory for His wonderful ways and for His work in Bella's life and in my life too. It is truly an occasion of joy unspeakable and full of glory.

CHAPTER 30

SKYPING WITH CHERISE

When Bella was in high school, and at my prompting, she expressed that she would like to come to America for a visit. I sent her a formal invitation which is required from the potential host of a Chinese person. Because the timing for the visit was shortly after the tragic events of 9/11, she had trouble getting a visa. As the weeks went by and the delay seemed endless, we decided it might be better to wait until a later date for her visit.

During this time, however, I felt it might be important for me to contact her mother, Cherise. I asked Bella for her mother's email address and sent her a cordial letter of introduction. Cherise, at that time, was an English teacher at a university in China and was the one who had taught Bella such perfect English. I was pleased when I heard back from her, knowing she would have been able to read my email with ease. Although Bella's hoped for a trip to America did not come about, her mother and I began corresponding regularly. I found that I enjoyed communicating with her as much as I had with Bella and soon we formed a warm friendship through email.

In time, she shared with me her desire to also start an English school to give young, grade school students in her community the opportunity to learn English. She felt knowing English was a necessary requirement for Chinese people as China was moving more toward the global marketplace. It was Cherise's desire to help raise the standard of those whom she taught and to nurture them into positive and productive citizens with an entrepreneurial and international outlook. At that time, she had about forty students whom she taught on weekends. She had done a remarkable job of teaching English to her own daughter, and now she was making a difference in the lives of many more young students in China.

When she mentioned that she needed books written in English for her students, I began scouring garage sales collecting children's books. Mailing them to her in an M-bag, a special post office bag, brought the cost down to $11 for each eleven pounds. It was snail mail, to be sure, and took about six weeks or so to arrive in China, but it was a way I could contribute to her library without exorbitant postal costs.

Right from the start of my relationship with Cherise, I spoke to her about the Lord, how I was a Christian and enjoyed Bible study. I could tell by her inquiries that she was intrigued. Later, I discovered that, although she was not a Christian herself, she had many Christian friends in China. I was sure, since some of them were missionaries, they were also talking to her about the Lord.

It wasn't long before Cherise asked me if I would teach her the Bible online, first on Instant Message and later on Skype. I was delighted with her interest, and when we both established that our computers were able to do video chats, we began weekly meetings. It amazed me that I was able to talk with and even see someone on another continent while we both sat in the comfort of our own homes.

Our first study was through the Gospel of John. I felt since she didn't know anything about the Bible, and really nothing about Jesus, that John would be a great introduction to Scripture. She would learn about Jesus' teaching, His character, His miracles, His

193

healing power, His crucifixion and resurrection. Hopefully, when she became acquainted with Jesus, she would fall in love with Him as I had many years ago and her daughter had more recently.

After much time with her in Bible study, she expressed that she was drawn to Jesus, even sensed His presence and felt comforted by His words. For several years, I continued to teach her from the Bible. There were many sweet times when I could sense God with us in our meetings.

In our time together, she did believe Jesus was who He said He was and acknowledged His stories rang true. She gained a lot of knowledge about Jesus and even tasted of His goodness, but a life commitment was not a desire she had. Although difficult, I respected her right to choose or not to choose a relationship with Jesus.

Each week, after our cordial hellos, I would have her read a passage of Scripture. We were in the Gospel of John, chapter six during one visit and had just read verse 35 where Jesus said, *"...I am the bread of life; he who comes to Me will not hunger, and he who believes in Me will never thirst."*

Cherise enjoyed thinking through the meaning of that statement and always had thoughtful questions. I explained that just as bread can give us physical life, Jesus offers Himself as spiritual life that will fill, nourish and satisfy our souls.

When I asked if she knew how a person came to Christ, her interest was piqued, so I shared the gospel message. Her aspiration was to know and understand the Bible, a noble goal. She was curious to know about God. We read and discussed Jesus words when He said, *"I am the way and the truth and the life. No one comes to the Father but through Me,"* (Jn. 14:6).

I spoke to her about how Jesus wants us to receive Him as evidence that we believe in Him. *"But as many as received Him, to them He gave the right to become children of God, even to those who believe in His name,"* (Jn. 1:12). I led her to Romans 10:9, *"that if you confess with your mouth Jesus as Lord, and believe in your heart that God raised Him from the dead, you will be saved."* I pointed out that the resurrection of Jesus from the dead is the proof that He is who He says He is. I told her that Christianity is the only religion where the founder raised Himself from the dead, that indeed, He is alive today.

Although she affirmed that she believed what I was telling her, she was not ready to commit her life to Jesus. I had to admit that she had every right to make her own decision.

A good illustration I once heard was this: If you were sick with a disease and I gave you a bottle of medicine that would cure you, what would you need to do? You could do a couple things. You could leave it in the bottle and put it on a shelf and not take it. Or you could receive it, open it and take the medicine and get well. Salvation is similar. Jesus offers eternal life, but we must receive it. I'm reminded of John 5:39, *"You search the Scriptures because you think that in them you have eternal life; it is these that testify about Me."*

Cherise and I have enjoyed a warm friendship for many years. I think as much as her quest for Bible knowledge, she also enjoyed the opportunity to have conversation with an English speaking American. We chatted about many subjects over the years and developed a close relationship, albeit we were thousands of miles apart.

During those years, I made another trip to China, this time to visit her since we had not yet met in person. Later, she also came to our home. On my trip to China, Cherise invited me to stay in her home. I gladly did so for a little over a week enjoying her amazing hospitality. Although we did not speak much of spiritual matters, we had a wonderful visit.

As an aside, I want to tell you about one evening in China after a busy day at her college, when we were to meet some of her friends for dinner. We waited two and a half hours. I was exhausted, but finally, they arrived and we were escorted to an exclusive VIP room where nine of us were served an unusual dinner of various foods that I had never been exposed to, including squid with suction cups all over it and some kind of unusual fish. No doubt, these were delicacies in China but totally unfamiliar to me. I identified a piece of crab after I figured out how to get it out of the shell and also recognized some celery and ate it along with either algae or kale. Anyway, it was dark green and I needed some veggies. Upon putting a heap of familiar looking noodles on my plate, I observed some horrible looking creature in the midst that looked like a tape worm. I almost passed out. Cherise said it was fish. It did not look like a fish. It was almost as scary as a later dinner where a parasite looking creature with horns somehow appeared on my plate. *(When my daughter, Kim, was editing this book, in a side note she highlighted this passage and wrote, "Ewwwww! Just had to react. No editing required.")*

On another occasion, Cherise and I walked to a very busy downtown restaurant. I found a table and waited while she went through the cafeteria line. Already seated at this table was an older woman who noticed I was wearing a cross. I had been told that Christians can wear a cross in Communist China. It is a way for other Christians to recognize us without setting off alarms. Indeed, this woman immediately noticed my cross and indicated that she, too, was a Christian. I wanted to communicate with her, but how? I did not know Mandarin, the language of China.

A strange thought went through my mind that I could sing to her. This had to be the prompting of the Holy Spirit because I do not sing solos in public. But before I knew it, I was singing Amazing Grace...loudly. I am sure she recognized the tune because she began to smile and clap her hands. Surprisingly, when Cherise returned to the table with our food, the lady excitedly chattered with her. Cherise interpreted to me that she was inviting us to her house church. I wish we could have gone, but our schedule did not allow for it.

Dinner was foreign to me again...a sesame bun filled with jellied rice. Oh, and for the dessert...peanut soup, a very watery, sweet broth with soggy peanuts. If you go to China, do not order peanut soup although I can tell you that it seems to be a favorite in China.

Interestingly, I have found that sometimes we are served unusual foods in foreign countries because they have heard that Americans like certain foods. Once in Switzerland, Bill and I were served baked ham with mashed, cooked bananas. They thought they were being thoughtful to serve us so-called American food. Just another example of a combination you never want to pile on your plate but I do credit their kindness and thoughtfulness.

One of the highlights of my trip to China was that Cherise invited me to teach her college students for a week and gave me free rein to speak about anything I wanted. We talked about what would be appropriate, and she agreed I should talk about American holidays. What an opportunity! I did just that, including, of course, Christmas and Easter and the real meaning behind those holidays. It was a wonderful week of ministry.

At one point, Cherise prompted me to write our American Pledge of Allegiance on the chalkboard, which I gladly did. Then, she had everyone stand up, place their hand on their heart and repeat it with me: "*I pledge allegiance to the flag of the United States of America and to the Republic for which it stands, one nation under God, indivisible, with liberty and justice for all.*" She left this on the board, and it was still there the next day. I wonder what Communist Party officials would have thought about that. Cherise didn't seem to think it would be an issue.

At the end of the week, the students gave me gifts to show their appreciation. One girl brought in two bottles of wine and commenced to offer a drink to anyone who would like a glass. To be cordial, I took a taste...much too sweet. But I had the oddest thought...it kind of seemed, in some ways, there was more freedom in this Communist university than there is in any American school.

On Sunday, I told Cherise I would like to go to church. She graciously agreed to take me to a government run church. In fact, she excitedly called several of her friends and invited them along. None of them normally attended church but agreed to go along with us. It was a novel experience for all. There was a Three Self Patriotic Government church in her town, so we made plans to attend a service followed by an English speaking service at a nearby location. Being government run, the Three Self church, which means self support, self governance and self propagation, is completely controlled by the government. Those who go must register their names. It is the only legal Protestant denomination in China.

As we sat through the Chinese service, Cherise was quick to kindly interpret the message for me. I found it to be somewhat biblically sound but more about how to live life out of our own strength and power than about Jesus living through us.

Teaching of many doctrines is forbidden, things such as Jesus' resurrection and second coming. The Communist party decides what can and cannot be preached. Evangelism is staunchly prohibited. In churches where government is the rule of law, I was told many do not even preach the gospel. Instead, they exploit the Bible by advocating another gospel which is just a set of social rules.

In China, public school teachers cannot be Christian. Soldiers cannot be Christian. Police officers cannot be Christian. Children and teenagers cannot be Christian. No one under the age of eighteen can be baptized. Being a Christian in China still often means lack of promotion, and even demotion or termination of employment. Perhaps, those are reasons why some have not accepted Christ. Perhaps that is why Cherise was hesitant to accept Jesus. She worked for a public university.

After the service, we had planned to attend an English speaking service, but due to a holiday, it had been cancelled. Though disappointed, another idea instantly came to mind. Some of the ladies had Bibles with them, as did I. I noticed there was a McDonalds across from the church, so I suggested we all go over there and have a Bible study. After purchasing drinks, I sent up a quick prayer as to what I should teach them. The Holy Spirit led me to the Gospel of John, the gospel message, and the book of Colossians.

On a piece of paper, I drew the chasm between God and man and talked to them about how man is on one side of the chasm and God is on the other side, and how no one can reach God by his own effort. Then, I drew the cross of Christ bridging the way from God to man across the chasm. I explained that, through Jesus shed blood on the cross, God provided a way for us to know Him. I shared how Christianity is not a religion but a personal love relationship with God. In Christianity, God reaches down to man for relationship. All other religions require man to try to reach God through keeping rules and laws, but through Christ's finished work on the cross, He has taken the initiative to make a way for us to have a relationship with Him.

On to I Corinthians 15, I explained how Jesus raised from the dead after dying on the cross. Then, I showed them in the Bible the sightings of Jesus after his resurrection, how He had appeared to many people.

I Corinthians 15:3 -8, *"For I delivered to you as of first importance what I also received, that Christ died for our sins according to the Scriptures, and that He was buried, and that He was raised on the third day according to the Scriptures, and that He appeared to* **Cephas** *(Peter), then to the twelve. After that* **He appeared to more than five hundred brethren at one time,** *most of whom remain until now, but some have fallen asleep; then He appeared to* **James,** *then* **to all the apostles;** *and last of all, as to one untimely born, He appeared to* **me** *(Paul) also."* (*Parenthesis and highlights are mine*)

I shared my personal testimony of how I came to Christ and talked to them about practical ways the Bible applies to marriage and family. I have found that personal stories are often one of the most effective ways for sharing my faith. We also talked about how the Bible was written and put together. I had a Gospel of John with me which I gave to one of them.

When we were done, one of the ladies approached me privately and whispered that she had recently been on sabbatical in the United States for six months. During that time, someone had shared the gospel with her and she had accepted Christ. She explained further that she hadn't been taught much. I think she appreciated our time in the Bible that day. I ended up praying with her. What a joy!

The stunning thing about this encounter was that I had to remind myself that I was in Communist China. People are persecuted and imprisoned for openly acknowledging Christ. Yet, there we were in McDonalds having a Bible study, and no one seemed especially fearful. It was later I learned that there are cities in China where they are very strict in forbidding Christianity, cities where churches are shut down and Christians are persecuted. But, there are other cities that are more lenient, cities where officials turn the other way and allow for some Christian expression so they will appear tolerant. I think we were in a more accepting part of the country. In fact, a missionary I met there said that underground churches in that town were safe. That was certainly not the case in all cities in China.

On my previous visit to Cherise's city, I noted it was quite large. As we traveled the city, we had seen that it appeared to be a third world country emerging into the first world. While modern skyscrapers were being built, interestingly, the scaffolding was made of bamboo sticks. Outside our hotel window, men were clearing the earth, not with machinery, but by hand. Large boulders were being lifted by hand onto trucks.

On that visit, I had spent time looking in store windows. All of the merchandise, including clothing, looked like it had come out of the 1940's or 1950's. Much of it was very plain. While I was drawn to the incredibly low prices, nothing caught my eye. The exchange rate was an amazing six to one at that time which meant what cost $60 in America was only $10 in China. But with outdated styles, I had no desire to purchase anything.

On this second trip to China, it was completely different. The malls were incredible. The styles could easily compete with American attire. In fact, I found many of their clothes more appealing than what our stores offered. I didn't buy anything, however, because if you think of American sizes compared to Chinese, Chinese women are very petite. I probably would have needed an XXXLT to fit my usual medium size in America. Somehow, even the thought of that made me uncomfortable.

After one shopping expedition with Cherise and a friend of hers, we decided to stop for dinner. I was thinking I couldn't handle another Chinese meal when Cherise suggested we eat at Kentucky Fried Chicken. Yes! A familiar eatery with food I understood. At KFC, we were all furnished plastic gloves to eat our sandwiches. People don't touch their food in restaurants. That suited me just fine as unclean hands are one of my fetishes. I don't like to touch food either, and this was certainly easier than washing my hands frequently. I had to appreciate this Chinese custom.

One evening, we were invited to the home of an American couple for dinner. It turned out they were another Christian couple among Cherise's friends. Hearing I was a Christian too, they engaged me in animated conversation about the second coming of Christ. It was a delightful evening with discussion on one of my favorite topics. I wondered what Cherise thought. She was always gracious and may have learned some things about the Lord that night that we had not covered prior to that.

On another evening, we went to visit another university campus where Cherise had friends. The coed who showed us around the campus caught sight of my cross and asked if I was a Christian. Once again, I felt a bond of kinship with a fellow believer.

That evening, after a very spicy dinner at an Indian restaurant on campus, one so hot my nose ran, we were off to an English Corner. I had always thought they were just opportunities on street corners for English speaking people to engage in conversation with locals interested in learning our language. This one was actually held in the apartment of some of Cherise's friends. The apartment was small and sparsely furnished but there were about a dozen students who came. After they introduced themselves in English, we played a game where each person had a character quality pinned on his or her back and had to guess what theirs was. I thought it was a good mixer, a fun opportunity for them to practice speaking English.

Then, the host asked me to tell them about myself. In the process, I mentioned that I was working on my Master's in Biblical studies. Aware of what I was saying, I wondered if that would pique anyone's interest. It did, and I ended up sharing my personal testimony of how I came to the Lord.

Then one young man, whom I felt the Lord was clearly drawing, asked me to summarize the Bible in five minutes. What a great opportunity to share the gospel message. He said two of his friends were continually preaching to him, and it sounded like he was irritated by it, but there he was at the English Corner hearing again about the love of Jesus. Once more, I emphasized that Christianity is not a religion but a love relationship with Jesus Christ. Another opportunity to plant some seeds.

The week before I had flown to Cherise's town, I had been in Beijing with my friend, Sue Werschky, and her daughter, Aly. I now flew back to Beijing so that Sue and I could fly home together. In the airport, I shared with them and their driver about the many wonderful experiences I had enjoyed with Cherise, how the Lord had opened many doors and what a joy it was to share Christ with people along the way. The driver had not accepted Christ yet but listened intently to our conversation. More seeds planted.

As Sue and I awaited the plane, the lady next to us in the air-port was listening to our conversation about all the Lord had done. When she saw my Bible, she asked if we were Christians. She had been in Beijing too and was interested in the doors the Lord had opened for me. I was only too glad to share.

Looking back at my trip to China, I feel it was anointed from the time we arrived until we got home. My experience in China was truly the most amazing trip of my lifetime.

After I arrived home, Cherise and I continued our Bible les-sons on Skype once again. Sometime later, I began to sense that God was bringing our teaching time to a close. While certainly not wanting to end my relationship with her, after much prayer, I did, however, feel it was time to stop teaching her the Bible. It was a hard decision. Her schedule had also picked up and she, too, was finding it harder to commit time to study with me. Yet, when I did end our discussions, she was very disappointed and I certainly felt a sense of loss as well.

Since then, we have kept up our relationship through occa-sional email. After a few years, Cherise's husband became quite ill and was hospitalized with an aggressive form of cancer. In China, when someone is hospitalized, a family member must be there with them during their stay. They are responsible for food for the pa-tient and for taking care of other illness related matters. Cherise, a devoted wife, could not leave her husband's bedside to even attend Bella's wedding which took place in another country. That must have been a sad day for her.

Following months in the hospital, Cherise's husband passed away. In my previous story about Bella, I mentioned that, happily, Bella had the opportunity to share Christ with her father while he was on his death bed and he had accepted Jesus. What peace that gave Bella, knowing she would one day see her father again in heaven.

Cherise's niece later came to America to attend a university here. Since she would be returning to China, I contacted her asking if she would mind taking copies of my books, "Mother Has Alzheimer's," and "Speak to Me, Lord, I'm Listening" back home with her to give to Cherise. She agreed to do that, so I mailed them to her, certainly cheaper than sending them directly to China. Cherise was to pick them up at her niece's home on her yearly trek to her part of the country during the winter holiday. Interestingly, it was during her time of grief over her husband's death that she finally received both books and read them.

As a result, she expressed she was encouraged by how I had found hope in God during my mother's demise with Alzheimer's. She also noted the peace I had found in the Lord during that time. Perhaps, having recently lost her husband, she was revisiting the importance of faith in God. So, she decided to get into a Bible study in her community. I prayed she would find Jesus to be her all in all during that difficult time in her life as she grieved the loss of her husband.

Several months after Cherise's husband's death, I felt led to search the New Testament for verses on who Jesus said He was. In Appendix A of this book, you can read those verses. Appendix D is a document on verses to pray for an unbeliever. There is something special about praying Scripture. You can know that you are praying directly in God's will.

As for my dear friend, Cherise, as I mentioned before, that is not her real name but I have used it here, not only to protect her privacy, but because of what that name means. It means "dearly beloved" or "cherished one". I like that the word "cherished" is similar to the name Cherise and in my heart, Cherise is a special, dearly loved lady whose friendship I will always cherish. In a book on meanings of names, Cherise is also accompanied with a Bible verse. Hers is Zephaniah 3:17, *"The Lord your God is with you, He is mighty to save. He will take great delight in you, He will quiet you with his love, He will rejoice over you with singing,"* (NIV). That is my prayer for Cherise.

Publishing of this book had been delayed and now I believe it was for an interesting reason. Recently, I received an email from Bella where she shared with me photos of her new baby boy. While I rejoiced with her about his birth, I had further reason to celebrate. She also shared with me about another "birth." Her mother, Cherise had not only joined a Bible study and was attending a church but, at last, she had accepted Jesus as her Lord and Savior. What a thrilling email to read. It was incredibly exciting for me to receive this information that Cherise had been "born again". Bill and I both wept tears of joy over this news. Since then, we have reconnected on WeChat online and are again resuming Bible study together.

Once more, I was reminded of John 4:37 *"For in this case the saying is true, 'One sows and another reaps.'"* I may never know who had the privilege of reaping but I am so thankful I had the opportunity to plow the soil of Cherise's heart and sow the seeds of Christ's love into her heart for so many years.

CHAPTER 31

A PREPARED HEART

Being a very social person, Cherise had introduced me to a number of her friends during my visit to China. One friend, in particular, stands out. I'll call her Katina. She worked in the computer science department at the same university as Cherise. Clearly, she was a very sharp young woman. Like many Chinese people, she was interested in improving her English and treasured any time she could spend with me. Her English was actually quite good but, like Cherise, she was full of questions regarding what different words meant and how to say things correctly.

I came to appreciate Katina and saw her frequently during that week as she and Cherise were close friends and spent much time together outside of class. Katina warmed right up to me, and in a sense, took me under her wing, wanting to make sure I was comfortable in various situations. I was especially grateful when she sat next to me at dinner parties, eager to take on the task of translating conversations for me. This thoughtful gesture helped me feel connected and able to communicate with others in the group. I think it also made her feel special to be translating for an American.

On Saturday morning, before we met with Katina, Cherise and I took a bus to Cherise's old neighborhood where she taught a children's English class. At that time, most Chinese did not own a car so buses or cabs were their sole modes of transportation. The neighborhood where Cherise taught youngsters was older and the apartment she used for teaching was through a back alley. It was dark and I admit I felt a twinge of fear. If I had been in such a neighborhood in America, I would probably have been more alarmed, but in China, guns are forbidden and crime is punished swiftly. With this deterrent, even some questionable neighborhoods are actually safe.

The apartment where she held her classes was up several flights of stairs and had actually been her former home before moving to their charming apartment near the sea. In this apartment, there were rooms set up for teaching with tables, chairs, and a blackboard. I noticed a book shelf in one room and recognized many of the books I had sent over the years.

Most of the students were in late grade school. Their alert, shining faces revealed they were eager to learn. Clearly, they were also excited to have a visitor from America and I enjoyed answering their enthusiastic questions. I learned about their holidays and again, as I had in the college class, I shared about American holidays with freedom to mention Jesus as the center of Christmas and Easter.

One very alert and vivacious student, Trisha, who was about twelve years old, stood out as especially eager to learn. She reminded me of Bella as a youngster, very sweet and precocious. After class, we returned to Cherise's home and Trisha came with us. Her mother, also a colleague of Cherise, had asked if she would watch Trisha for the afternoon. She was such a delightful child, I was happy for the opportunity to get to know her. Katina also met us later at Cherise's home for lunch.

After a delicious meal, Cherise went upstairs to lie down leaving Katina, Trisha and myself alone for the afternoon. As we sat visiting in the living room, all of a sudden, Trisha said, "Betsy, can you tell me what the Bible is about?"

"Yes," chimed in Katina, "I'd like to know about the Bible too."

What a great opportunity! I felt so honored that here in China, these two young women wanted to hear about Christ. I began in Genesis and for the next hour and a half moved through the Old Testament and on to Jesus' life, death on the cross, resurrection, ascension and prophecies about His first and second coming. Katina was very interested and said she believed it but wanted to know more before she received Jesus as her Lord. Her open and honest response was heartwarming. She knew that I had been teaching Cherise the Bible online and asked if I would also teach her when I got home. Happily, I agreed.

In the evening, we joined a number of other friends and went out to dinner. I was learning more about Chinese food and even tried pig's tongue. Even today, I can't believe I did that, but my recall was that it wasn't too bad. The meal was topped off with peanut soup and sugar cane juice which were still both way too sweet for my taste.

Katina joined Cherise and me on several of our outings. As we walked along the beach of the China Sea one afternonon, Katina noticed a wedding couple getting their pictures taken along the shore. Before I could stop her, she ran right up to them and asked if I could be in a photo with them. What could I do? So, I smiled and wondered if I was on Chinese candid camera. The moment was a delight for Katina but rather embarrassing for me. I am not sure what the couple thought but they played along. In later years, I am confident the presence of an unknown American in their wedding pictures will be a mystery to their families and friends.

As we stopped to rest at a table along the beach, I noticed that while there were hundreds of people on the beach, no one wore a swim suit and no one was in the water except for a few people sitting inside a round pool toy. This seemed odd since it was a beautiful, warm, sunny day. Since the weather was similar to Florida, I knew the water would be warm as well. Upon asking why no one was in the water, Cherise explained, "Oh, you can't swim in the sea. It's too toxic." That seems to be an issue in China. Some people can't even eat the fish anymore since they are full of chemicals. The sea is not the only toxic issue in China.

Before flying to Cherise's home, I had spent a week with friends in Beijing. The smog in that city was so thick you could barely see the buildings. My trip was a month or so before the Olympics and some athletes were debating whether to compete due to the deteriorated air quality. I could only imagine how such extreme pollution would affect an athlete's lungs. Then I heard how China planned to fix the problem. They would shut down all industry and only allow public transportation on the roads for a month before and during the Olympics. Voila! Clean air. It worked, but after the Olympics, it was back to business as usual.

Katina also joined us for lunch at Pizza Hut one afternoon. That was an experience to remember. We entered a bank building and took an elevator to the top floor, and there was the Pizza Hut overlooking the entire city on one side and the China Sea on the other. Fabulous views only to be found in five star restaurants in America.

What tickled me, though, was that neither Katina nor Cherise had ever been to a Pizza Hut and had never seen a salad bar. Salads are not part of Chinese cuisine. It took me quite awhile to explain with great detail how to go through a salad bar line. We ordered pizza first, but Chinese are used to numbers of dishes on a table so they wanted to order spaghetti as well. Fortunately, I talked them out of it since I knew it would be way too much food for the three of us.

On to the salad bar where they shared a single salad plate and wanted to know if I would like to join them, a threesome with one plate. With a grin, I declined, picked up my own plate, and we three proceeded through the line. I have never seen a plate so full as the one they shared. Fruit and vegetables kept falling off the over burdened plate as we traveled down the bar. All the while, they were oblivious.

After lunch, we went to the only Bible book store in town. Yes, there are Bible bookstores in China, but in this town of at least two million people, there was only one. I was not surprised to learn that Cherise, who had many Christian friends, knew the owner, a delightful woman who spoke English well. I had told Cherise that I would like to buy Katina a Bible, so she had phoned the owner ahead of time. In China, it is unlawful to buy a Bible anywhere except in a government church. All Bibles must be registered, but the bookstore owner secretly kept a few in the back for friends. So, for about 60 RMB (about $7), I purchased a lovely Bible that in America would have cost about $50. It had English on one side of each page and Mandarin on the other. That way, Katina could self translate when necessary.

This was her first Bible, so I wrote Jeremiah 29:11 in the front cover and signed my name. *"For I know the plans that I have for you,' declares the Lord, 'plans for welfare and not for calamity to give you a future and a hope.'"* I wanted Katina to know that God had plans for her life. She had not yet received Christ, but I felt someday she would, perhaps as we studied together over the internet. She was thrilled to have a Bible and wanted her picture taken with both of us holding up the Bible, a memory I will always cherish.

I also bought her and Cherise each a book about Jim Elliot's life written in Chinese. It was strange to see authors I recognized but not be able to read any words. The bookstore also carried some books by James Dobson among others. It was odd to see so many books, trinkets, cards, etc. but no Bibles in a Bible bookstore. The owner told me that it is very hard to have a Bible bookstore in China with so many government rules that change with a whim. Yet, I found it interesting that there was one at all. With the official religion of China being atheism, I was surprised they would tolerate a Christian bookstore, but I suppose that is part of the pretense of tolerance.

While they espouse freedom of religion, clearly, it is not the kind of freedom we enjoy. After I left Beijing, the church our friends had been going to was shut down. Peculiar, because it was an expat church only open to foreigners. Chinese people were not even allowed to attend. Cherise's town, like Beijing, also had a number of government churches, some quite large. Chinese believers can be part of these churches, but they are closely monitored and, as I mentioned in my story about Cherise, many biblical subjects are taboo. As a reminder, pastors are not allowed to preach about Christ's resurrection or second coming, and it is against the law to speak of Christ to children under eighteen. Proselytizing is also forbidden. Sadly, churches are made up mostly of women and older people.

All too soon, my visit in China came to an end. It had been a remarkable time that I will never forget. Fortunately, my online friendship with Katina would soon begin. When I arrived home, I immediately began meeting with Katina through Skype. Being a computer teacher at the university, she was very tech savvy and had no trouble with internet chats. We began by reading the Gospel of John, one chapter per week. We discussed the meaning of each section and she began to understand who Jesus is.

On our third week, we were partially into John, chapter three, having read Jesus words from verse three where He said, *"...Truly, truly, I say to you, unless one is born again he cannot see the kingdom of God."*

Suddenly, Katina burst out, "This Jesus is amazing! I want Him in my heart!"

Wow, I didn't expect that response so fast.

"Katina, do you feel you are ready to pray and invite Jesus into your life?" I queried.

"Yes, I want Him right now!" she excitedly responded.

With joy, I led her in the sinner's prayer and that night she became a Christian. She did, however, have one question before praying. "Betsy, will this mean I am no longer Chinese?"

I had to smile, "No, Katina, you will still be Chinese. The kingdom of God is made up of people from all over the world. In fact there are upwards of eighty million Christians in China right now." (Today, some organizations claim the number is closer to two hundred million.) "Katina, Christianity has nothing to do with nationality. There are Christian believers from every country." With that settled, she readily came into God's Kingdom.

Katina and I met for several years. In that time, her enthusiasm to know God continued to grow. She was a zealous student who loved her new relationship with God and how He met her in the midst of her life circumstances. Many times, she was aware of God's intervention in various situations and excitedly shared them with me in our online meetings. Her most fervent prayer was that God provide a husband for her. She so desired marriage and a family.

Eventually, however, her work schedule became so full that she had trouble fitting in our study appointments. She hated missing our arranged times to chat, but work was demanding, so I encouraged her to find a local Bible study. It seemed like it was time for both her and Cherise to have fellowship in their own community. I prayed a lot about my decision to end our chats, but it was clear that my China assignment was drawing to a close. Since then, God has answered Katina's heartfelt prayer. She has married and now has a child. I pray she is continuing her walk with God. Her enthusiasm at hearing about Jesus remains one of my sweetest memories. Oh that everyone could hear of Him and respond so openly and quickly.

CHAPTER 32
ON THE BRINK OF DEATH

During the time my mother had Alzheimer's, the time came to move her to Michigan to be closer to us. God found a perfect place for her to stay. I had been browsing a local weekly Shopper's Guide when my eyes fell upon an ad for an adult foster care home. I had never heard of this type of home but I had been praying about where to put my mother when we moved her here. Perhaps, this was God's answer. I had immediately called to inquire then driven over to take a look. It was exactly what I had hoped for. A beautiful home formerly owned by a doctor. It had a warm homey atmosphere, not the feel of an institution.

Along with the caretakers, there were five elderly ladies living there. With one bedroom left, I felt it would be an ideal location for Mother. After she moved in, I visited my mother often and soon became acquainted with the other ladies in the home. Near the back door entrance, where we usually entered the house, was Kathryn's room. Hooked up to an oxygen tank twenty-four hours a day, Kathryn spent much of her time in bed. Seeing people come and go past her door provided her meager socialization. At best, her existence was tedious, often accompanied with labored breathing. My heart went out to her and we began regular visits as time allowed.

Since I went by her room on every visit to Mother's room, Kathryn and I often greeted each other and chatted a bit. To pass the time she relied on television, reading, and a rare guest. Telling visitors about the latest old movie she had watched helped distract her from the dreariness of her long days. I couldn't help but think how wearisome and monotonous Kathryn's life had become in her later years.

As I prayed at home one morning, a thought I recognized as being from the Lord dropped into my mind, *Why don't you tell Kathryn about Me?* Each time I prayed after that, the same thought recurred. Up to that point, my conversations with Kathryn had been rather surface and mundane. Would she even be interested in spiritual conversation? And how would I start such a dialogue with her?

Ok, Lord, give me a clear opportunity and I will guide the conversation to You, I promised the Lord.

In a hurry one day, I dashed over to see Mother and stopped by for a quick hello to Kathryn. She began to tell me about her life as a younger woman. Progressing quickly to her present bleak situation, she ended with a statement that jarred me. "I wish I would just die," she lamented. "Living has become so difficult."

I know now that there are many elderly people who share this same sentiment but that was my first time to hear such painful words. Realizing this was God's open door, I carefully moved the conversation to the Lord. "Kathryn, may I ask you a question?" With her affirmative nod, I continued. "Do you know for sure that you will go to heaven when you die?"

With a heavy sigh and downcast eyes full of despair, she replied, "I don't know that I would, Betsy. I hope so but I don't think I'm good enough." Her dejected and hopeless demeanor tugged at my heart. How tragic that she was facing death imminently, yet had not settled the most important question in life. Even sadder was that she was not informed about how a person gains eternal life. She had lived over seventy years and had never really understood the gospel message.

I shared some of God's plan at that time, but feeling rushed I asked if I could come another day and share some Bible verses with her. Smiling, she said she'd be pleased to have me come back.

Several weeks passed and I thought of Kathryn often. On days I thought I might visit with her, she either had company or her door was closed which meant she was asleep. Still, I began to sense an urgency to go back and continue our conversation. I almost sensed the Lord planned to keep her alive just long enough for her to re-solve some important spiritual issues in her life.

Finally, the opportunity presented itself and we moved right to meaningful, spiritual dialogue. "Kathryn, I've been thinking about the last time we visited and how you said you didn't think you were good enough to go to heaven. I want you to know that I have some good news for you. Your access to heaven is not depen-dent on how good or bad you've been. God has a different and bet-ter plan to offer. Would you like to hear about it?" With a look of curious eagerness, she responded, "Yes, I sure would like to hear."

I then proceeded to read aloud Billy Graham's pamphlet, *"Steps to Peace with God."* (See Appendix B) "Salvation," I explained to Kathryn, "is not dependent on what we do but on whom Christ is and what He has done for us. Kathryn, have you ever accepted Jesus as your personal Lord and Savior?" I asked.

"Yes, many years ago," she whispered with a far-away look in her eyes, "but I've never read the Bible. Please read more of the pamphlet to me," she pleaded.

Recalling her earlier comments about lack of assurance of her salvation, I read I John 5:11-13, *"And the witness is this that God has given us eternal life, and this life is in His Son. He who has the Son has the life; he who does not have the Son of God does not have the life. These things I have written to you who believe in the name of the Son of God, in order that you may know that you have eternal life."* (See Appendix G)

"Kathryn isn't it wonderful that we can know that we will go to heaven when we leave this earth?"

She smiled as we prayed together, and I noticed a peaceful glow spread across her face as she thanked me and we said good-bye. I saw Kathryn briefly on one more occasion. She again expressed her gratitude to me for sharing the good news of Christ with her.

"I've read the pamphlet over and over," she exclaimed. "The verses of assurance have meant so much to me."

Kathryn went to be with the Lord the next week. God's timing had been perfect. I have no doubt she confidently entered the Kingdom of Heaven and today is living in the presence of God. She met Jesus knowing that He would accept her not on her own merits but because of His shed blood on the cross for her sins.

I was thankful that I had listened to God when He had nudged me to talk with Kathryn and share His love for her before she went home to meet Him. It was gratifying to know that her heart was settled and prepared for her home coming.

(This story appears in my book, *"Mother Has Alzheimer's,"* available at Amazon.com or contact me).

CHAPTER 33

ONE SOWS AND ANOTHER REAPS

I t was a typical, muggy July day when I stopped by Leslie's home to deliver a book she wanted to read. As we chatted over a cup of tea, she explained how she and a mutual friend, Nancy Groff, had met and how much she enjoyed their many conversations. Nancy was a close friend of mine, too, and a devoted Christian woman with many stories of how God had used her to witness to people. So, when Leslie shared with me that Nancy had talked with her about being a born again Christian, I was not surprised. However, as far as I knew, Leslie had not taken that step into salvation.

Not knowing how their conversations had progressed, I asked, "Leslie, do you understand what Nancy meant by the term 'born again' Christian?"

"No, I'm still not real sure of that terminology," she responded.

"Well, may I explain it to you?" I enthusiastically asked.

When she agreed, I then explained the simple gospel message by sharing the booklet, "The Four Spiritual Laws." This is a booklet put out by Bill Bright's ministry and is similar to *"Steps to Peace with God."*

I continued by sharing that the term "born again" is found in John 3:3-5. A man named Nicodemus, a Pharisee and ruler of the Jews, stealthily approached Jesus one night with some questions. Apparently, his interest in Jesus had been stirred as he watched His ministry. Jesus cut right to the chase when He responded, "...*Truly, truly, I say to you, unless one is born again he cannot see the kingdom of God.*" These were powerful words that left Nicodemus in a contemplative mood. Jesus was telling him that unless he was born again, he had no hope of being part of God's kingdom. To a Jew who depended on good works and following the law, that must have shaken his theology. Yet, Nicodemus stayed to hear more."

When considering the idea of good works, which many people believe will determine their eternal destination, I sometimes use an illustration because it is amazing how many people feel they have to "do" something to earn salvation. Suppose all the people of the world were lined up on the beach of the Atlantic Ocean with a goal of swimming to Europe. Invalids and those in wheelchairs would obviously have no chance as just getting into the water would be a challenge. Children and non-swimmers might make it out a few yards in the water, not wanting to get in over their head. Champion swimmers might swim out further but the point is that no one would make it to Europe on their own. It is impossible to swim that far. It is the same with our good works. No matter how good we try to be, we will come up short. No one can meet God's perfect standard. Only Jesus is perfect. Only Jesus met God's requirements. Christ alone. Yet, sometimes people put themselves on a treadmill of good works to which the obvious question would be, "*How many good works will it take to please God and earn salvation?*" Soon realizing, it is an impossible task. It would never be enough. But when we choose to believe in Jesus' finished work on the cross, we qualify for heaven based on His shed blood alone. This truth offers a sure hope. Not by works, but by faith, we receive salvation.

I went on to describe to Leslie what Jesus meant by the term, "born again". "Leslie, when a person is born again, she receives

Jesus into her heart. At that moment, the Holy Spirit comes to live in her. This is salvation based on faith. It requires abandoning the belief that we are saved by works, but rather by faith, embracing the finished work of Christ on the cross. Jesus, while on the cross, said, '*...It is finished...,*' (Jn. 19:30), which meant the debt owed for sin was now paid in full," (Col. 2:14).

Interestingly, I had been reading a book by Bill Bright entitled, *"How to Witness without Fear"* and had asked God to give me more opportunities to share my faith. Upon sharing the good news of Christ, I asked, "Leslie, have you ever prayed to receive Christ as your own personal Lord and Savior?"

"No, but I would like to," she quickly responded.

Wow...that was so easy, I thought. Later, after leading her in prayer, I almost felt guilty because I knew Nancy had been witnessing to Leslie for two years, planting seeds and watering them. I just happened to walk in when she was ready to accept Jesus. Some might say the fruit was ripe and ready to pick. God had already drawn her and laid a foundation through Nancy's nurturing. I Corinthians 3:8 says, *"Now he who plants and he who waters are one; but each will receive his own reward according to his own labor."*

I love how God does not distinguish between the one who sows seeds into a person's life and the one who reaps the harvest. There have been people that I have labored over for months and even years and never seen them accept the Lord. And there have been others whom I seem to walk in the door and they immediately want Jesus. In those cases, perhaps other people have sown seeds, some have watered them, and I just had the joy of reaping. In reality, it is all His work and we are simply tools in His belt.

John 4:37-38 says, *"For in this case the saying is true, 'One sows and another reaps.' I sent you to reap that for which you have not labored; others have labored and you have entered into their labor."* From God's point of view, we are all in it together...sometimes sowing, other times reaping. There is no room for ego. It's all God's work.

CHAPTER 34

TWO WAYWARD SOULS

My life intersected with Jodi and Tara in different circumstances and each for only a brief period of time. I don't know if they went on with the Lord or if they permanently fell by the wayside. I only know that God asked me to be faithful in presenting the gospel to them, to mentor them, to love them, and to be there for them. Sometimes, we think that God's favor is only judged by results, but in reality, our faithfulness to what God asks us to do is what He is looking for. That is all God asks, just that we be faithful. As I've said before, that is His definition of success.

Both of these women had been prostitutes. Both also had drug/alcohol addiction issues in their immediate past and each dealt with monstrous problems from their former lifestyles.

I can only imagine what their home lives must have been like during their formative childhood years. For Jodi, poverty, neglect, and sparse parental guidance defined her upbringing. Many girls like her end up raising themselves on the streets, not exactly an environment for cultivating "goodness" and a positive outcome.

"In high school," Jodi explained, "I was very angry, aggressive, and in lots of fights." Other girls taunted me because, although I am a black girl, my skin color is a little lighter."

To me, a white lady, this was new information. Although she looked dark to me, she was quite serious in her explanation.

"Yes, Betsy," she continued in all seriousness, "people of color are ranked according to the darkness of their skin. Dark is good and lighter is not as acceptable. People will tease you if your skin color does not conform to the acceptable norm."

This was interesting to know but there was more.

"Another thing, Betsy, is that black women judge their peers by their hair as well. Now, I have good hair because mine stands straighter and taller than other girls."

Her serious brown eyes held mine as she tried to help me understand the gravity of these issues. While our conversation was completely foreign to me, I made an effort to listen attentively and respectfully. I wasn't even sure what she meant by hair that stood taller. My own hair is naturally flat. The concept of tall hair was new to me. I found myself puzzling: *What is tall hair? Were these comparison issues just hers or really true in her traditions?* Whichever, this was how she perceived it. I felt I was getting a cultural education.

Jodi was living in a halfway house in our community when I first met her at church one Sunday. Having been on just about every drug out there, crack was the final blow. She couldn't get off it by herself. She had needed help and had bravely sought it out. Now, a new creature in Christ, her eyes were clear and all she talked about was Jesus. It was truly sweet to listen to her child-like faith. I began to understand in a new way what Jesus meant when he said in Matthew 18:4-5, *"Whoever then humbles himself as this child, he is the greatest in the kingdom of heaven. And whoever receives one such child in My name receives Me."*

"There is a new lady moving into our halfway house," Jodi advised me one day as we sat together in our local coffee shop, "and I am very concerned about it."

"Why is that, Jodi?"

"Well, she is also a black woman and I am afraid she might give me a hard time because my skin color is lighter."

"Jodi, the new lady is probably afraid too," I suggested. "She will be the new kid on the block and probably hopes she will fit in and that no one will treat her in a way that she feels ostracized. Jodi, this is an opportunity for you to show her Christ's love by accepting and welcoming her."

That was a new thought. Jodi was learning new ways to respond to people. We talked about how to talk to people and to make a commitment to choose to walk in the wisdom of Ephesians 4:29. *"Let no unwholesome word proceed from your mouth, but only such a word as is good for edification according to the need of the moment, so that it will give grace to those who hear."* She found that to be a profitable verse.

We prayed about the pending situation, and thankfully, the new lady embraced her kindness. I had never dealt with this level of fear. I could only observe her feelings and try to understand this cultural difference between us. I can't even imagine what her life has been like.

When we prayed, again showing her child-likeness, she wanted to hold hands. I have to admit, what flashed through my mind was the thought, *these hands have been involved in unimaginable sin for many years.* For a split second, I felt hesitant to take them in my own but just as quickly, God reminded me that, now with Christ, she was as pure as the driven snow...forgiven, cleansed, and in the process of experiencing God's healing power. I felt humbled as I considered my own sin nature and how we are all on the same level at the foot of the cross. With joy, I embraced her.

Jodi and I met for several months while she recovered from her former choices. Then, she moved south to be near her relatives. I pray she is still clinging to Jesus. It was God who brought her into my life for a season, a season where I believe I learned as much about God's kingdom from her as she did from me. In this life, I may never know where her travels took her, but I believe we will see each other again on the other side.

Then, there was Tara who had been a "call girl" in her former life. My encounter with Tara was a brief eight months. She was a single mom with two children, one, a baby and the other a toddler. I'm not sure she knew who the fathers were but being a single mom was very difficult for her. She didn't work, was on welfare, and was barely making ends meet. This was certainly different than the more glamorous lifestyle she had left.

A Christian friend, Mary, who lived near her had introduced us and had asked if I would be willing to talk to her about the Lord. She informed me that Tara was determined to make changes and she felt getting to know Christ would be a good start. I agreed. Mary had already been talking to her about Jesus but hoped I would also meet with her and help her to understand what it meant to be a Christian.

During our first meeting, Tara indicated she was eager to know Jesus personally. She knew she needed changes in her life and was especially struggling with how to care for her children. After sharing the gospel message with her, she was ready to invite Jesus into her life. Because she sincerely wanted to change, I began meeting with her weekly, teaching her the Bible and praying with her. Hungry to grow, she strongly desired to become a godly woman. Happily, she was coming along well and making better choices. Difficult though her life was, she focused diligently on becoming the woman God created her to be.

After months of intense discipleship, however, I began to notice Tara was starting to drift. The challenges of life and motherhood had become wearisome. Memories of her old life with money to spare and so-called "freedom" began to beckon her back. Her old life was calling her once again. Mary and I tried to encourage her to stay the course. She knew that in her new life in Christ, she was enjoying a freedom and peace of mind that were unlike anything she had ever experienced before, but the trappings of her former life were beckoning more loudly every day. Before long, she once again found herself in the bondage of Satan's snare.

Within a short time, she was declared an unfit mother and her children were put in foster care. Interestingly, she was relieved. Raising children alone was just too burdensome and more responsibility than she could manage. Later, she gave them up for adoption and moved back to Florida. Sadly, the last we heard, she had fallen back into her old way of life.

Although Tara was not exactly a story of victory and triumph, we have to be realistic. We aren't going to win some people for the long term. So, how do we emotionally process people like Tara? While I am thankful I had the opportunity to speak into her life for a season, during that time I chose to hold her tightly and yet loosely all at once. I am grieved that she chose to return to a life of sin, yet I know that seeds were planted deep within her soul by a God who loves her more than she knows. As long as she is alive, there is room for better choices. Someday, she may return. I may or may not know about it. Again, God only asked me to be faithful to what He had called me to do. I have no control over other people's choices. I do know, however, that God's word, when it goes forth, does not return void. It always accomplishes what He sent it to do. Isaiah 55:11, *"So will My word be which goes forth from My mouth; it will not return to Me empty, without accomplishing what I desire, and without succeeding in the matter for which I sent it."* By faith, I believe that to be true for Tara. Not by sight, but by faith.

Tara's situation reminded me again of the parable of the sower, (Mk 4:3-8; 14-20). Remembering this parable helps me keep perspective when someone chooses to walk away from God. I try to optimistically believe that God isn't finished with them yet. It's not for me to judge another person's walk with God, but for Tara, it would seem the seed may have landed among the thorns. She heard the word but her desire for other things deceived her and choked it out. I pray that someday she will come to her senses and return to God just as the prodigal son did.

At times like this, in my own journey, I try to remember that I am responsible "to people but not for them". They are responsible for their own choices. I did what I could to influence Tara toward right choices, but in the end, each person has the responsibility to make their own decisions.

With both Tara and Jodi, God gave me the unique opportunity to observe up close the consequences of people's choices. I saw how their lives without Jesus as Lord left them destitute in a corrupt lifestyle, a lifestyle that plunged them into profound bondage where their lives were not their own. For Jodi, I think she may have made it out. God is all about redemption and second chances. For Tara, I pray she will one day find her way back to God and realize that a life of sin has brutal consequences. God, however, is no respecter of persons. He loves them both dearly.

CHAPTER 35
OUR 51ST ANNIVERSARY IN JAIL

It was December 21st, our 51st wedding anniversary, and we were in jail. We had never been in jail before, but here we were in the LaGrange County, Indiana jail. Before you start picturing us in jailhouse uniforms with chains on our ankles, I should say we were not really there as prisoners but with a team from our church to visit and minister to those who had been incarcerated. Our pastor had arranged for several teams of five to visit on a Sunday afternoon during the holiday season.

Originally, I had not planned to go. Bill was going but I had told him I wasn't interested. Then, a friend, Carolyn Hostetler, asked, "Why don't you join us, Betsy? We have enough men going, but we could use one more woman."

At the time, I had no idea that God was speaking to me through Carolyn's encouragement and I considered pushing the idea aside. With no real desire to go, it was not even on my radar. But I do enjoy Carolyn's company, so for that reason, I decided to join the team. My plan was to just observe, but later, because of what God did on that first visit, I realized He was in it all along and there are no mistakes with God. He knew exactly what He wanted accomplished that day, and He hand-picked our team to do it.

As we checked into the jail, there were three teams of men, each with five men from our church and one team of five women. As we entered the jail and were ushered through a series of locked doors down a winding hallway to cell block "C," it felt like I had entered a different world. The surroundings felt cold and bleak. There were no pictures on the walls, no sign of human activity, just one barren concrete hall after another. As we passed a number of windowless cells, I could only imagine the devastated lives that were behind each door.

At the end of one hallway, we were led into a stark, echoing room they referred to as the common area for the women inmates. These were ladies for whom Christ had died, now living in this sterile, lonely block of cells. As the metal door clanged shut, it seemed to accentuate desolation throughout the room. There were four round metal tables, each having four cold metal stools, all nailed to the floor. Two floors of cells were connected by a concrete staircase. The echo of our voices as they reverberated off the walls made it almost impossible to hear what anyone was saying.

The women, seven of them that day, all dressed alike in tan pants and matching shirts, were excited to see us. Truly, we were the highlight of their otherwise bleak day. Even with no makeup and unkempt hair, their faces were aglow at the idea of having visitors enter their sad existence, breaking up the monotony of the day. Each lady had a large open box for personal items and received a bag of cookies we had brought. Of course, the cookies had to be emptied from the bag as a guard watched and collected the bags. Later, the ladies would take the treat back to their cells for a snack, thankful someone had remembered them during the Christmas season.

If they opted to come to our jail church meeting, it meant they were locked out of their cells for the entire afternoon. Since they never knew for sure if anyone from the outside would be available to come for church, they found ways of socializing by bringing cards, paper, and books to the meeting area.

Out of the seven women, several were clearly Christians. They brought Bibles and eagerly looked up any Scripture that was mentioned during our visit. Two ladies, however, sat off to the side. They were new with less than a week in jail. I could tell they were feeling unsure of how they fit in. Their discomfort and insecurity were palpable as their frightened eyes darted around like trapped animals in these new and strange surroundings.

After some small talk with the ladies, we led them in some Christmas carols. Being in jail during the holiday season was especially hard for these women. Although most were unmarried, they all had children now living with their parents, grandparents or boyfriends. Of course, they especially missed them as they thought of not being home for this festive time of year. Their pain made its way to their eyes as they wiped away tears of sadness as we sang. Carols, although joyful, were a harsh reminder of where they were.

I tried to imagine what it must be like for them. There were no Christmas trees, no decorations, no aroma of turkey dinner or gleeful laughter of children opening gifts. This alone should surely be enough for some of them to commit to do better in life when they were released. Truly, the emotional punishment of not being with family for Christmas and trying to endure some semblance of holiday joy with strangers was a difficult experience. But then, maybe they never enjoyed a family Christmas like we do. Since most of them were in jail for drug related crimes, maybe their idea of Christmas was less appealing. Perhaps now, being in jail and being sober, they were rethinking choices they had made and realizing what they had given up. It's hard to say. I only know they were all lonely and missed their children terribly.

After singing, one of our ladies, Michelle Porter, gave a meaningful message on the topic of "choices". I thought… *what an appropriate subject for these ladies.* I can only imagine that these women were probably agonizing as they considered the events and decisions that had led them to this point in time, to this place. "Choices in life matter," Michelle explained. "Choices we made years ago can build to right or wrong choices today." It was a powerful message that gave the ladies a lot to ponder.

As we divided up for personal conversation, I sensed the singing and message had softened the ladies hearts. They were open to talk about their lives and where God might fit in. Laura James, one of the ladies from our church, and I sat with the two new ladies. Following some small talk, Laura moved right into intentional ministry by sharing how she had come to Christ. She made it short and to the point and, although I had planned to just observe, I found myself taking the cue from her and also shared my personal story. When I finished, a thought nudged my heart...*why don't you ask the ladies if they have ever accepted Christ as their personal Lord?*

First, I asked the lady to my left who answered, "Yes, I did that some years ago." I could tell she wasn't interested in discussing it, so I turned to the other lady, Kim, with the same question. "No," she replied. "I've never asked Jesus into my life." Nudged by God again, I asked, "Would you like to do that?" Without hesitation, she eagerly said, "Yes".

Taken aback by her quick response, I cautiously reiterated... "Would you like to invite Jesus into your heart right now?" Again, her decisive answer confirmed she was unwavering and hungry for something spiritual, something to give meaning to her life. Upon agreeing that she was a sinner in need of a Savior, I had her follow my lead as we prayed the prayer of confession and invitation. I told her the angels in heaven were rejoicing over her decision to follow Christ.

Before we left, I read several verses to her affirming what she could now know. I John 5: 11-13, assured her new position in Christ. Truly, God used our whole team to bring hope to a group of ladies, to encourage them to make fresh choices in line with His will. One of our team had led Christmas carols, two gave short messages followed by personal ministry, and Laura and I shared our testimonies. God had spoken to each of us to go and bring good news to the captives, just as had been prophesied of Jesus in Isaiah 61:1 -3, *"The Spirit of the Lord God is upon me, because the Lord has anointed me to bring good news to the afflicted; He has sent me to bind up the brokenhearted, to proclaim liberty to captives and freedom to prisoners; To proclaim the favorable year of the Lord and the day of vengeance of our God; To comfort all who mourn, to grant those who mourn in Zion, giving them a garland instead of ashes, the oil of gladness instead of mourning, the mantle of praise instead of a spirit of fainting. So they will be called oaks of righteousness, the planting of the Lord, that He may be glorified."*

We had made a choice too.

With such a positive beginning, I decided to sign up for jail ministry so that I could regularly visit with the ladies to bring them encouragement in the Lord. After being vetted, on my next visit to the jail, I was happy to see Kim, the lady who had come to the Lord on my last visit a few weeks prior. There were also a couple of new ladies. Following a lesson given by my ministry partner, Michelle, I again asked if there was anyone who would like to receive the Lord that day. Kim leaned over to one of the new ladies and nudged her. I took the cue and asked her if she would like to receive Christ. After briefly explaining the gospel to her, she was ready to pray the sinner's prayer. I was so excited and my heart was warmed to know that Kim was already ministering to the other inmates about her new faith. Together we had the privilege of bringing another soul before the throne of grace as we introduced her to Jesus.

At that time, the jail had two separate sections for women but usually only one section asked for visitors. This day the other section also wanted us to stop by. There were two women in the cell and while we usually meet in a common area with the other women, in this section, we met in their cell. It was a small concrete room with one little, unreachable window and tiny TV near the ceiling. There were also two cots and an open toilet with no privacy at all. Each bed had a blanket but no pillow. They explained that inmates are denied pillows because they could be used to smother another inmate. I had no frame of reference to even process that kind of thinking.

One of the women I had seen before. Her whole family was in jail, all in separate sections. The family business, a meth lab, had been raided.

Both ladies were smiling as we entered, so glad to have visitors. Each had her Bible out and was eager to learn. After sharing some verses, I asked if they had received Christ. Yes, they both had. The meth lady's roommate had brought her to the Lord. I noticed the roommate had Christian books, a Bible, and lots of papers with notes she had taken as she studied the Bible on her own.

She shared with me that she had been in and out of jail since she was thirteen. She was now about thirty-four. She expressed how relieved she was to be back in jail. I had never considered that someone would actually be happy about being incarcerated. "When I'm in jail," she explained, "it gives me time to think, to focus and press into God. When I'm out of jail, my life spirals downward to the point where I can't even think straight. I really need the structure of jail to be good with the Lord." What an interesting perspective!

She was so eager to grow now that she was back in jail that she had lots of questions, took notes and absorbed our every word. She was one of the most teachable women I have met. How sad that she could only find God when she was behind bars.

During a visit several weeks later, the ladies wanted to sing hymns. Another jail ministry had typed hymns on a group of papers that had been hand sewn together with yarn since they couldn't have anything sharp, not even a staple in their reading material. We sang our hearts out to the Lord. I don't think I've ever heard music sung so utterly out of tune while at the same time with such complete abandon and exuberance. Truly, a joyful *noise* to the Lord.

That day, I spoke to the ladies about putting off the old from Ephesians 4:22. *"That, in reference to your former manner of life, you lay aside the old self…,"* and putting on the new from Colossians 3:12, *"So, as those who have been chosen of God, holy and beloved, put on a heart of compassion, kindness, humility, gentleness and patience; bearing with one another, and forgiving each other, whoever has a complaint against anyone; just as the Lord forgave you, so also should you."*

There were no first time commitments to the Lord that day, but later, I received the nicest note from one of the inmates who had been transferred to another facility. She wrote: *I'm sure the girls appreciate you coming in this Sunday. I know I really enjoyed your visit last Sunday. You helped me and the girls have an amazing day and rest of the week! You definitely helped us lift our spirits and I just wanted to take the time to thank you for that! I will keep you in my prayers.*

Since it was becoming clear that God was calling me to this ministry, this note especially warmed my heart. It was further affirmation that God had a plan for my time with these dear ladies. It amazed me how quickly I had become attached to them and how much I missed them when they left. I know that one of the traits of jail ministry is that there is a swinging door. Most women are there for a short few weeks but some are there for months. We were forming some sweet relationships, and I found my heart was actually sad when one of my new friends left. I so wanted them to succeed on the outside but would I ever see them again? Probably not for most of them, although over time some were readmitted.

Sometimes, my heart melted at the kindness and respect they showed me. After I finish with Guideposts magazines, I bring them to the jail to share with the ladies. Of course, I remove all the staples that hold the pages together as nothing sharp is allowed in the jail. One time, I had not noticed that some of the issues had my name and address on them. Since most didn't, I had not noticed that some did. I had not told the ladies my last name as we were encouraged, as a protective measure, not to. Candace, one of the long-term inmates, quickly noticed my name and address on several of the magazines. Instead of taking note of it, she quietly got a magic marker and blotted out all personal reference to me. I was so touched by her gesture. She could have taken advantage of the moment but, instead, considered my concern for safety and anonymity. The next time I saw her, I again thanked her for her kindness and conveyed to her how thoughtful and considerate she was to have had my back. She knew I didn't feel comfortable letting the girls know my last name and address so she had taken it upon herself to protect me. I was deeply moved.

There have been ups and downs with the inmates I have met. It's hard when I hear later that a lady has chosen to continue in drugs after leaving the jail. Stacy was a delightful lady who seemed to be a team leader among the inmates. She was serious about her faith and even spoke to me about the possibility of returning to the jail someday to do what I do in ministering God's word to them. I was delighted when she said she was done with drugs and had learned her lesson.

You can imagine my distress when I got the message several days after she got out that she had overdosed on heroin and died. I can't help but wonder what happened. Perhaps she was fooled into thinking that one more shot wouldn't hurt or maybe she thought she could start up where she had left off. She had been clean while in jail and her body wouldn't have tolerated the dose she tried that one night. I will never know what happened but the sadness of her death swept through the jail. The ladies who were left still cried weeks later as I'm sure her children do too. Hopefully, her untimely death will be a wake-up call to other inmates who think they can continue drugs with no consequences.

On the other hand, Pam, a sweetheart of an inmate was moving into her 50's when she found herself, not for the first time, in jail and later prison for her involvement with meth. She was determined not to continue in her former lifestyle. A life in and out of jail and prison was getting old. Pam had a genuine encounter with the Lord while in jail, however, and after her stay in prison, she checked into a halfway house for a number of months. Continuing her walk of faith, she is now back in the real world and tells me her focus is still on the Lord. My heart is comforted to know there are people like Pam who make the transition and stay with Jesus. My prayer is that someday God will use Pam in jail ministry encouraging women in their walk of faith. That would be full circle.

I have found most of the ladies I have met are delightful people, definitely not hardened criminals. I have no idea what they are like when they aren't in jail or when I'm not there, but something about being in jail causes their hearts to soften. They are pliable and seem to really want to change, make better choices and follow the Lord. I'm not naïve enough to think they will all continue when they are back on the outside, but while in jail, I get to see the authentic, real people that God meant them to be, people untethered from drugs, humbled by their circumstances and wanting a better life. It has been a joy to bring many searching women to the throne of grace over the years.

CHAPTER 36
JAIL MINISTRY CONTINUED...

On one particular visit to the jail, there were four ladies who had asked for ministry. I felt the Lord prod me to talk to them about forgiveness. I know there are many hurts and wounds in their lives that likely go back to their childhoods. I acknowledged that they had probably been wounded by someone from their past but asked if they had been able to find forgiveness in their hearts. We talked about the importance of forgiveness and how the alternative, bitterness, would affect every area of their lives. At the same time, I explained that forgiveness doesn't mean what people had done to them was right. It absolutely was not. I remembered an adage, however, I had heard that to not forgive is like taking poison and expecting the other person to die.

One of the sections of scripture that I enjoy using over and over in jail ministry is out of Colossians 2:13-14, *"When you were dead in your transgressions..., He made you alive together with Him, having forgiven us all our transgressions, having canceled out the certificate of debt consisting of decrees against us, which was hostile to us; and He has taken it out of the way, having nailed it to the cross."*

When I told them a story behind this verse, it resonated with their situations and gave them a sense of peace and acceptance.

I told them that in those days when a person was arrested and put in jail, a list of their offenses was written out and attached to their jail cell door. Anyone could see the things they had done. After they had served their sentence, however, the warden would write across the list, "Paid in full". So, when the inmate was freed, if anyone questioned him, he would show the document that explained he had served his time and had paid for his crime.

In a similar way, when Jesus was dying on the cross, His last words were, *"...It is finished...!"* (Jn. 19:30). What He meant was that by dying on the cross, He had paid for all of our sins. Because of that, our certificate of debt consisting of decrees against us had been cancelled. He had atoned for all of our sin. Written across our sin issues were the words, "Paid in full".

When I shared this good news with the ladies in the jail, there was almost an audible sigh of relief as they realized Jesus forgave them. He had paid their debt by dying on the cross and all of their sins were nailed with Him. They could know that He loved and accepted them.

After my teaching, I asked if anyone would like to forgive someone from their past just as Jesus had forgiven their sins and cancelled their debt. Almost in unison, they all said, "NO!"

I had to smile. They are such babes when it comes to how to live life successfully. We talked about how they probably wouldn't "feel" forgiveness, but would they be willing to take the first step by an act of their will? They agreed that they could do that, so we prayed. I explained that forgiveness can be a process, sometimes a long one and I gave them an example from my life, and how when I finally forgave, I was set free.

Again, I asked if anyone would like to receive Jesus. The two new ladies quickly agreed they wanted to. So, I led them in the *"Steps to Peace with God"* pamphlet I had brought along for each of them and at the end, they prayed to receive Christ.

Once more, I don't know what will come of their decision but seeds were planted and I can know that God will now take over and give them every opportunity to allow Him to do the work in their hearts as only He can do.

God has been gracious to provide me with other workers to help with ministry. Diane and Janet have been valuable helpers. Recently, Marcie, Tina and Rita, came on board, all clearly called of God for this kind of work (and it is definitely a calling). These women all fit in seamlessly with the inmates. Their love, care and kindness are so appreciated.

One Sunday, I was teaching out of I Peter 3:8-11. We were defining each word in the passage and explaining what the verses meant. It may have been verse 9 that convicted one of the ladies where it says, *"Not returning evil for evil or insult for insult, but giving a blessing instead; for you were called for the very purpose that you might inherit a blessing."*

I'm not sure what may have transpired between her and Amber, another of the inmates, but she immediately turned to her and said, "I have to stop here and tell you I'm sorry for what I did. What I did was wrong."

Amber, who was new to the jail, began to tear up and nodded that she would forgive the inmate who had apparently hurt her.

It was a poignant moment because of what I later found out. After my teaching, we divided up into groups and I had each of my helpers take a group. I opted to sit at another table with Amber who had just forgiven her fellow inmate. I could tell she was feeling shy and out of place with the other seven ladies who all seemed to know each other so I approached conversation in a lighthearted way.

"So, tell me about yourself," I began. Upon hearing that she has five children, we talked about them for a few minutes. Then I asked her if she had ever invited Jesus into her life.

"No, I never have," she answered.

"Would you like to hear more about Him?" I asked.

"Yes, I would," she quickly affirmed.

I gave her the gospel message and when we came to the prayer of salvation, she practically leaped into the Kingdom of God. She was so ready. After accepting Christ and His finished work on the cross, I asked if it would be ok for me to tell the others. She quickly agreed.

"Attention ladies, I have an announcement. Amber has just accepted Jesus into her heart so you now have a new sister in Christ."

With that, they all applauded enthusiastically and welcomed her.

When it was over, I wondered, if the inmate who had offended her had not asked forgiveness, would that have hindered Amber from coming to the Lord. The whole scenario seemed so God-driven. I believe it happened just as He had planned. I left that day exhilarated at God's goodness and rejoicing with the angels over another new sister in Christ.

In contrast to Amber, however, while most of the women seem so child-like and soft, I came across Angie some time ago, another new inmate, who had more of a resistant look on her face. At first, I wasn't sure what that was about. I could tell, as I engaged the ladies in a lesson one afternoon that Angie was not totally with us.

Coming out of their cells to attend Bible study (which they all call church) is voluntary. Angie had chosen to attend but her demeanor suggested that something in her was fighting the idea of a loving God. Her eyes were hard, somewhat defiant, questioning, maybe even challenging the gospel, but at the same time, pleading to be loved. I wondered what had happened that would put her in such opposition. When I asked her at the end of the lesson if she had received Jesus yet, her eyes dropped and she seemed uncomfortable, unable to answer. Her cellmate quickly came to the rescue by explaining that she was talking to Angie about the Lord but Angie wasn't quite ready to accept Him because of what had happened to her. Since most of the women in jail are there for drug related crimes, I assumed Angie was there for that reason as well. With that in mind, I also assumed I was about to hear about something that had happened to her with drugs.

With piqued curiosity, I asked Angie if she could tell me what happened. I was not prepared for what she said. Looking vulnerable and wounded, Angie opened up. "I did attend a church for awhile," she explained. "In fact, I was even baptized. Then the church found out I had a 'bastard child' (her exact words) and they shunned me and wanted nothing to do with me. So now, I'm not sure about Jesus."

I was shaken by Angie's testimony and felt the tears well up in my eyes as I considered what she had experienced. With a quiet voice and all sincerity, I lamented, "I am so sorry that happened to you, Angie. That is not how Christians are to treat anyone. You need to know that God is not like that. God will not shun you and He does not see your son as a bastard. He loves you and your son. You are both precious to God. There are many churches that would embrace you with love. I hope you will give God another try. His arms are open to you. Try not to throw God out because of what people did to you."

That day, I felt God had sent me to the jail to minister truth to a wounded soul. I hope Angie was able to hold on to the words of life that were imparted to her on that occasion, not only by me but by several other sweet ladies. I know she is in good hands with her roommate who has made a sure commitment to Jesus. Her love and acceptance will speak volumes to Angie.

It seems more than coincidence to me that more than once God has strategically placed some more mature believers in with the women, sometimes even in their cell. Pam was one such woman. She had a gift for affirming not only the other inmates, but also we who went in to minister on Sunday's. All of my workers considered her a rare asset in the jail and we were so encouraged by her cheerful demeanor and her single minded focus on Jesus. She eventually left the jail and served extended time in prison. Then she moved on to a faith based halfway house. Everyone missed her when she left. I hear she is still following the Lord and I sincerely hope that one day she will return not as an inmate but to minister to others in a jail setting. She's a woman of impact, one who left meth and other drugs in exchange for a powerful relationship with the Savior of her soul.

It is interesting for me to look back at my prayers before I started jail ministry. For some time I had been questioning God about a desire I had to witness to people and introduce them to the Lord. Until I began at the jail, I was feeling that prayer had been answered with *not now*. This seemed odd to me since God wants us to share our faith. I had never dreamed that the place this prayer would be answered with a resounding "yes" would be in a county jail. I had often read, John 4:35 where it states in part, *"...Behold, I say to you, lift up your eyes and look on the fields, that they are white for harvest,"* and I had wondered where these fields were in my life. Now I know. For me, one of the fields that are white for harvest has turned out to be jail ministry. God is so endlessly creative.

CHAPTER 37

RENEWING AN OLD FRIENDSHIP

Caroline was a friend from the past. She had recently moved to a popular retirement community in Florida and one winter, when I was vacationing nearby, we met for lunch at a restaurant in Orlando. After ordering our food, we picked up conversation as though we had never been apart, even though we had been for many years. I was quickly reminded of how much I had enjoyed her, and although I was thrilled to see her again, I admit I had a pang of sadness that we had not seen each other in so long. Reconnecting with her now reminded me of how much I missed her fun, upbeat personality.

It is interesting how, with some friends, you can instantly pick up where you left off and once again thoroughly enjoy their company. Caroline and I had once attended the same church where we had been confirmed together, sang side by side in choir, and attended various other church activities with one another. Over the ensuing years, however, our minimal contact had sadly dwindled to yearly Christmas letters.

Meeting with Caroline after so many years apart was truly a joy for me. We launched right in to reviewing our life experiences and reminiscing about old friends. Then, we went on to our present lives, our families and current interests. Soon, the conversation took a turn when she asked me a question.

"Betsy, I've noticed that over the years, you have continued to attend church while I have not. I seem to have drifted away from church. I have occasionally attended a Congregational church, but it got to the point where I just didn't feel it was meeting any need. I grew discouraged and decided to just stop going. I am wondering what it is that has kept you in church."

I was delighted with her question and immediately felt this meeting was an appointment from God, an opportunity to share my faith with an old friend who seemed to be searching for something more in her own life. In a way, it was sad she had missed the very things that had made my life so full and meaningful. For me, although church was important, it was more about discovering an exciting life through trusting Jesus as my Lord. That relationship was what had changed and enriched my life.

"Caroline, I appreciate the opportunity to answer why I remained in church. I'm glad you asked. The reason I continued to attend church was because I came to a point where I felt a need for something more in life. I had done everything my parents had expected of me...finished college, gotten married, and had two children. I came to a point where I felt there had to be more to life than what I was experiencing. While I had always attended church, when we moved to California, God led us to a church where, for the first time, I heard about a personal relationship with Christ. As a result, I invited Him to be my Savior and Lord. That meant that He now had control and would lead me in His plan for my life. With that decision, I discovered that I needed a church body which would help me grow in my faith and would offer fellowship with people of like mind. Whereas, in the past, I had gone to church because it was just what we did on Sundays, now church was where they helped me get into the Bible, learn more about Jesus, and grow in my faith."

Caroline listened with interest and I could tell she was thinking when she interjected, "I have heard people explain that all religions lead to the same god and that we all serve the same god but come to him from different ways, kind of like a wheel where God is the hub and different religions are the spokes."

I pondered a moment and then plunged in, "Hmmm, I guess I would have to disagree with that assessment, Caroline, and here are some reasons why. Did you know that around the Muslim Dome of the Rock in Jerusalem, there is an inscription that says, 'Allah does not have a son?' If that is true of the Muslim faith, then Allah cannot be the same as the God I serve. My God has a Son and His name is Jesus. Also, because Muslims do not believe in Jesus' deity, they also deny the trinity. That is one more reason why the Christian God is not the same as Allah.

"There is also an issue with the Hindu religion," I continued. "They have many gods. My God says He is the only one true God. Christianity is a monotheistic religion while Hinduism is polytheistic. All through the Old Testament, God warned the people not to follow other gods. For instance, the Bible says, *"You shall not follow other gods, any of the gods of the peoples who surround you,"* (Deut. 6:14). Over and over, God was very clear on that point.

"So, can you see that the spokes of the Muslim and Hindu faiths both fall short of leading to the same god. They worship different gods than the Christian God." I reminded her of Jesus' words when He said, *"I am the way, the truth, and the life. No one comes to the father but through Me,"* (Jn. 14:6). According to that verse, Jesus claimed that He was the only way.

"Caroline, according to the Bible, the only way we can come to God is through Jesus." With a smile, she saw the sense of that argument and said she had to agree with my point. She conceded that all roads do not lead to the same god.

Undaunted, however, she challenged me with another question that had gone unanswered in her mind. "If Jesus is the only way to God, what about all the people who have never heard of Him?"

Again, that was a great question and I was eager to pitch an answer. "Caroline, I have heard that same question many times. Here are some things to consider. First, God is all knowing and powerful enough to reveal Himself to anyone who is truly seeking Him. While He enjoys using Christians to bring the good news to people, we must remember that He is perfectly capable of bringing enlightenment to people all by Himself. In fact, here's something you might find interesting. I have read recently, in a number of sources, that missionaries in Muslim countries are observing an unusual phenomenon. They are finding that many Muslim people are having dreams about Jesus. It has become so common that in some places, missionaries are approaching Muslims with a simple question, 'Have you had a dream?' The answer is usually 'Yes, I dreamed about Jesus, but I don't understand my dream.' This has been a perfect opening to share the gospel, the good news of Jesus Christ, with a searching soul."

This seemed to answer her question, but I admit I wished I had time to share more with her on that topic. I could have reminded her of Paul's experience on the Damascus Road as told in Acts 9. Paul had been persecuting Christians and heartily agreed with their torture. But, as he walked on the Damascus Road, he experienced Jesus first hand. No one told him about the Lord. He had a personal encounter with Him and it changed the course of his life forever. In that encounter, verse 5 is revealing, *"And he* (Paul) *said, "Who are You, Lord?" And He said, "I am Jesus whom you are persecuting."* (Parenthesis mine) While many Muslims are having dreams today, the Bible reveals that Paul had a vision of Jesus.

I could have also talked to Caroline about Romans 1:19-21 where the Bible talks about the fact that God has personally made Himself 'evident' within every human being. The word 'evident' means obvious or apparent. That is, what we can know, that God has made Himself obvious to everyone. Within our hearts, every person knows deep down that there is a God and by observing creation, it is clear God exists. Psalm 19:1 expresses it well, *"The heavens are telling of the glory of God; and their expanse is declaring the work of His hands."*

Granted, some have seared their conscience and deny the obvious, but no honest person can look at creation and miss the attributes, nature, and power of God. Just a study of the human genome is incredible proof of a higher Being. It is clear that there is a God.

But I didn't have a chance to expound on this subject further because Caroline was full of questions and eager to move to her next one. She had been talking to a religious friend who explained to her that we can't believe all the Bible stories are literal truth. We have to look at each one and consider its believability. While I did agree that there were times that the Bible used various ways of expressing truth such as metaphors, parables, or hyperbole, I disputed that we mortals could decide which stories were true and which ones were myths. To question such stories as Jonah or Noah is to question the authority of Jesus Himself since He confidently supported their credibility in the New Testament. Noah is actually referred to eight times in the New Testament.

"Look at it this way, Caroline, if I am the one who decides what parts to acknowledge as truth and what parts to reject, then who has become the authority, God or me? If I am the one who makes decisions regarding the truth or error of the Bible, I have set myself up as the one having the last word. Clearly, we must esteem the whole Bible as truth or toss the whole thing out. It is not within our jurisdiction to argue with God's word. It would seem to me it would be arrogant for me to proclaim I knew better than God what truth was and what was not."

Several times in our discussion, Caroline almost breathed a sigh of relief. "Betsy, it is so nice to finally find someone who is willing to honestly address my questions about God. Over the years, I have approached other people with my questions but have been disappointed that their only comment was that I should read the Bible. That was so frustrating because I didn't even know where to start. It seemed intimidating. How would I have any idea where to find specific answers? It is such a relief now to actually have some explanations that make sense to me."

This led to her next query. "Speaking of the Bible, if I were to read it, where should I begin?"

"When I'm talking to people who are unfamiliar with the Bible," I answered, "I always direct them to read the book of John. This is the book where you will get to know Jesus. Jesus is the One you want to know." Really, knowing Jesus helps explain the rest of the Bible.

She continued to show interest so I proceeded, "May I ask you a question?"

She agreed that I could. "Have you ever invited Jesus into your life? I remember in my own journey to faith, when we were in church together, I understood that Jesus had died on the cross for my sins. That part was clear. What I never heard or understood was that He wanted to be Lord of my life that He wanted to be on the throne, the one in control. I wonder if you have ever invited Him into your life."

"No, I have not taken that step," she replied.

This was all so new to her and I could tell she needed to research Jesus and faith, so I left her with a question to ask God.

"Caroline, I believe God wants you to know Him, so why don't you go home and begin asking Him to reveal Himself to you."

"Well, what if He doesn't?" she pondered.

"Oh, He will," I responded.

"But how will I know when He reveals Himself?"

"Oh, you'll know. There won't be any doubt." I smiled.

When God reveals Himself to a person, it is like the fog lifting or like a veil being removed from our face. What was there all the time, we can finally see. II Corinthians 3:16 explains it best, *"But whenever a person turns to the Lord, the veil is taken away."*

With that we departed. I am now praying that God will reveal Himself to her. I hope we are able to chat more in the future but for now, I will leave her in God's care. I have no doubt He is capable of revealing Himself in due time. Sometimes, the first step toward salvation is finding answers to valid questions about God. I pray Caroline will continue her journey toward the Lord.

CHAPTER 38

GENEALOGY MYSTERY

Sitting at my computer, I was ready to take another dive into my family's past. For about a year, I had been working on my genealogy through Ancestry.com. Entering facts onto my tree, I had accumulated names of grandparents, great grandparents, and as many relatives in the history of my family as I could locate. Using census records and other documentation, my tree was coming along nicely.

Recently, as I had been looking over the many names and dates, a thought had surfaced in my mind, one I had been pondering. *Why was I doing all this ancestry work anyway? Yes, I was enjoying it, but what was the point? These people were all deceased. I would never meet any of them in this life.* Yet, I felt driven to continue.

While I have always enjoyed research of any kind, I wondered if that was what my interest in ancestry boiled down to…just something to study. But the question seemed curious enough that a few weeks earlier, I had sent up a quick prayer. *Lord, why am I so interested in this? Is there a reason I am not seeing yet?*

Being a curious person by nature, God has often led me to interesting and intriguing discoveries in life, whether a new scripture, a fresh perspective, a way to pray, or a satisfying adventure.

Although I found a degree of fulfillment in researching my family's genealogy, as I booted up my computer that day, I was unaware that something incredible was about to happen.

Before going to the ancestry site, I usually took a quick look at my email. That day, there was a curious post that had come through Ancestry's site. While they don't give out email addresses, fellow researchers can contact each other through their private site. *Hmmm,* I thought, *I wonder who this email is from.* As I opened it and began to read, my mouth literally dropped open.

> *Dear Betsy,*
>
> *I saw some information you posted on Ancestry that seems related to research that I am doing. I noticed your grandparents were Guy H. Dixon and Nell E. Lyons. I have been told that is the name of my grandparents on my father's side. I believe my father, Richard, was their son. He was married to my mother in 1942. They were divorced in 1945, and my mother never told me anything about my father or his family. Is there any chance we are related or that you know anything about my family? Thank you for any help you can give me. I have been longing for information about my father most of my life, what he was like, if I have other family.*
>
> *Mike -----*

My heart was pounding as I focused on this unexpected query and tried to understand what I was reading. Guy and Nell Dixon were indeed my grandparents and their son, Richard, was my uncle. He had been married to my Aunt Angie and they had two boys. That was all I knew of Richard and his family. Had my uncle been married before and had a son I knew nothing about? If so, that meant it was possible his two boys were half-brothers to this Mike I had just met through a website. Was Mike a relative I had known nothing about?

My mind was swirling. What should I do? Before I could gather my thoughts, another email came from Mike asking if I might like to see the only photo he had of his father holding him as a baby. Would this help me to know if he had contacted the right family of Guy and Nell?

I talked with Bill before writing back. We had heard so many stories about internet scams. This Mike could be anybody, but going through Ancestry.com somehow seemed like a safe and protected way to approach this situation.

In the end, I responded, "Yes, it would ease my mind to see a picture."

When the photo arrived in my inbox, it was definitely my Uncle Richard and I did not recognize the baby he was holding. The drama quickly became a dilemma as to what I should do now. Mike wanted to meet his father and I would have the unfortunate task of telling him that he had passed away many years ago. Richard's wife, my Aunt Angie, however, was still living. Perhaps, she could fill in some of the blanks of Mike's life. I had not seen Angie in quite some time since she lived in another state, but at eighty years of age, she was still sharp as a tack, still leading an active life.

Then, of course, there was the obvious dilemma of whether Angie even knew Richard had been married before her. It was beginning to feel like a soap opera. How could our family not have known that Richard had another wife and a son that we knew nothing about? If other family members knew about this, they had surely kept it a secret all these years. Then, I had a flashback to something my mother had said right before her demise with Alzheimer's. "Betsy, someday, I will tell you about Richard."

I had been curious but, at the time, that was all she offered.

After agonizing how to approach Angie, I took a deep breath, offered up a prayer for wisdom and punched Angie's number into the phone.

"Hi Angie, this is your niece, Betsy."

After some reconnecting pleasantries, I decided to use a direct approach as I carefully continued. "Angie, I have an unusual question for you due to something that has happened. I have to tell you right off that I feel uncomfortable even asking it."

I felt I was about to rock her world and I was nervous about doing so.

"Oh?" she said, with piqued interest.

"Yes, I've been doing some research on Ancestry.com and I have been contacted by a man who is claiming that your late husband, my uncle Richard, is his father."

Before she could answer, I forged ahead. "Now, to my knowledge, you are the only wife Richard had. Do you know anything about another wife?"

I waited. There was a long pause. I hoped I hadn't offended Angie or brought up a subject she would rather not talk about. After an awkward moment, she sighed and said, "Actually, Betsy, Richard did have a wife before me."

Stunned by this news, all I could squeak out was, "Really?"

Taking another deep breath, I ventured forward with hesitation and a pounding heart. "Well, do you happen to know if there were any children from that marriage?"

Quietly, she replied, "Yes, there was a son."

"Oh my, Angie, I think I've been corresponding with him by email. When would he have been born?"

"Let's see...it would have been about 1942," she answered.

Gulp! That seemed to be further confirmation. Mike had told me he had been born in 1943. "Well, Angie, his name is Mike and he would like to connect with family. Is there any chance you would be willing to talk to him?"

Another pause, then, "Sure, Betsy, I could do that. Give him my number."

This was going better than I had imagined. Angie was one brave lady and seemed willing to give me information. She had even agreed to talk to Mike. I was starting to relax but I had one more question to ask her, perhaps a more difficult question, one that had the possibility of complicating the situation. "Angie, do your boys know they have a half-brother?"

Another awkward moment... "No, I've never mentioned it to them," she breathed with a sigh.

"Would you possibly consider telling them?" I asked. "I know Mike would be thrilled to know he has brothers. He was brought up as an only child, and with his mother's passing, he literally has no family now outside of his own children and his wife's family."

"I'll think about it," she cautiously responded, "but I'm concerned it might upset them."

I could certainly understand her concern, and wanting to respect her boundaries, I didn't push. She needed time to process our conversation. It was a lot to take in. Of course, she was concerned about how her boys would react to knowing they had another brother. Would they be angry at her for not divulging this information in years past? Would this news damage their relationship with her? Would it taint their memory of their father?

All I could express to her as she pondered how this information could change her life was, "I understand, Angie. Let me know what you decide. Meanwhile, I will have Mike call you."

About a week later, Angie called to say she and Mike had a lovely phone visit and she had been able to answer many of his questions about his father. Angie is a good conversationalist, so I was not surprised to hear they had spent an hour on the phone.

She said she had also thought about approaching the subject with her boys. "I'm still apprehensive about what their reaction will be but I have decided they deserve to know they have a half-brother."

First, she told her oldest son. Happily, with great enthusiasm, he was delighted to know he had another brother. She then told her younger son who was also thrilled. Angie breathed a sigh of relief. The secret was out and the boys were ok with it, even excited. The brothers proceeded with phone conversations with Mike and plans were made to meet.

Before my correspondence with Mike began, Bill and I had planned a trip to California to visit friends. As we learned more about Mike, we realized that his home was only a half an hour from the town where our friends lived. This seemed more than a coincidence. God was leading us to meet one another. Bill and I were delighted to get together with Mike and his gracious wife who invited us to share a lovely lunch with them at their home.

As a gift, I had made a scrapbook by printing copies of old pictures from my photo albums, photos of "his family," our shared relatives. It was a treasured gift that brought tears to his eyes. Not being in his shoes and having a wonderful family myself, I can only imagine the pain that must go with the loss of all family, of not knowing anything about them. Yet, on that day, as I watched Mike turn the pages of the scrapbook, I was blessed to experience the joy he felt seeing so many family members for the first time, realizing that he had a heritage, knowing now where his roots lay.

As for me, I no longer had to wonder, *why am I doing research on ancestry?* The answer was clear. God had bigger plans than writing statistics about people long gone. His plan had been to connect a man to his family, a man who had spent his life longing to know his father and his side of the family. God, through Ancestry.com, gave me the joy of giving Mike this gift.

To be continued...

CHAPTER 39

A HAPPY REUNION

As expected, Mike was warmly received by both of his brothers and they have met several times over the years. They had much to talk about. After several years, when one of their wives passed away, it was Mike who played the role of "big brother" and stayed for a week after the funeral to lend support to his new found relatives.

The funeral was unique and I had really never attended anything quite like it. The half-brother and his wife had been nominal Catholics so the funeral was led by a Catholic priest who had been imported for the occasion. The church, as expected, was packed with family, friends and well-wishers.

The priest began his message by informing the entire congregation that none of us had anything to worry about. We were all going to heaven. "Yes," he said, "God has guaranteed that we will all be there."

I was stunned at his misinterpretation of scripture. I couldn't help but think of my nominal Catholic cousin, my Christian Scientist Aunt, and Mike, whom I didn't know where he was spiritually, all hearing such false statements from a man of the cloth. Then I had to chuckle inwardly as I thought of God looking down with a raised eyebrow wondering what planet this priest came from. Had he never read the Bible? Nowhere does it say we are all going to heaven. In truth, that idea is blasphemous since it bypasses the cross of Christ. Why would Jesus have bothered to endure the excruciating experience of the cross and shed His blood for our sins if everyone gets a free ticket without even acknowledging Him? *Sigh...*

I thought back to when I had first begun talking to Mike years before. Right from the beginning of our fledgling relationship, I had decided to be upfront about my Christian faith. Each time we talked, I would bring up the Lord's name and talk about how important God was in my life and the life of our family. Mike listened politely and responded kindly but gave no indication that he was a believer. Realizing he was a laid back type of person, however, I grew to appreciate his open heart and took opportunities to plant seeds here and there as I quietly prayed for his salvation.

After some months went by, he shared with me one day that a man he worked with had been talking to him about Jesus. Upon hearing about their conversations, I began to recognize that God was at work and had brought this man into Mike's life. He was a member of a church that I was familiar with, so I encouraged Mike to listen to him, and I continued to pray.

A year or so passed and again, Christianity came up in conversation with Mike as he told me that his granddaughter, Jessa, had invited him to go to church with her. Again, when I heard what church it was, I knew that he would hear truth there. So, I continued to pray.

Then, after the funeral, we had a wonderful discussion with Mike. Bill and I were glad for the opportunity to gently correct some of the misconceptions from the funeral service. Mike began to ask questions about baptism and about faith. At one point, I had a sense that Mike may have accepted Christ since I had last talked to him. So, I asked, "Mike, have you ever come to a time when you received Jesus as your personal Lord and Savior?"

To my surprise he casually answered, "Yes, I recently did invite Jesus into my life."

"Really," I exclaimed with joy. "When did that happen?"

"Well," he answered, "I started attending church with my grand-daughter and at the end of the service, they have an altar call. I went forward one Sunday and accepted Jesus into my life."

I was so excited to hear of his decision I wanted to jump up and down. Another family member who was now born again, another family member who would spend eternity in God's presence with us. What a joyful time and just like God's quirky sense of humor to have me find out at a funeral, of all places. I could almost hear the angels surrounding us with shouts of joy.

Although I was not the one who eventually brought Mike to the Lord, I knew that my prayers had been answered. Sometimes, we underestimate the power of praying when, in truth, praying can be our most strategic approach to winning a soul to Christ. The indisputable fact is that God had heard every cry of my heart for Mike's soul and He had arranged just the right people at just the right time to plant seeds that would one day bear fruit for His Kingdom.

Since that time, Bill and I began Facebook correspondence with Mike's granddaughter, Jessa, the one who had taken Mike to her church. When we realized she also shared our abiding faith in the Lord, we invited her to Michigan for a visit. During that visit, we had the pleasure of introducing her to our family, now her family as well. She was thrilled to know that she has so many cousins who love the Lord as she does. Her mother, Alysa, has also spoken with us by phone and concurred that it is so great to know there are other Christians in her family.

Looking back to the day I first decided to join Ancestry.com, I now see that the hand of God was in it all along. He is the One who nudged me with a desire toward genealogy. He is the One who just happened to have Mike starting his own search on Ancestry at the same time. He is the One who just happened to have us visit California friends who lived close to Mike. God is the One who cared enough about Mike to reveal his family to him and now we have more extended family through him as well. It was God Who ultimately planted people in Mike's life to sow seeds and eventually win him to Christ. Really, it is all about Jesus, the One who reaches out to people and calls them into His family.

APPENDIX

Included in the appendix are seven helpful topics. When talking with people, it is good to be equipped with information so that we will be prepared for various situations that may arise as we witness. We are exhorted in I Peter 3:15 as follows, *"But sanctify Christ as Lord in your hearts, always being ready to make a defense to everyone who asks you to give an account for the hope that is in you, yet with gentleness and reverence."* This is a strong exhortation. To be ready is to be prepared to tell about Jesus to anyone who shows interest.

First and foremost, in Appendix A, you will become acquainted with what Jesus said about Himself. Then, it is also good to see what others said about Him. Their testimony can be helpful.

Appendix B gives a simple ways to share the gospel message. If you need help, you can start with two leading questions and then use the *"Steps to Peace with God"* pamphlet which can be purchased online. Of course, it is also good to weave in your own personal testimony.

Appendix C is crucial information regarding our identity in Christ. If a believer has not settled that issue, she will be hesitant to witness. Jesus wants us to identify with Him and to know who we are in Christ.

Appendix D is a helpful tool in knowing how to pray for unbelievers. Praying Scripture is critical because those prayers will be directly in the will of God. There is power in praying God's own words.

Appendix E points out a number of salvation verses that can be used as you witness. It will be helpful if you memorize some of them.

Appendix F presents a contrast between heaven and hell. Some people may show interest in knowing the alternatives before making a choice.

Appendix G is a comprehensive look at the topic of eternal security. Until a person reckons with this issue, he will approach Christianity from a fear based or works based theology. In order to continue in the freedom Christ offers, we must know that we are secure in Him.

(Any parentheses amidst quotations are mine throughout the appendixes.)

WHAT DOES JESUS SAY ABOUT HIMSELF?

W hat Jesus said about Himself is truly breathtaking. Using just the gospels of John and Luke, let's examine Jesus' own words about Himself.

1. Jesus claimed to be the Messiah.

John 4:25-26, *"The woman said to Him, 'I know that Messiah is coming (He who is called Christ); when that One comes, He will declare all things to us.' Jesus said to her, 'I who speak to you am He.'"*

2. Jesus claimed to be the Son of God, therefore deity.

Luke 22:70-71, *"And they all said, 'Are You the Son of God, then?' And He said to them, 'Yes, I am.' Then they said, 'What further need do we have of testimony? For we have heard it ourselves from His own mouth.'"*

3. Jesus used God's name, "I Am," to identify Himself.

The Jewish leaders knew exactly what He was referring to because they wanted to stone Him for blasphemy (Ex. 3:13-14).

John 8:58-59, *"Jesus said to them, 'Truly, truly, I say to you, before Abraham was born, I Am.' Therefore they picked up stones to throw at Him, but Jesus hid Himself and went out of the temple."*

4. Jesus claimed to be One with God.
In John 10:30-33, 36-38, Jesus said, *"'I and the Father are one.' The Jews picked up stones again to stone Him. Jesus answered them, 'I showed you many good works from the Father; for which of them are you stoning Me?' The Jews answered Him, 'For a good work we do not stone You, but for blasphemy; and because You, being a man, make Yourself out to be God….do you say of Him, whom the Father sanctified and sent into the world, 'You are blaspheming,' because I said, 'I am the Son of God'? If I do not do the works of My Father, do not believe Me; but if I do them, though you do not believe Me, believe the works so that you may know and understand that the Father is in Me, and I in the Father.'"* What works was He referring to? The miracles, the healings, delivering people from demons, changing water to wine, and raising people from the dead.

5. Jesus agreed He was a King.
John 18:37, *"Therefore Pilate said to Him, 'So You are a king?' Jesus answered, 'You say correctly that I am a king. For this I have been born, and for this I have come into the world, to testify to the truth. Everyone who is of the truth hears My voice.'"*

6. Jesus claimed He could forgive sins.
Luke 7:48, *"Then He (Jesus) said to her, 'Your sins have been forgiven.'"*

7. Jesus claimed He gave people eternal life.
John 10:27-28, *"My sheep hear My voice, and I know them, and they follow Me; and I give eternal life to them, and they will never perish; and no one will snatch them out of My hand."*

John 6:40, *"For this is the will of My Father, that everyone who beholds the Son and believes in Him will have eternal life, and I Myself will raise him up on the last day."*

8. Jesus offered people peace.

John 14:27, Jesus said, *"Peace I leave with you; My peace I give to you; not as the world gives do I give to you. Do not let your heart be troubled, nor let it be fearful."*

9. Jesus spoke seven 'I Am' statements in the book of John. He said:

    A. I am the bread of life (6:35).
    B. I am the light of the world (8:12).
    C. I am the gate (10:7, 9).
    D. I am the good shepherd (10:11, 14).
    E. I am the resurrection and the life (11:25).
    F. I am the way, the truth, and the life (14:6).
    G. I am the true vine (15:1, 5).

Through these significant statements by Jesus, we see that He was confident in who He was and is. He did not mince words or leave room for question. He knew He was the awaited Jewish Messiah, the Son of God, King of kings and Lord of lords. He had no doubt that He could offer people forgiveness from sin, eternal life and peace.

What Others Said About Jesus

1. They said Jesus offered eternal life and was the Son of God.

John 6:68-69, *"Simon Peter answered Him, 'Lord, to whom shall we go? You have words of eternal life. We have believed and have come to know that You are the Holy One of God.'"*

John 19:7, *"The Jews (Jesus' antagonists) answered him, 'We have a law, and by that law He ought to die because He made Himself out to be the Son of God.'"*

2. They said they saw Jesus' resurrection body.

After Jesus was crucified, He raised from the dead. No other person has ever brought himself back from the dead. I Corinthians 15 tells us that **over** 500 people saw Jesus in His resurrection body. This is a documented historical fact.

3. They recognized Jesus was the Lord and God.

John 20:26-31, *"After eight day,"* (8 days after Jesus' resurrection), *"His disciples were again inside, and Thomas with them. Jesus came, the doors having been shut, and stood in their midst and said, 'Peace be with you.'"* (Only God can offer peace.) *"Then He said to Thomas, 'Reach here with your finger, and see My hands; and reach here your hand and put it into My side; and do not be unbelieving, but believing.'"* (Remember Jesus died on a cross...His hands and feet were nailed to the cross so in His resurrected body, there were holes where the nails had been. His side had also been pierced with a sword.) *"Thomas answered and said to Him, 'My Lord and my God!'"* (Thomas was a disciple and Jesus accepted his worship.) *"Jesus said to him, 'Because you have seen Me, have you believed? Blessed are they who did not see, and yet believed. Therefore many other signs Jesus also performed in the presence of the disciples, which are not written in this book; but these have been written so that you may believe that Jesus is the Christ, the Son of God; and that believing you may have life in His name."* (This is the point of the Bible that you may believe Jesus is who He said He is and thereby have eternal life.)

Jesus claimed to be the Messiah, the Son of God, a King. He claimed He was one with the Father, even took God's name (I AM), claimed He could give eternal life to people, forgave sin, offered peace, raised Himself from the dead, and accepted worship. These are just a few of His claims.

What conclusion can we make from the empirical, historical evidence? Either Jesus was a lunatic or a sociopathic liar...OR He was exactly who He said He was. There is no other way to look at it. If He is a lunatic or a liar, then more good has come into the world from a madman than from any other known historical figure.

If, on the other hand, He is who He said He is, then what does He want from us? He wants us to know how much He loves us, that He forgives our sin, and wants to be Lord of our lives.

APPENDIX B

SHARING YOUR FAITH MADE SIMPLE

There are two questions you can use to discern where a person is spiritually.

One: Do you know for sure that you are going to be with God in heaven?
Two: If God were to ask you, "Why should I let you into My heaven," what would you say?

The only acceptable answer to this question is this: Jesus blood shed on the cross paid for all my sins. I have received Christ into my life, therefore His blood covers my sin.

A tool I often use in witnessing is a booklet called, *"Steps to Peace with God,"* by Billy Graham. This can be purchased through Christianbook.com. In this booklet, Graham takes the reader through four steps to salvation. Here is an abbreviated version.

Step One: God loves you and wants you to experience peace and life- abundant and eternal (Rom. 5:1, Jn. 3:16, Jn. 10:10).

Step Two: We choose to disobey God and go our own willful way. This results in separation from God (Rom. 3:23, Rom. 6:23).

Step Three: Jesus Christ died on the cross and rose from the grave. He paid the penalty for our sin and bridged the gap between God and people (Rom. 5:8, Jn. 14:6, Eph. 2:8, 9).

Step Four: We must trust Jesus Christ as Lord and Savior and receive Him by personal invitation (Jn. 1:12).

If the person shows interest in accepting Christ, a simple prayer follows.

PRAYER: Dear Lord Jesus, I confess to you that I am a sinner and I know that you died for my sins. I ask forgiveness for my sins and invite you to come into my heart. I want you to be my Lord and Savior. Amen.

A good follow-up for assurance of salvation is I Jn. 5:11-13.

APPENDIX C
IDENTITY IN CHRIST

One of the most important issues that Christians must have in place is their identity in Christ. Every human being has formed an identity of some sort, usually a compilation of good and bad. Sometimes, we take the labels that have been assigned to us from childhood and we determine our worth and value by these words spoken over us as youngsters. These could involve physical, personality or behavioral labels. A child could hear such things as: "You are so stupid; You're such a slob; You're too fat; You're too thin; You're such a bully; You're so shy; Cry baby, cry baby; Can't you do anything right?"

Sadly, these negative words can become permanent marks on the child's soul. Negative words impact a child and often leave a deep scar. Any of these kinds of expressions can penetrate and become an identity carried throughout life. Many people form their entire identity based on a perceived weakness, flaw or negative aspect that was drilled into their psyche as children.

In his book, "The Bondage Breaker", Neil Anderson says: "No person can consistently behave in a way that's inconsistent with the way he perceives himself. If you think you are a no-good bum, you'll probably live like a no-good bum. But if you see yourself as a child of God who is spiritually alive in Christ, you'll begin to live in victory and freedom as He lived. After years of working with people who were in deep spiritual conflict, I found one common denominator: None of them knew who he or she was in Christ. Satan can do nothing to damage your position in Christ. But if he can deceive you into believing his lie—that you are not acceptable to God and that you'll never amount to anything as a Christian—then you will live as if you have no position or identity in Christ." (Neil T. Anderson, *Bondage Breakers,* (Eugene, Oregon: Harvest House Publisher, 1990).

When you received Christ as your Lord and Savior and He came by His Holy Spirit to take up residence in your heart, He made you a new creature. *"Therefore if any man is in Christ, he is a new creature; the old things passed away; behold new things have come,"* (II Cor. 5:1). When we come to Christ, our old way of identifying who we are passed away. Whatever names or brands, we or someone else had attached to us, were removed at the cross. We are now a new person "in Christ".

We no longer have to identify ourselves by our weaknesses or labels. That is not who we are. None of us need to carry a label because we are new and clean in Christ and our identity is now in Him and everything He stands for. He made the exchange of all our filthy rags for His clean white garment. We are not only forgiven, we are righteous. Why? Because He is righteous and we identify with whom He is. When we think of ourselves, we now think of a righteous person.

Who we used to be has been *"...crucified with Christ; and it is no longer I who live, but Christ lives in me; and the life which I now live in the flesh I live by faith in the Son of God, who loved me and delivered Himself up for me,"* (Gal. 2:20).

It is incredible to think about, isn't it? *"He made Him who knew no sin to be sin on our behalf, that we might become the righteousness of God in Him,"* (II Cor. 5:21). We are holy because He is holy, and He dwells in us.

This means that Christ took all our filthy rags of identification and exchanged them for His pure, holy righteousness. When Christ went to the cross, He became sin. The Living Bible puts it this way: *"For God took the sinless Christ and poured into Him our sins. Then, in exchange, He poured God's goodness into us."* The King James version says, *"For he hath made him to be sin for us, who knew no sin; that we might be made the righteousness of God in him."*

This means that on the cross, the sinless Christ, although He never personally sinned Himself, actually became bitter, angry, jealous, abusive, greedy, lawless, quarrelsome, a homosexual, a drug addict, a liar, a prostitute, an idolater, a drunkard, a fool, a glutton, a slanderer and more. By taking all of our sin on Himself, He made an exchange so that we might become righteous, compassionate, humble, gentle, patient, pure, forgiving, lovers of God and people, peaceful, forbearing, thankful, self controlled, faithful, good, worshipful and more.

With this monumental exchange, we gained a completely new identity. Our old fleshly identity with its passions and desires was crucified with Christ. We can now come before His throne of grace confidently knowing He sympathizes with our weaknesses, (Heb. 4:15-16).

Knowing who we are in Christ frees us up to make right choices in life. The way it works is this: When our identity is settled, we are free to choose actions that line up with our identity. Whatever weaknesses of soul that may have been behind our former behaviors, ones we formerly identified with, we can now choose not to act on because it does not line up with who we are in Christ. Life, then, is a series of Spirit-controlled decisions where we become more and more like Christ in our words, attitudes, and actions so that what we DO lines up with who we ARE. As we understand more clearly who we are, then our actions and thoughts will line up more easily.

It might be an interesting exercise for you to prayerfully make a list of things that identify you. For example: I am righteous and holy. I am hidden with Christ in God, I am a new creation. I am a temple for the Holy Spirit. I am a child of light, not of darkness. As you read your Bible, you can add other things to this list or refer to the list at the end of this article.

There are many distortions and lies that we have believed about ourselves. How we view these lies will determine how we approach our relationship with God and other people. In the best scenario, parents love, cherish and nurture their child in truth so that he feels valued and secure. Safe and protected, the child is able to value and respect others and eventually pass on positive qualities to his own children.

For many people, however, the following is more accurate... a life where value is stolen and expunged leaving the child to internalize lies about his worth. A devalued child, although born with God-given worth, only receives negative input. Lies saying he is no-good, stupid, and worthless begin to feel like the truth. With no skill set to sort truth from lies, he believes what he is told. The resulting void in his soul often culminates in an unbiblical lifestyle. With no solid ground of truth, the lies then perpetuate to the next generation.

But God, in His grace and mercy, offers a way to regain lost value by renewing of the mind. A devalued person may feel confused and unable to sort out his life, but with Jesus Christ, there is hope. Although lies have corrupted the child's soul, exposure to God's Word can impact change for good. By embracing God's truth about his worth, an adjusted mindset is possible and can be passed on generationally.

At times children experience rejection or even abandonment and have a skewed identity as a result. Satan is a master deceiver and is adept at "identity theft". He rejoices when he can convince a person of a false identity, one apart from our true God given uniqueness. Our value and sense of connection, however, can be re-claimed. It starts when we believe God's truth about who He says we are.

The biblical perspective concerning identity in Christ is found in John 15 where God gives us a picture of the vine and the branches. He says, *"I am the vine and you are the branches...."* A branch is connected to the vine. It is a part of the vine. It can be likened to Jesus' "sap" flowing through us because we are "in" Him, just as a branch is "in" the vine. We produce fruit because He energizes and controls us. We are nothing until He is in us and we are in Him. This is intimacy, connectedness at its finest. This is our identity in Christ.

Sometimes we forget that we are continually connected to the Author of Life Himself. That bond is a firm and sure connection and it is eternally secure. Jesus says in John 10:30, *"I and the Father are one."* That means they are connected. And He invites us into that unity, that oneness, that connectedness. Jesus is "in" the Father and the Father is "in" Jesus. As believers, we are also "in" Christ and He is "in" us, our hope of glory, (Col. 1:27). What gratitude a believer can have for this wonderful gift!

To change our identity, we must change who and what we identify with. If we are rooted in Christ, and He Himself is actually the root of our life, then everything that springs from that root has to be holy, good, right, loving, and pure because there is no unrighteousness in Him. A branch in a tree is dependent on the root system of the tree and whatever comes up into the branch flows up from the root. Likewise with Christ. Because Christ is completely righteous, His flow of nourishment into our life is continual and always righteous.

Romans 11:16 says, *"...if the root be holy, the branches are too."*

Colossians 2:7 also talks about roots, *"...having been firmly rooted and now being built up in Him and established in your faith...."* Our roots and therefore our identity are firmly grounded and rooted in who He is, and all the attributes and character of Christ are at our disposal when we are "in Him" and He is "in us". This is intimacy at its utmost, and this is our identity in Christ. This is the closeness of relationship that the Lord offers us, the root of our identity.

Webster's Dictionary says identity means, "the condition or fact of being the same in all qualities under consideration; sameness; oneness."

In John 17:11 Jesus prays, *"...Holy Father, keep them in Thy name, the name which Thou hast given Me, that they may be one, even as We are."* I believe Jesus was praying about our identity here, that our identity be in His name, that we be one with Him and the Father. Then in verse 21, *"...that they may all be one, even as Thou, Father, art in Me and I in Thee, that they also may be in Us...."* and vs. 23, *"I in them and You in Me, that they may be perfected in unity, so that the world may know that You sent Me, and loved them, even as You have loved Me."*

Jesus fervently prayed that we know who we are, that we be clear about our identity in Him but it goes beyond just us. He is passionate for the world to know that He loves them. With our new identity secure, knowing we are loved, we are in a position to witness. This is His will for us, and He cried out to the Father that it would be so.

Knowing that our true identity is in Christ, there is NO WAY we can say that weak tendencies, whether mental or emotional, whether fleshly thoughts or names others branded us with, are our identity. They don't fit with the identity we have in Christ. Yes, we all have weaknesses associated with our flesh nature, but as new creatures in Christ, our identity is no longer associated with our flesh. Our identity is in the Spirit. We are righteous because He is righteous, and He has imputed His righteousness to us. Therefore, we are rooted in righteousness. We are holy because He is holy. We love because He is love and as believers, He lives in us and loves others through us.

Realistically, there are times we choose to act or think apart from the context of our true identity. We sometimes choose to walk in the flesh, but our deeds do not change the fact of who we are in Christ. Our flesh can rise up and do or say unloving things, hurt people or hurt God, but that is not out of our God-given identity.

It's important to remember that for every Christian, there is a "condition" and a "position." Our "condition" is that we were born with a flesh nature and that we will have it until our bodies are glorified at Christ's return. But, in Christ, we have a new "position" that is in the heavenlies, seated on the throne "in Christ". Our lives now optimally operate out of our new position, (Eph. 2:6).

For your reference, here is a partial list of our identity in Christ. In answering the question, "Who am I?" here is your true identity in Christ.

Identity in Christ Scripture
I am a child of God, (Jn. 1:12).
I am the salt of the earth, (Matt. 5:13).
I am the light of the world, (Matt. 5:14).
I am part of the true vine, a channel of Christ's life, (Jn. 15:1,5).
I am Christ's friend, (Jn. 15:15).
I am chosen and appointed by Christ to bear His fruit, (Jn. 15:16).
I am a slave of righteousness, (Rom. 6:18).
I am a joint heir with Christ, sharing His inheritance with Him, (Rom. 8:17).
I am a temple-a dwelling place-of the Holy Spirit, (I Cor. 3:16 and 6:19).
I am a member of Christ's Body, (I Cor. 12:27, Eph. 5:30).
I am a new creation, (II Cor. 5:17).
I am reconciled to God & a minister of reconciliation, (II Cor. 5:18-19).
I am a saint, (Eph. 1:1, I Cor. 1:2, Phil. 1:1).
I am God's workmanship, created for good works, (Eph. 2:10).

I am born again, (Jn. 3:3,7).

I am righteous and holy, (Eph. 4:24).

I am a citizen of heaven, seated in heaven now, (Phil. 3:20, Eph. 2:6).

I am hidden with Christ in God, (Col. 3:3).

I am chosen of God, holy and dearly loved, (Col. 3:12, I Thess. 1:4).

I am a son of light and not of darkness, (I Thess. 5:5).

I am one of God's living stones, being built up in Christ as a spiritual house, (I Pet. 2:5).

I am a member of a chosen race, a royal priesthood, a holy nation, a people for God's own possession, (I Pet. 2:9-10).

I am an alien and stranger in this world in which I temporarily live, (I Pet. 2:11).

I am an enemy of the devil, (I Pet. 5:8).

I am what I am by the grace of God, (I Cor. 15:10).

APPENDIX D

PRAYING SCRIPTURE FOR UNBELIEVERS

1. **That they will see a need for faith in God.** Hebrews 11:6, *"And without faith it is impossible to please Him, for he who comes to God must believe that He is, and that He is a rewarder of those who seek Him."*

2. **That they will be convicted that they are sinners.** Romans 3:23, *"For all have sinned and come short of the glory of God."* John 16:8, *"And He, when He comes, will convict the world concerning sin, and righteousness, and judgment;"*

3. **That Satan will be bound.** Matthew 16:19, *"I will give you the keys of the kingdom of heaven; and whatever you shall bind on earth shall be bound in heaven, and whatever you shall loose on earth shall be loosed in heaven."*

4. **That Jesus will knock on the door of their hearts. That they will open the door of their hearts to the Lord.** Revelation 3:20, *"Behold, I stand at the door and knock; if anyone hears My voice and opens the door, I will come in to him, and will dine with him, and he with Me."*

5. **That the Holy Spirit will draw them.** John 12:32, *"And I, if I be lifted up from the earth, will draw all men to Myself."* John 6:44 *"No one can come to Me, unless the Father who sent Me draws him; and I will raise him up on the last day."*

6. **That they will count the cost.** Luke 14:28, *"For which one of you, when he wants to build a tower, does not first sit down and calculate the cost, to see if he has enough to complete it?"*

7. **That Jesus will reveal Himself to them.** Luke 10:22, *"All things have been handed over to Me by My Father, and no one knows who the Son is except the Father, and who the Father is except the Son, and anyone to whom the Son wills to reveal Him."*

8. **That the Father will grant them salvation.** John 6:65, *"And He was saying, 'For this reason I have said to you, that no one can come to Me, unless it has been granted him from the Father.'"*

9. **That they will see Jesus as the only way to God.** John 14:6, *"Jesus said to him, 'I am the way, and the truth, and the life; no one comes to the Father, but through Me.'"*

A few other thoughts about praying for unbelievers would be:

- That God would lift the veil from their eyes for revelation and enlightenment
- For the Holy Spirit to hover over them and protect them
- For godly people to be in their path each day
- That God will cast down anything in their lives that would exalt itself against the knowledge of God, specifically pride and rebellion
- That God will take down all known strongholds – thought patterns, opinions on religion, fear
- To bind Satan from taking them captive; to bind all wicked thoughts and lies Satan would try to place in their minds
- That God will send workers into the harvest of their lives

APPENDIX E

SALVATION VERSES

John 3:15-16, *"So that whoever believes will in Him have eternal life. For God so loved the world, that He gave His only begotten Son, that whoever believes in Him shall not perish, but have eternal life."*

Romans 10:9-10, *"If you confess with your mouth Jesus as* <u>Lord</u>, *and believe in your heart that God raised Him from the dead, you will be saved; for with the heart a person believes, resulting in righteousness, and with the mouth he confesses, resulting in salvation."*

Psalm 86:5, *"For You, Lord, are good, and ready to forgive, and abundant in lovingkindness to all who call upon You."*

Romans 3:23-24, *"For all have sinned and fall short of the glory of God being justified as a gift by His grace through the redemption which is in Christ Jesus;"*

Romans 3:28, *"For we maintain that a man is justified by faith apart from works of the Law."*

Romans 6:23, *"For the wages of sin is death, but the free gift of God is eternal life in Christ Jesus our Lord."*

Romans 4:4, 5, *"Now to the one who works, his wage is not credited as a favor, but as what is due but to the one who does not work,* but believes in Him who justifies the ungodly, his faith is credited as righteousness...."

Romans 10:13, *"for whoever will call on the name of the Lord will be saved."*

Romans 11:6, *"But if it is by grace, it is no longer on the basis of works, otherwise grace is no longer grace."*

Acts 4:12, *"And there is salvation in no one else; for there is no other name under heaven that has been given among men by which we must be saved."*

Ephesians 2:8-9, *"For by grace you have been saved through faith; and that not of yourselves, it is the gift of God; not as a result of works, so that no one may boast."*

Titus 3:5-6, *"He saved us, not on the basis of deeds which we have done in righteousness, but according to His mercy, by the washing of regeneration and renewing by the Holy Spirit, whom*

He poured out upon us richly through Jesus Christ our Savior,"

II Timothy 1:9, *"who has saved us and called us with a holy calling, not according to our works, but according to His own purpose and grace which was granted us in Christ Jesus from all eternity...."*

I John 5:11-13, *"And the testimony is this, that God has given us eternal life, and this life is in His Son. He who has the Son has the life; he who does not have the Son of God does not have the life. These things I have written to you who believe in the name of the Son of God, so that **you may know** that you have eternal life."*

Salvation, forgiveness of sin, is a free gift offered by God to all who believe. It all boils down to faith. Life is short. Our time here on earth is less than a hundred years. In terms of eternity, that is just a drop in the bucket. I believe our time here is a testing ground to prepare us for eternity. We could be gone in an instant. Where will we spend eternity? God wants us to know we can have eternal life...but, of course, the decision is ours to accept or reject. God is *"not wishing for any to perish but for all come to repentance,*" (II Pet. 3:9). To reject His invitation is to go into an eternity void of God. This is a serious choice. People sometimes laugh when they talk about heaven and hell. One man who rejected God said he was looking forward to a grand game of golf in hell. We need to understand that God does not send people to hell. People choose to go there by rejecting God's offer of eternal life through Jesus Christ.

APPENDIX F
HELL OR HEAVEN?

I debated whether to include the following verses in this book but I feel for some, they could mean the difference between an eternity with God or one without Him. I will let them speak for themselves. For some, this may be a wake-up call, a sober warning of things to come apart from salvation and forgiveness in Christ. Each verse speaks of the future Jesus died to save us from. The choice is ours to make. Any wise decision in life should be done with all the facts so consider these verses describing hell.

Matthew 8:12, "... *cast out into the outer darkness; in that place there will be weeping and gnashing of teeth.*"

Psalm 6:5, "*For there is no mention of You (God) in death; In Sheol (hell) who will give You thanks?*"

Isaiah 38:18, "*For Sheol cannot thank You, Death cannot praise You; Those who go down to the pit cannot hope for Your faithfulness.*"

Ecclesiastes 9:10, "*Whatever your hand finds to do, do it with all your might; for there is no activity or planning or knowledge or wisdom in Sheol where you are going.*" (This is a very sobering thought to consider.)

Ecclesiastes 9:5, "*...the dead do not know anything, nor have they any longer a reward, for their memory is forgotten.*"

Habakkuk 2:5, "*... like death is never satisfied....*"

Isaiah 66:24, *"For their worm will not die and their fire will not be quenched;"*

Psalm 18:5, *"The sorrows of hell compassed me about...."*

Luke 16:23, *"In Hades (hell) he lifted up his eyes, being in torment...."*

II Thessalonians 1:7-9, *"...Lord Jesus will be revealed from heaven with His mighty angels in flaming fire, dealing out retribution to those who do not know God and to those who do not obey the gospel of our Lord Jesus. These will pay the penalty of eternal destruction, away from the presence of the Lord and from the glory of His power,"*

Hell is a dark, empty place with scorching fire, a place of sorrow and torment, of nothingness where there is continual weeping. It is a place with zero activity of any kind, no planning, knowledge or wisdom, no satisfaction, and no memory of anything. It is a place of perpetual darkness void of God and empty of hope. Surely, no one would choose such a destiny. Yet it is a choice.

God desires none to perish (I Tim. 2:3-4), yet some people consider God mean and hateful when they hear about hell and that there is only one way to avoid it. They find God intolerant when they hear that people of other faiths aren't included in the eternal life He offers. After all, they shriek, don't all paths lead to God?

Here is a word picture that could help with that line of thinking. Suppose you were on the 4th floor of a burning building where all the known exits are blocked by heat, smoke and flames. It's night and the room you are in is dark as the electricity has gone out. The elevator is inoperable and the stairs are blocked by debris and flames. You hear the crackling of the burning walls and realize you are out of options as the fire ignites all around you. Suddenly, someone bursts into the room and beckons you to follow them. They know of a remote stairway that is still open, one that you were unaware of. To get to the stairway will require you to follow this person's directions so as not to get lost. You have a choice. Trust the man to lead you out or stay behind in the inferno.

Would you accuse this person who is trying to save your life of being mean and hateful for asking you to carefully follow his directions? Would you write him off as intolerant because he asserted there was only one way out of the building? Of course not. You would be grateful that he cared enough to seek you out and lead you to safety. (The idea for this illustration came from: (Dr. Robert Jeffress, *Not All Roads Lead to Heaven*, (Grand Rapids, Michigan: Baker Books, 2016) 31.)

Matthew 7:13-14, *"Enter through the narrow gate; for the gate is wide and the way is broad that leads to destruction, and there are many who enter through it. For the gate is small and the way is narrow that leads to life, and there are few who find it."*

Entering into an eternal covenant with God, whereby heaven is a guarantee, is a faith decision yet one with a sure hope. Hebrews 11:1, *"Now faith is the assurance of things hoped for, the conviction of things not seen."*

Heaven is also a very real place. It is where God dwells, a glorious place filled with light, joy, and peace, a place where there is purpose, meaningful activity, knowledge and wisdom, a place with an abundance of all that is good and right, where there is continual access to God. It is a place filled with music where thanksgiving, praise and worship flow continually. Heaven is a place where holiness exists in all purity.

John 14:2, *"In My Father's house are many dwelling places; if it were not so, I would have told you; for I go to prepare a place for you."*

Hebrews 11:16, *"But as it is, they desire a better country, that is, a heavenly one. Therefore God is not ashamed to be called their God, for he has prepared for them a city."*

Revelation 21:19-21, *"The foundation stones of the city wall were adorned with every kind of precious stone. The first foundation stone was jasper; the second, sapphire; the third, chalcedony; the fourth, emerald; the fifth, sardonyx; the sixth, sardius; the seventh, chrysolite; the eighth, beryl; the ninth, topaz; the tenth, chrysoprase; the eleventh, jacinth; the twelfth,*

amethyst. And the twelve gates were twelve pearls; each one of the gates was
a single pearl. And the street of the city was pure gold, like transparent
glass."*

Psalms 97:2, *"...Righteousness and justice are the foundation of His
throne."*

Revelation 7:11, *"And all the angels were standing around the throne
and around the elders and the four living creatures; and they fell on their
faces before the throne and worshiped God, saying, "Amen, blessing and
glory and wisdom and thanksgiving and honor and power and might, be
to our God forever and ever. Amen."*

I Corinthians 2:9, *"Things which eye has not seen and ear had not
heard, and which have not entered the heart of man, all that God has prepared for those who love Him."*

Revelation 21:27, *"And nothing unclean, and no one who practices
abomination and lying, shall ever come into it, but only those whose names
are written in the Lamb's book of life."*

Revelation 7:16-17, *"They will hunger no longer, nor thirst anymore;
nor will the sun beat down on them, nor any heat; for the Lamb in the center of the throne will be their shepherd, and will guide them to springs of the
water of life; and God will wipe every tear from their eyes."*

Revelation 21:4, *"He will wipe away every tear from their eyes, and
death shall be no more, neither shall there be mourning, nor crying, nor
pain anymore, for the former things have passed away."*

Revelation 22:5, *"And there will no longer be any night; and they will
not have need of the light of a lamp nor the light of the sun, because the Lord
God will illumine them; and they will reign forever and ever."*

John 10:28, *"And I give eternal life to them, and they will never perish;
and no one will snatch them out of My hand."*

We can gain entrance into this glorious kingdom by praying
something like this... *Jesus, I need You in my life and by faith I am coming to You in prayer. Thank You for dying on the cross, for taking my sins
away and offering me Your forgiveness. Thank You for giving Your life that
I might be one of Your children. I receive You by faith and accept Your death*

that I may be saved from an eternity in hell. I ask You to be my Savior and my Lord. Forgive me and take control of the throne of my life. Make me who You want me to be. I recognize and accept You as my Lord.

Jesus desires relationship with each of us but it is on His terms. When we invite Him to be Lord in our lives, then He will be our Savior. Acts 4:12, *"And there is salvation in no one else; for there is no other name under heaven that has been given among men by which we must be saved."*

APPENDIX G

A CASE FOR ETERNAL SECURITY

The Great Exchange

Jesus has done everything necessary for salvation. The blood of Jesus paid for it all. Our response is simply faith. It is on the basis of faith alone, nothing added. If we add anything, we are saying that His blood was not good enough or powerful enough. All of our sins past, present, and future were paid for at the cross. We did nothing to earn salvation. If we think our sin causes us to lose salvation and we have to be saved anew, then in essence we are saying that Christ's blood wasn't good enough the first time. We have to ask ourselves: *Which sin is not covered by the blood? Which sin is so big that the blood cannot atone for it?* And the answer is that no sin is too big. His blood covered them all. This is why we can rest. We rest in God's finished work on the cross. We no longer have to strive for salvation. It is a free gift, never to be revoked. Rebirth occurs only one-time. Nowhere in the Bible does it say that a person can or needs to be reborn again and again.

No sin can enter heaven and we know that Christ is coming for a pure, spotless bride. But we also know that none of us is pure and spotless on our own. When God looks at us, He sees us through the filter of Jesus' blood. We are righteous because of Jesus' righteousness in us. On our own, our flesh is corrupt and we all deserve death if we depend on anything we do or don't do, think or don't think, say or don't say. It is when we realize the total depravity of our own soul that we began to understand how amazing His grace is toward us. Our salvation is based solely on the blood of Christ and the finished work of the cross. He did it all. We simply respond in faith and say, "Yes" to Him.

Just as we have no righteousness of our own that can gain us salvation, so we have no unrighteousness of our own that can hinder us from salvation. We know that all our deeds are as filthy rags from Isaiah 64:6 and that our hearts are more deceitful than all else and desperately wicked from Jeremiah 17:9. We also know that there is none righteous, no not one from Romans 3. If this is the state of our heart, and it is, and Romans 5:6 says that while we were yet sinners, Christ died for us, then logically, our sins were paid for long before we received Him. We don't need to clean ourselves up before we come to Him. We come as we are, sinful and broken and He will begin the process of cleansing. The key is accepting His finished work at the cross.

Romans 10:9 is a simple salvation verse that does not involve any cleaning up on our part. *"If you confess with your mouth Jesus as Lord, and believe in your heart that God raised Him from the dead, you shall be saved."* When we invite Him into our lives, He begins the process of cleaning us up. Bill took years to come to the Lord because he thought he had to clean himself up before God would accept him. And he found that the harder he tried the worse he became. We can't clean ourselves up.

We come to Him as wretched sinners. All we have to offer Him is a broken life. He takes us in our brokenness and sin. We give Him our sin and He gives us His righteousness. That is the great exchange. Whatever righteousness we have is from Him and in Him we are 100% righteous. Whether we feel guilty, depressed, isolated or worthless, in Christ we are still 100% righteous in our spirit regardless of our performance. His blood has already cleansed us of every sin and continually cleanses us now and into the future. So, by His blood we are justified (just as if we had never sinned). For the believer, sin will not be the issue on judgment day. Romans 5:9 and I Thessalonians 5:9 both promise that we shall be saved from the wrath of God to come. As believers, we never need to fear God's wrath. His blood has covered us and His wrath will bypass us just as the plague judgment of death bypassed the Israelites whose door posts had the symbolic blood over them. We remember how rebellious and willful the Israelites were, yet the blood protected them, not their works or performance. Our flesh is and always will be completely unrighteous. When we choose to walk in the flesh, we have become carnal Christians, Christian in name only, not in deed.

We are not looked at according to what we do. God looks at us for who we are and we are the righteousness of Christ if we are in Him. All of us will still sin at times, some willfully and some not willful, but our identity is that we are the righteousness of Christ, solely based on His finished work on the cross. If we lost our salvation every time we did something wrong, we would not be able to keep up with ourselves. Our lives would become sin and repentance centered rather than Christ centered. We can be thankful that He covers it all. For instance, would we lose our salvation if we felt bitterness in our heart, if we were angry with someone, if we gossiped, if we argued and had trouble controlling our tongue? Would we lose salvation if we were selfish, or complained and grumbled? After all, one of the major sins God was upset about with the Israelites was grumbling, (I Cor. 10:10). What if we procrastinated, told lies, or swore? Do you get the point? Sin is sin and we all do it and we are sometimes willful about it. Our sin just shows us how desperately we need a Savior. But as we grow in the Lord, many sins diminish. More and more, as we mature as Christians, our goal is to allow Christ to transform us so that we choose to line up our words and deeds with who we are in Christ. Righteous deeds because we are righteous. This is the sanctification process that goes on in our soul. Remember, our spirit is where Jesus dwells and from which our righteousness emanates. It is our soul that needs sanctified, needs to daily reckon itself as dead to sin and this can only be accomplished by the work of the Holy Spirit within us.

Aren't we glad Jesus doesn't throw us out when we find ourselves caught in the snare of the trapper? If ever we needed an advocate and Savior, it is in those times. Aren't we glad He works with us and pulls us out of the miry clay and sets us again on the Rock? Instead of pushing us out, He waits patiently and gathers us into His loving arms when we realize we have walked out of fellowship with Him. Never for one moment does He abandon us. He is always there waiting for us to come to the end of wallowing in our selfish desires.

Not only did Christ die for all sin but also He crushed the power of sin. He paid the penalty for sin in the past, delivers us from the power of sin today and will deliver us from the presence of sin in the future.

The prodigal son is a perfect example of a person who lost fellowship with his father. But he never lost relationship. He was always his father's son and while his father grieved and lamented his son's choices, nowhere does scripture say that he disowned him as a son. He waited and watched for him to come back and have fellowship restored.

It's kind of like our children. They will always be our children, no matter what they do. They are our children by birth or adoption. The relationship is there. No matter where they are, they are related to us. In a similar way, we are God's children by rebirth. We share His blood. We are Jesus' blood relatives.

Amazing Grace

Hebrews 7:25 says that Jesus always lives to make intercession for us. Do you know what Jesus is doing when we are caught up in sin? He is interceding on our behalf to the Father. He is continually applying His blood to our sin. His grace abounds to us as He pleads our case before the Father day and night. *"...Where sin increased, grace abounded all the more,"* (Rom. 5:20). *"And if anyone sins, we have an Advocate with the Father, Jesus Christ the Righteous and He Himself is the propitiation (satisfaction before God) for our sins...,"* (I Jn. 2:1). Jesus' blood sacrifice satisfied God the Father for all the sin that we have experienced. This is why His grace is so amazing, so divine, so awesome, so powerful. This is what He chose to do for us while we were wallowing in sin. This is how much He loves us.

When we truly understand how awesome God's grace is and how liberally He applies it to our sin, we are left with only one conclusion, the same conclusion Paul came to in Romans. 6:1, *"What shall we say then? Are we to continue in sin that grace might increase? May it never be...."* and again in 6:15, *"What then? Shall we sin because we are not under law but under grace? May it never be!"* When we really understand the incredible magnitude of grace, we can only exclaim, "Wow!" as we realize any sin we commit is covered.

The obvious question Paul had was that if all sin is covered, then shall we go ahead and give ourselves permission to sin? But, of course, we hopefully come to our senses quickly and realize that even though it would be covered, we will choose not to sin because we love God so much we don't want to offend Him or hurt our fellowship with Him. We don't want anything to come between us and God. We remember we are in a love relationship with our Creator and love does no wrong.

Yet, who among us has not let our liberty be an occasion for sin? Because we are at times disobedient, the Word says that at those times, we didn't love God, (Jn. 14:15, 21). But praise God He loves us to the end and nothing separates us eternally from Him.

He woos us back and we again choose to love Him as shown by our obedience.

He even offers more in Hebrews 4:15-16, *"For we do not have a high priest who cannot sympathize with our weaknesses, but one who has been tempted in all things as we are, yet without sin. Let us therefore draw near with confidence to the throne of grace, that we may receive mercy and may find grace to help in time of need."*

He understands that we are weak and sometimes get off track. He knows the lure of sin. He, too, was tempted. He is not surprised when we fall. But He waits with open arms to restore us because He has a vested interest in us, an eternal interest, a promised interest, a covenant interest. So, He waits and if we are truly His, I John 3:9 says, *"No one who is born of God practices sin,* (the actual Greek says **continues** to practice sin), *because His seed abides in him; and he cannot* (continue) *sin, because He is born of God."* The length of time that we sin may vary but eventually if we truly belong to God, the Holy Spirit won't allow us to continue in sin. Yes, it is possible to grieve and even quench the Spirit in our lives, but that does not preclude lost salvation.

Assurance Verses

"My sheep hear My voice, and I know them, and they follow Me; and I give eternal life to them, and they shall never perish; and no one shall snatch them out of My hand," (Jn. 10:27-29).

Jesus said in John 18:9, *"...Of those whom Thou hast given Me, I lost not one."*

I John 5:11-13, *"And the witness is this, that God has given us eternal life, and this life is in His Son. He who has the Son has the life; he who does not have the Son of God does not have the life. These things I have written to you who believe in the name of the Son of God, in order that you may know that you have eternal life."*

Do you notice that again in these verses the only criteria for eternal life is belief, not our deeds, good or bad? It clearly says we can **know**, not guess, hope, or wonder, but know that we have eternal life and it is based only on belief in the Son. After we accept Christ as Lord, when we are in sin, do we still believe in Jesus? Of course we do.

And beyond that we were sealed with the Holy Spirit of promise. When we first believed in Jesus, we were sealed for eternity. Nowhere does the Bible say we become unsealed. The Holy Spirit of promise came to live in us and it is for eternity. *"In Him, you also, after listening to the message of truth, the gospel of your salvation, having also believed, you were sealed in Him with the Holy Spirit of promise, who is given as a pledge of our inheritance...,"* (Eph. 1:13-14).

The Holy Spirit is a pledge or promise from God of our inheritance. God never reneges on a promise. The Holy Spirit bears witness to our spirit that we are children of God. We are called God's own possession in verse 14. He owns us. We have been bought with a price. We sometimes grieve the Holy Spirit. We are sometimes unfaithful. But He remains faithful to the end.

Symptoms of Lack of Security

Eternal security is so foundational to our lives that to deny it will automatically mean an outcropping of certain symptoms in individuals and corporately in the church which can hinder growth. Here are some of the symptoms that can be noticed:

1. Motivated by fear
2. Driven to perform
3. Works oriented life
4. Controlling attitude
5. Sometimes, a harshness
6. Feelings of condemnation and judgment
7. Lack of true freedom
8. Rules and rigidity leading to legalism
9. Feelings of never being good enough, even a failure

10. Feelings of sadness, low self esteem and depression
11. Stunted growth because focus is on sin and fear of doing something wrong
12. Tendency to give up
13. Feeling that you can't please God
14. Insecurity that will creep into every area of life

These symptoms are simply the natural result of a doctrine at a tilt that I have observed in people I have talked to over the years and in churches which subscribe to a no eternal security doctrine. I liken this doctrine to a child coming home after school. The child left in the morning to go to school. While at school he got into some trouble that was his fault. He sinned. The child returns from school only to discover his family has moved in his absence with no forwarding address. This would be so hurtful. No security, no chance for reconciliation to right fellowship. But really, isn't that what a skewed doctrine denying eternal security teaches? Children must be secure in their family life to function in a healthy way on a daily basis. In like manner, Christians need to be secure in their salvation to fully embrace God and the plans He has for them.

They must know that when they sin they will not be abandoned. Deuteronomy 31:8, *"The Lord himself goes before you and will be with you; he will never leave you nor forsake you. Do not be afraid; do not be discouraged."* Joshua 1:5, *"No one will be able to stand up against you all the days of your life. As I was with Moses, so I will be with you; I will never leave you nor forsake you."* Psalm 94:14, *"For the Lord will not reject his people; he will never forsake his inheritance."*

Jesus said: "Of all that He has given me, I lose nothing."
John 6:12 is in the midst of the story about Jesus feeding over 5000 people. In verse 12, Jesus says to the disciples, *"...Gather up the left-over fragments that nothing may be lost."* It would be easy to wonder why this was so important and the reason, I believe, is because

this miraculous sign was followed closely in the same chapter with words of eternal security. Picking up all the scraps so that nothing was lost became a visual sign of what Jesus wanted his disciples to grasp about their eternal security. In verses 37-39 of the same chapter, we see the spiritual meaning of the visual sign. *"All that the Father gives Me shall come to me...,"* (remember from verse 44 we see that) *"no one can come to Me unless the Father who sent Me draws him; and I will raise him up on the last day."* (a sure promise) *"...and the one who comes to Me, I will certainly not cast out. For I have come down from heaven, not to do My own will, but the will of Him who sent Me. And this is the will of Him Who sent Me, that of all that He has given Me, I lose nothing, but raise it up on the last day. For this is the will of My Father, that everyone who beholds the Son and believes in Him may have eternal life; and I Myself will raise him up on the last day."*

Do you see here that it is God's will that Jesus lose nothing. If something is God's will for Jesus, we can know with certainty that Jesus will fulfill that will in full obedience. Jesus will not allow us to be lost. He fulfills all of the Father's will continually. Verses 48, 54, and 57 again confirm that if we believe, we have eternal life. It's a "done deal" based solely on our belief with no strings attached. Period. Eternal security has absolutely nothing to do with our deeds, good or bad, willful or blindly executed. John 5:24 again confirms this, *"Truly, Truly, I say to you, he who hears My word and believes Him who sent Me, has eternal life, and does not come into judgment, but has passed out of death into life."* No hidden clause about works but simply belief.

The Judgment Seat of Christ

We who believe will stand before the judgment seat of Christ. We will be judged by one and only one work when it comes to our eternal life. That work will be our saving faith. The only sin that can keep a person out of heaven is unbelief. In John 6:28:29, the disciples asked, *"Therefore they said to Him, 'What shall we do, so that we may work the works of God?' Jesus answered and said to them, 'This is the work of God, that you believe in Him whom He has sent.'"*

As mentioned earlier, sin will not be an issue for the believer on judgment day. There are many judgments that are to come when the Lord returns. Some Christians get mixed up and lump all the judgments together. Unless we understand who is being judged, we could suffer unnecessary fear regarding our salvation. Some of the judgments spoken of in scripture are the following:

The judgment of Israel
The judgment of Satan and demons
The judgment of the nations
The Great White Throne judgment (only for unbelievers)
The Bema Seat judgment known as the judgment seat of Christ (only for believers)

This last one, the judgment seat of Christ, is for believers. It has nothing to do with sin and salvation. Usually, when we think of judgment, we correlate it with punishment. When we, as believers, are judged before Christ's throne, however, it will not involve punishment because this judgment has nothing to do with sin. Remember, our sins were taken care of at the cross. Salvation is secure. *"Truly, truly, I say to you, he who hears My word, and believes Him who sent Me, has eternal life, and does not come into judgment, but has passed out of death into life,"* (Jn. 5:24).

What, then, will this judgment entail? The Bema seat judgment will be a judgment of rewards. Think of the Olympics. Each contestant is rewarded according to how he performs. Those who practice and perform well receive a medal, while those who may not have been as diligent suffer loss.

The judgment seat of Christ is not for salvation but rather a judgment of what works we have done after salvation while here on earth. Yes, there is a place for works…after salvation. The works or deeds we have done after we were saved that were in Christ will be rewarded and we will rejoice over these good works and rewards. The works we have done that were not in Christ will be burned out of our lives and we will sense a loss because of unprofitable choices. How we conduct ourselves while here on earth will have eternal consequences according to our works. Our works judgment is after salvation is secure. Knowing we will all face this particular judgment should give us incentive to follow Christ wholeheartedly, to seek to hear His voice, to walk in obedience.

This is all clearly explained in I Corinthians 3:10-15. Now, remember, this judgment has nothing to do with our eternal destiny but is simply a rewards judgment for a job well done. *"According to the grace of God which was given to me, as a wise master builder I laid a foundation, and another is building upon it. But let each man be careful how he builds upon it. For no man can lay a foundation other than the one which is laid, which is Jesus Christ."* Jesus is to be the foundation stone in our lives but we are responsible for choices of cooperating and allowing Him to build on that foundation.

"Now if any man builds on the foundation with gold, silver, precious stones, wood, hay, straw, each man's work will become evident; for the day will show it because it is to be revealed with fire, and the fire itself will test the quality of each man's work. If any man's work which he has built on it remains, he will receive a reward. If any man's work is burned up, he will suffer loss; but he himself will be saved, yet so as through fire."

If we build our lives on gold, silver and precious stones, those metals symbolize works that will bear up in the fire. They will be refined and purified by fire when Christ returns and will go with us into eternity. They represent the works we have allowed the Lord to do in and through us.

On the other hand, wood, hay and straw are works which will not stand in the fire but will burn up and be gone. These represent works done outside of God's will, works not done by faith, works done in the flesh. They won't last. When set to flame, they will be completely consumed and to that I say, "Great". I wouldn't want that stuff clinging to me anyway. It is His mercy that gets rid of all of our dead works forever.

That will be the day He will burn out all that we did in the flesh and I say "Burn away". He does this in preparation of our entering eternity. Nothing impure can enter heaven and this will be the time when all unrighteousness will be completely eradicated from our lives forever. We will be completely cleansed and purified.

To be clear, there is a judgment called the Great White Throne judgment. This judgment is not for believers but is for those who do not know Christ. No born again believer will ever undergo the Great White Throne judgment which does involve punishment. Unbelievers, because they have not entered into a faith covenant with God, will be judged only for their deeds and, as we have noted, all deeds apart from Christ are filthy rags. Refusing to apply the blood of Christ to their sins, none will be covered; therefore, not one deed will be found "in Christ." Entry into God's eternity will be unattainable.

Can We Lose Salvation?
So, you might ask, "Is there any way a person can lose his salvation?" Clearly, in this paper we've been straightforward in the truth that God is a God of covenant. When He makes a covenant, for His part, it is permanent. It is sealed. Based on our faith and His grace, He has made a pledge to us that our eternal destiny is secure and not precarious. He has done everything necessary to seal our redemption, (Eph. 1:13-14, 4:30).

If God will never end His covenant relationship with us, is it still possible to lose salvation? This is a much debated subject. In my opinion there is only one scenario where that "might" happen. That would be if we shake our fist in God's face and declare that we do not believe in Him and do want Him in our life. If we knowingly, intentionally, and purposefully banish God from our life, the covenant relationship might end, not by God's choice, but by ours. This would be a serious, heartfelt, willful unbelief and hatred of God. This kind of apostasy would likely be a down-hill, long, difficult and dark road with many sign posts calling us to repent. But to think that salvation can slip through our fingers if we commit any other sin than total unbelief would be cause for such insecurity as to potentially paralyze our Christian walk.

Where do we draw the line? One might wonder if a person continues to walk in willful sin, were they really saved in the first place? Was Jesus ever really Lord if a person continues in sin with no repentance and no fruit? Still, one thing is very clear: God will not abandon His commitment to us. This tells us He will do whatever is necessary to keep our foot from slipping. He is for us, not against us. For His part in our relationship, it is total, all out devotion to us. We do not have to ever be concerned that God will initiate ending our relationship. It is not going to happen. We can be fully assured that we are eternally secure.

I Peter 1:3-5, *"Blessed be the God and Father of our Lord Jesus Christ, who according to His great mercy has caused us to be born again to a living hope through the resurrection of Jesus Christ from the dead, to obtain an inheritance which is imperishable and undefiled and will not fade away, reserved in heaven for you, who are protected by the power of God through faith for a salvation ready to be revealed in the last time."* In this we greatly rejoice!

Chosen, Dearly Loved and Eternally Secure

AUTHOR'S BIOGRAPHY AND CONTACT INFORMATION

 Betsy Tacchella lives in Sturgis, Michigan with her husband of over fifty years. She has three children, nine grandchildren, two great grand-daughters on the way, three grand-puppies and two grand-cats. Betsy has been teaching the Bible for over forty five years and has a Master's degree in Biblical Studies from Trinity Theological Seminary. She also mentors women and if you are looking for a speaker for your group, she enjoys public speaking. Betsy has also written two other books, "Mother Has Alzheimer's," a book of hope in the midst of loss and "Speak to Me Lord, I'm Listening," on hearing God's voice. Both may be purchased through Amazon.com. You may contact the author through her website/blog at www.betsytacchella.com, her Facebook page, https://www.facebook.com/HearingGodsVoice/ or through email at tacchella@hotmail.com.